Peace, not War

A Decade of Interventions in the Plateau State Crises (2001-2011)

Ignatius Ayau Kaigama

Published in 2012
Ignatius Ayau Kaigama
Copyright © 2012

ISBN 978-978-49329-1-2

Cover:
- A contrast between peace and war.
- A dove hovering over the map of Plateau State indicating a longing for peace after war.
- The rocks in the map are the rich endowments of the state.

Printed by
Hamtul Press Ltd
Print Villa, Bisichi-Jos, Plateau State.

Dedication

To men and women of goodwill committed to dialogue,
reconciliation and peace in Plateau State and beyond.

Contents

Title Page i
Dedication iii
Contents iv
Acknowledgements viii
Preface ix

Section One
Introduction
1

Section Two
Plateau... the Beautiful
5

- Moving Plateau Forward: An Agenda for Peace. – *5*
- A Word with Chairman of Plateau State Traditional Council. – *21*
- Stakeholders in Plateau Peace Project. – *24*
- Dialogue of Life: An Urgent Necessity for Nigerian Muslims and Christians – *29*
- The Challenges of Political and Religious Conflicts to the Church in Plateau State – *32*
- January 17, 2010 Jos Crisis: Is Religion the Cause? – *39*

Section Three
Counting our Losses
44

- In the beginning...September 7, 2001 Jos Crisis – *44*
- Sharing the Pains of Victims – *50*
- The 2004 Yelwa Crises: February 22-24; May 2, 2004 – *53*

- Our Peace Mission to Yelwa – *61*
- Namu Crisis: An Overview. – *66*
- Uniting Goemai and Pan Nations. – *68*
- Brief on the 2008 Jos Crisis – *73*
- A Word of Caution to the Media – *75*
- Sallah Greetings after the November 28, 2008 Crisis – *77*
- Memo to the Nunciature, Abuja – *79*
- Solidarity Mass/Healing for Victims of Plateau Crisis – *81*
- Dogon Nahawa Mass of Solidarity/Healing – *83*
- The 2010 Christmas Eve Bombings – *84*
- Solidarity Mass for Bomb Blast Victims: Courage! Rise up and Walk – *90*
- Civil Disturbances in Jos North LGA– August 29-30, 2011 – *94*
- What Manner of Crises in Jos? – *98*
- Waiting for another 'Religious Riot'? – *107*

Section Four

Attempts at Inter-Religious Harmony

115

- Our Mission of Peace and Reconciliation in Plateau State –*115*
- In the Saddle as Chairman of Inter-Religious Council on Peace and Harmony – *119*
- Christianity as a Tool for Crises Management and Peace Building – *123*
- Overcoming Evil with Good – *133*
- We are God's Children rather than Northerners, Southerners, Muslims or Christians – *140*
- Muslims and Christians Living and Working Together – *144*
- Better to Light the Candle than to Curse the Darkness – *147*
- The Plateau State Government's Commitment – *150*
- Do all You Can to Live in Peace with Everyone – *153*
- Brother and Friend– Emir Haruna Abdullahi of Wase – *162*

Section Five

Memoirs/Interventions
167

- Christian/Muslim Relations in Jos and Nigeria: A Personal Experience – *167*
- Religion and Post Conflict Peace Building in Northern Nigeria – *178*
- The State of Emergency Imposed on Plateau State – *180*
- A Word of Encouragement – *186*
- In the Name of our Benevolent God, Stop the Violence – *188*

Section Six

Devotion to the Creator
190

- A Call to Sober Reflection, Prayer and Fasting – *190*
- Call to more Intense Prayer – *191*
- Prayer for Political, Ethnic & Religious Peace in Plateau State – *193*
- Prayer for Peace (complied for a group in Germany) – *1194*

Section Seven

Letters/Correspondence
195

- Francis Cardinal Arinze – *195*
- Peter Cardinal Turkson – *196*
- Ivan Cardinal Dias – *198*
- Cardinal Tarcisio Bertone – *199*
- Senator (Alhaji) Ibrahim Naziru Mantu – *200*

- Pauline K. Tallen, Hon. Minister of State for Science and Technology – *201*
  - British High Commission, Abuja – *202*
    - Bishop of Awka – *203*
  - Bishop of Kandi, Benin Republic – *204*
    - Roger E. Simon, Canada – *205*
  - German Bishops' Conference – *206*

Section Eight

Conclusion

208

Appendices

219

- Interview with *Punch* – *219*
- *Vanguard* Report: St. Finbarr's Church – *223*
  - *The Word of Life / Christ und Welt* – *229*
    - *The Word of Life* – *230*
  - Healing Wounds on the Plateau – *231*
    - Eighth General Assembly – *234*

Index

240

Acknowledgements

To God who can do infinitely more that we imagine I give honour, glory and praise. This book is the fruit of his numerous blessings.

I appreciate the role of my private secretaries since 2001, who not only taught me the use of the computer but helped to type my speeches and discourses and in many cases made good input. In this regard I thank Fr. Vincent Diyong, Fr. Joshua Daffa , Fr. Alexander Dung, Fr. Gideon Pwakim and Fr. Daniel Pwajok. The late Fr. John Gyang, Fr. Paulinus Nweke and Fr. Stephen Akpe were part time secretaries who were helpful in many ways. My office secretary, Ms Tina Igbokwe, ever loyal and hard working deserves special thanks.

I commend and thank Mr. Godfrey Danaan at whose insistence this work began and was completed. He was committed to seeing my speeches, discourses and interventions during the crises from 2001 to 2011 made into a book. He did so much for this and also wrote the Introduction.

Prof. David Jowitt did not only gladly read and edit the texts but also kindly wrote the Preface. I owe him a debt of gratitude.

I must mention the constant support of the Priests, Religious and Laity of the Archdiocese of Jos with whom we keep collaborating on matters of pastoral progress and interreligious dialogue and harmony.

A special appreciation to my Muslim brothers, especially the Sultan of Sokoto, His Eminence, Muhammad Sa'ad Abubakar III and my bosom friend, the late Emir of Wase, Alhaji Dr. Haruna Abdullahi and other Emirs, Imams and Sheiks who kept encouraging me with the words: "continue doing the good work". God bless and keep us all in His peace.

Preface

His Grace the Catholic Archbishop of Jos, Ignatius Ayau Kaigama, has established a well-deserved reputation at home and abroad for his untiring efforts to bring about lasting peace in Plateau State, Nigeria. This book is a memorial to these efforts, consisting mostly as it does of a number of speeches on the subject that he has made over a period of many years.

Plateau State has officially been described as "the home of peace and tourism", but for at least a decade, and especially since 2001, it has been prey to a series of outbreaks of violence. In these are embroiled the ethnic groups dwelling in the State, with those who can claim to have been there since a relatively remote time in the past on one side, and more recent arrivals on the other; but because the former have to a great extent embraced Christianity and the latter are Muslims, issues of land ownership and employment have been ineluctably tied up with those of religion.

Archbishop Kaigama is one of those who have bravely affirmed that the recurring 'crisis' is fundamentally not one of religion. He has also persistently tried to involve 'Christians' and 'Muslims' in dialogue to bring about a permanent solution; and, as he points out, he has sometimes been attacked by fellow Christians for his faith in dialogue, just as Muslims who also believe in it are often denounced by their co-religionists. Archbishop Kaigama clearly regards the warm friendship he established with the late Emir Abdullahi of Wase as a model of the kind of harmony that dialogue should naturally lead to.

At the same time, reading between the lines, and especially in his graphic accounts of some of the troubles of which he had first-hand experience, one feels that he has no illusions as to where the provocative behaviour leading to yet another crisis emanates from. This does not deter him from his chosen course, one that no doubt he regards as demanded of him by his Lord and Master, who said 'Blessed are the peacemakers, for they shall be called sons of God'.

The Archbishop comes over in these discourses as a man of great faith, humanity, insight, and overall integrity, and so well-equipped with the resources needed to face great challenges. One of the most difficult of these, perhaps, though it is one which no spiritual leader should find strange, is to offer convincing words of comfort to those who have been bereaved. One of the discourses shows him discharging this duty with particular courage, when he preached at a Solidarity Mass held at St Jarlath's church, Bukuru, in the wake of the brutal killing of Berom women and children at the village of Dogo Nahawa just outside Jos in March, 2010.

As a contribution to the continuing debate about the causes of and possible solutions of the Plateau State crisis, to interfaith dialogue in the world at large, and to the literature of Christian perspectives on issues of social conflict, the publication of this book is a major and most welcome event. It deserves the careful and sympathetic attention of a wide readership, within and outside Nigeria.

Your Grace, hearty congratulations!

DAVID JOWITT ,
Professor of English,
University of Jos,
Plateau State,
Nigeria.

Section One
INTRODUCTION

Those familiar with Plateau State before its protracted crisis began will recall the days when people of all ethnic extractions coexisted peacefully with their host communities, whose character of accommodation attracted Muslims, Christians, Hindus, Buddhists and non-believers to the land. Their desire was to remain united and chart a common cause. Unfortunately, violence erupted, resulting in renewed hostilities which lasted for a decade. The bloodshed escalated beyond the capacity of internal security agencies and the might of the military was deployed at various times to contain the situation.

However, the Catholic Archbishop of Jos, the Most Rev. Ignatius Ayau Kaigama, was on hand to keep hope alive as he chose the path of dialogue and insisted that the attempt by the political class to mystify the crisis was needless. His firm belief in genuine dialogue reigns supreme. In an interview which he granted the *Punch* newspaper on April 2, 2011, he declared that "Plateau crises won't end even if you attach five soldiers to every family". The implication is that if the heart is rebellious, poisoned and harbours hatred, very little can be achieved despite heavy security presence. In that regard, he believes that "all ethnic groups, all religions should transcend their tribal or religious sentiments to address real issues.... It is only when we are ready to listen to the voice of reason that there will be peace". This was what he stood for while the crises lasted. He initiated programmes to promote interfaith harmony and strengthen relationships, especially with the Muslim Ummah; he counselled the government at all levels and traditional rulers on reconciliation and peace-building efforts; he organized and hosted several interfaith meetings and workshops, among other things.

This book, *Peace, not War*, suggests that a new dawn beckons for Plateau State. It is a compendium of interventions in the Plateau crises by the Archbishop through peace-building efforts, dialogue and reconciliation in one decade: 2001-2011. The title reflects the philosophy of the author who, in his thirty-one years of priestly ministry, has promoted world peace, dialogue and reconciliation among people of all races and beliefs. He uses the term "Christian" or "Muslim" in the context of the crises in a generic sense as he believes that the crises cannot be simply reduced to Christian/Muslim issue; implying that there are multidimensional causes.

As Bishop of Jalingo Diocese, he intervened in the Jukun/Kutep/Tiv crises through dialogue with warring communities which ended the protracted war. Since 2000, when he became Archbishop of Jos, he has carried on with his mission of reconciling all citizens of Plateau State who once coexisted peacefully but chose to go the wrong way. In all these, he has advocated peace not war.

The first section highlights the exciting themes which the author discusses with tact and uncommon intellect. In Section Two, the situation in Plateau State is captured to provide background to further discourses. The author sets the agenda for stakeholders: politicians, government officials, media, traditional, religious and opinion leaders. He initiates a 'Dialogue of Life: An Urgent Necessity for Nigerian Muslims and Christians' to buttress its essence. He outlines the challenges of political and religious conflicts to the Church in Plateau State and suggests ways of ending the protracted war in the State.

The third section is a litany of losses resulting from the Plateau crises which had spread across the state like wild fire. These include the September 7 Jos crisis, the 2004 Yelwa crisis, the Namu crisis, the Dogon Nahawa attacks, the 2010 Christmas Eve Bombings, the civil disturbances in Jos North LGA. He expresses solidarity with all victims and prays for their physical and spiritual healing. In all this he asks: What manner of crisis in Jos? Waiting for another religious riot?

The fourth section showcases the Archbishop's character of mediation in interfaith matters, especially between Muslims and Christians living in Nigeria. His effort in bringing the adherents of both religions round the table and his wise counsel at different fora endeared him to the Muslim community, his Christian family, the government and other stakeholders, who have entrusted him with many leadership responsibilities. He brings to bear his experience on the society in his capacity as co-chairman of the Plateau State Inter-Religious Council on Peace and Harmony, Chairman of the Christian Association of Nigeria, CAN, and a commentator. He also remembers his bosom friend, the late Emir of Wase, with whom he strengthened interfaith dialogue in Plateau State and Nigeria.

In Section Five, the author sheds light on the Plateau crises in a parley with the international community. He advocates reconciliation and cooperation beyond the boundaries of religions, races and countries. He gives an insight into the Jos crises and tells the international community that the crises are multidimensional. This section also contains memoirs and personal reflections in which the Archbishop bears his mind on issues of common interest. He comments on religion and post-conflict peace-building in Northern Nigeria and the State of Emergency imposed on Plateau State; he encourages the clergy, religious and laity of the Archdiocese to remain faithful Christians in the prevailing circumstances.

Section Six contains devotion to the creator. His Grace calls for sober reflection, prayer and fasting. He initiates the prayer for political, ethnic and religious peace in Plateau State and composes a prayer for peace for a group in Germany.

Sections Seven and Eight feature correspondence from the Vatican and other agencies as well as the conclusion.

This book is incisive, objective, stimulating and simple.

GODFREY DANAAN,
Lecturer,
Department of Mass Communication,
University of Jos.

Pope Benedict with a Muslim leader

The author with Muslim leaders and development worker after a peace meeting in Jos

Section Two
PLATEAU... THE BEAUTIFUL

MOVING PLATEAU FORWARD:
AN AGENDA FOR PEACE

A paper presented at a Peace Colloquium organized by the Nigerian Institute of Public Relations, Plateau State Chapter on May 22, 2007 at Hill Station Hotel, Jos.

Introduction

May I begin by thanking the members of the Nigerian Institute of Public Relations (NIPR), at whose instance we are gathered to set an agenda for peace in Plateau State and indeed Nigeria. I thank NIPR for not only inviting me to be a participant at this peace colloquium but also challenging me with the task of being the guest speaker. This gathering of stakeholders, I must tell you, is very timely as it comes on the threshold of a new administration in Plateau State. In the recent past, Plateau State became a boiling cauldron with festering crises that took several dimensions. It is unfortunate that these seemingly intractable crises have had negative consequences for the moral, political, social, religious, economic growth and stability of the once beautiful Plateau. The morale of Plateau citizens is greatly dampened and the image of the State battered as a result of the prolonged hostilities.

I consider my function at this forum a sacred duty which my faith and ministry bestows on me. I have therefore responded to this invitation with all the patriotism it deserves. While there is palpable cynicism in the masses regarding the sincerity of the political class in addressing this hydra-headed monster, there is equally a deep-seated longing for a messiah who will salvage the state. The favourable responses characterized by the large turn-out of people at peace rallies, peace prayers, peace novelty football matches, and peace musical concerts attest to the desire of the Plateau citizenry for peace in the State. In fact, if you want patronage for any public event, tag it 'peace', and you will attract a mammoth crowd. There is also a corresponding growth of peace-related NGOs in the State.

As a patriotic citizen, who is very troubled by the crisis that bedevils Plateau State, I am very delighted to be part of this event. I consider my principal assignment in this colloquium as that of animating sincere, frank and constructive discussions on how to move our dear State forward. I may not be wrong, however, to presume that everybody in Plateau State knows that something went wrong and we have found ourselves at a crossroads. Even the present government realizes this; hence the new programme, 'Healing Point' broadcasts simultaneously on all arms of PRTVC.

My presentation will be a modest contribution to an issue that is wide and complex. This reflection will move along five broad headings. First, we shall go down memory lane to see how, before the creation of the state, the elders of Plateau State considered peace and stability as paramount factors in the existence of the State. Secondly, we shall highlight the peaceful nature of the average Plateau person. Then we shall briefly reflect on the upheavals of the recent past. Fourthly, we shall explore ways of moving Plateau State forward. Finally, we shall challenge various stake-holders on their contributions to peace-building in the State.

Birth of Plateau State

The history of Plateau State cannot be complete without a look at the good old days of Benue-Plateau. After seizing power in July

Joseph Deshi Gomwalk
Pioneer Governor, Benue-Plateau State

Chief Solomon Daushep Lar
1st Civilian Governor

Amb. Fidelis Tapgun (KSM/KSGG)
2nd Civilian Governor

Chief Joshua Chibi Dariye
3rd Civilian Governor

Da Jonah David Jang
4th Civilian Governor

1966, the then Lt. Col. Yakubu Gowon identified the existing structural imbalance in the country as one of the major obstacles to national cohesion. He felt that the existing division of the country into four regions did not allow minority groups to participate adequately in national development. Gowon also noticed that the domineering attitude of the majority tribes in the various regions was capable of generating tension and possible crisis in the polity, because the minority groups could some day revolt. Consequently, he scrapped the existing regional demarcation and divided the country into twelve states in order to safeguard national unity. On May 27, 1967, Lt. Col. Gowon announced the promulgation of a decree creating twelve States. Benue-Plateau State was one of those States created, and Chief Superintendent of Police, Joseph Deshi Gomwalk, a Plateau son, became its first military Governor. By this account, we can deduce that Benue-Plateau State was a product of the quest for national peace by the Gowon administration. According to Chief Anthony Goyol, one of the things considered by some Plateau elders who were contacted prior to the creation of the state was the guarantee of the freedom and of the compatibility of Plateau people with the province they were going to be merged with. Plateau province had the option of merging either with Bauchi or with Benue Province. The elders chose to merge with Benue as against Bauchi, because Bauchi Province had a large presence of the Hausa/Fulani stock, and for fear of domination, Benue was a better option.[1] This shows that Plateau citizens, by their nature, desire to co-exist peacefully.

As time passed, disaffection started looming in the state as political actors of both Plateau and Benue origin started accusing each other of marginalization and injustice on several fronts. The Plateau bloc expressed fear of domination by the Benue people because, as they argued, there was a great imbalance to the advantage of Benue people regarding population, education and employment in the State civil service. For them, this was enough

---

[1] Anthony Goyol, *J.D. Gomwalk: A Man of Vision* (Jos: LECAPS Publishers, 1996) p.45

reason for separation.[2] This dream came true when on February 3, 1976, the Late Gen. Murtala Mohammed announced the creation of more states and Benue and Plateau were separated. Again the Plateau people wanted to live peacefully on their own. Apart from other factors, the characteristic peaceful nature of Plateau State was a contributory factor to its hosting of the Social Democratic Party (SDP) and People's Democratic Party (PDP) national conventions in 1993 and 1999 respectively.

We Are Peaceful People
It was generally observed by early anthropologists and philosophers that Plateau people are generally peace-loving. One Sr. Marie de Paul Neiers, who taught philosophy at St. Augustine's Major Seminary, Jos, wrote;

> in the Jos region, life normally flows along in an atmosphere of harmony and serenity to be dreamt of and envied. What is the secret of this? —and the price to be paid for it? —for, when all is said and done, life really was and is happy there, in (sic) despite of the pinch of poverty. ... In Jos, of course, as anywhere else, things are far from perfect, but the chronic unease which is rampant in a world sick from its own over-civilization, brings no sleepless nights to the pagan nor does it come between him and the enjoyment to the full of the simple pleasures of the life which is his.[3]

Sr. Marie also added that they were very warm and accommodating because Jos[4] "is a cosmopolitan meeting place

---

[2] *Plateau State: The Heritage and Hope* (Jos: Plateau State Government, 2001) p.62
[3] Sr. Marie de Paul Neiers, *The People of the Jos Plateau, Nigeria: their Philosophy, Manners and Customs* (Frankfurt: Peter Lang, 1979) p.132
[4] The reference to Jos in her study is inclusive of other tribes because the scope of her research covered all the tribes of Plateau which she called *The People of the Jos Plateau, Nigeria*. The usage of 'pagan', though offensive

where the members of the various tribes represented tend to regroup themselves and live together in urban 'villages', in the midst of immigrants from every region in Nigeria and of a quite large non-African population".[5]

The Vision for Plateau State

The agitation for self-determination is a common phenomenon among human beings. It is always the desire of people to have the freedom to articulate and chart their destinies, especially politically. The concerted and genuine desire of Plateau people for peaceful emancipation and development saw to the creation of Benue-Plateau State and later, an independent Plateau State. Although many Plateau politicians jointly struggled for both the creation of Benue-Plateau State and subsequently a separate Plateau State, there was an icon whose personality crystallized the entire aspirations and dreams of the Plateau people. This was the late Joseph Deshi Gomwalk. J.D. Gomwalk rightly visualized Plateau as a land with immense potentials and he set out to harness these potentials. Within his eight years of leadership, J.D. Gomwalk distinguished himself as a man who saw beyond his age and was credited with outstanding commitment to the progress of his people. Going by the legacy he left behind, as manifested in the projects he initiated and executed, one cannot doubt his commitment to making the state a vibrant one in all ramifications. Benue-Plateau soon developed. That was why it was rated second by the Federal Government in April 1972.[6] J.D. Gomwalk laid an enduring foundation for the state through widespread developmental strides:

> The enduring foundation he laid included the State Civil Service, crucial road networks, water works in major towns and cities, schools,

in contemporary times, was commonly applied by early anthropologists and philosophers to practitioners of traditional religion.

[5] Op. cit. Sr. Marie de Paul Neiers, p.64
[6] Op. cit. Anthony Goyol, p.318

hospitals and health centres, hotels, a mass transit company, a construction company (Benue-Plateau Construction, BEPCO), an investment company, Standard Newspaper, Benue-Plateau Television (BPTV), University College, Jos, and a Marketing Board.[7]

J.D. Gomwalk was a visionary who was good to his dream. Although he never lived long enough to reap its fruits, his legacies testify to his vision for Plateau. It is worth noting that he was able to achieve this feat because of the existing peace in the state. We shall later talk about the relationship between peace and development.

If J.D. Gomwalk had this lofty dream for Plateau State, what went wrong and when did it go wrong?

Synopsis of Violent Conflicts in Plateau State
No matter how peace-loving people in a given society are, they could exhibit violent tendencies when some core values are tampered with. Sr. Marie de Paul knew another side of the Plateau People when she said that "the pagans of the Jos region have a remarkable sense of independence, self-confidence and pride, as well as a delicate sensitivity. They are extremely conscious of their rights and know how to employ any and every means to obtain them. This rather unexpected side of their character is in sharp contrast with their quiet and unresisting submission to authority duly established and recognized".[8] This implies that though Plateau people are generally submissive to authority, they have a serious aversion to injustice and suppression. In fact, apart from political factors, most of the crises we recently experienced could largely be traced to the fear of domination and perceived injustice in policy formulation and implementation.

---

[7] Op. cit. *Plateau State: The Heritage and Hope*, p.73
[8] Op. cit. Sr. Marie de Paul Neiers, p.74

As we seek to move Plateau out of the battlefield, it will be important to briefly highlight the various crises we experienced recently.

A) Pre 2001. Prior to the major violent conflicts that rocked Plateau State in 2001, the State had been an oasis of peace in the country, hence the title "Home of Peace and Tourism". Even when all the surrounding states of Bauchi, Kaduna, Taraba and Nassarawa witnessed several rounds of violence, the state remained calm. Except for the unease generated by the influx of refugees from other States, minor clashes over grazing areas between farmers and pastoralists, and land ownership tussles, all was well in the State.

B) 2001. March 17, 2001 blew the lid off for subsequent crises in the state. The once peaceful virgin was about to be ravished by violent conflicts. It was reported that between March 17 and September 7, 2001, Plateau State witnessed at least five serious armed conflicts in which many lives were lost and entire villages sacked. The most serious was that of September 7-12, 2001 when Jos, the capital city, experienced unprecedented carnage that changed the face of the once serene city.

C) 2002. The first mishap to befall the State in 2002 was the orchestrated burning of the Jos ultra-modern market in February. By May 22, 2002, Naraguta 'B' ward was boiling, while on June 26, Yelwa, a sprawling commercial transit town in Shendam L.G.C., was set ablaze. Many casualties were recorded. The Mavo, Lamba and Kadarko attacks were soon to follow between July 2 and 5, 2002.

D) 2003. There was no respite in 2003 as violence broke out in several villages in Langtang South, Langtang North and Wase Local Government Areas on April 13, June 3, and November 10 respectively.

E) 2004. The worst was soon to come. By early February, violence spread across villages in Wase, Langtang North and Shendam Local Governments. The greatest of them was February 24, 2004 and its reprisal on May 2, 2004. The level of carnage meted out on Yelwa-Nshar town attracted a lot of public attention, and the imposition of a State of Emergency on the entire state was its immediate consequence.[9]

F) 2006. With many peace initiatives by both the state government and non-governmental organizations, during and after the State of Emergency, relative calm returned to the State. However, with the creation of development areas on November 11, 2005 tension began to build-up in Namu, a commercial town in Qua'an-Pan L.G.C. Namu remained uneasy until April 11, 2006 when full-blown ethnic violence rocked the settlement. Since then, the community has been uneasy as suspicion is still prevalent in the community.

G) 2006 to 2007. The better part of 2006 up till now has been spent in political wrangling. The State has been held ransom by intra- and inter-party disputes. It has seen one litigation after another and the state has been at a standstill.

I have deliberately left out the nitty-gritty regarding the causes of individual crises because of want of time. However, the combined factors of wrong government policies, fear of domination, power tussles, poor response to security reports, politicization of religion and ethnicity, poverty and religious hate have played leading roles in the crises. As a result of these crises, we have suffered the loss of resources and manpower, stagnation and, worse still, a general apathy and loss of confidence by the masses in the affairs of government. Our people now find it difficult to trust government. There is great urgency for the

---

[9] Details of the dates and places of crises between 2001 and 2004 can be found in *"Making Peace: The Plateau Experience"* (Jos: Plateau State Government, 2004) pp. x-x

incoming administration to chart a new course in order to restore the confidence of people in government. Government must rekindle the dream and restore the pride of Plateau people.

Moving Plateau Forward

Our hosts at this colloquium have rightly identified peace as an agenda for moving Plateau forward. I strongly agree with their thesis that peace is the most basic instrument for building a virile Plateau State. Although there are other definitions of peace, I find the sociological description as very practical. It describes peace as "a condition of social harmony in which there are no social antagonisms. In other words, peace is a condition in which there is no social conflict and individuals and groups are able to meet their needs and expectations".[10]

Moving Plateau forward entails developing the state. There is, however, a close-knit relationship between peace and development. Peace is the most essential factor for development. Pope Paul VI in his great social encyclical of March 26, 1967, *Populorum Progressio* (On the Development of Peoples) said that development is another name for peace. Victor Adetula, while lamenting the counterproductive nature of conflicts, wrote that:

> Conflicts have the capacity to severely constrain development endeavours by destroying infrastructure, interrupting production processes and diverting resources away from productive uses.[11]

The following data on the Horn of Africa support Adetula's thesis:

> In the Horn of Africa, for example, civil wars in the 1980s and 1990s hindered development by affecting not only state structures but also other sectors. In three decades, life expectancy went

---

[10] Shedrach Gaya Best, ed., *Introduction to Peace and Conflict Studies in West Africa* (Ibadan: Spectrum Books Ltd) p.5
[11] Ibid. p.385

> down by 10-20 years; per capita income
> decreased by 50 percent; famine became
> endemic; and other welfare indicators such as
> health and education were worsened.[12]

Conflict stunts development because it creates humanitarian problems and resources are diverted to security, relief materials and reconstruction. In fact, conflict situations promote corruption because a lot of money can be diverted under the guise of security and relief. One can only imagine how much was spent by both the local and state governments during the crises and the State of Emergency period. I at least have an experience of the financial cost of resettling people after a crisis. This is because I know what it cost the Justice, Development and Peace Commission of Jos Archdiocese to distribute relief materials, resettle refugees, organize peace-building workshops etc. This money could have been used for some developmental purposes. One can equally imagine how much government has spent in prosecuting litigation as a result of the current political face-off in the state.

It is important to emphasize some key issues that must be taken into cognizance if we are to make progress.

1) Moral re-orientation for good governance. Morality is not simply a theoretical matter. It has to do with doing things the way they ought to be done. There is always a right way to do things, and if they are not done right, they are bound to fail. With regard to governance, we must return to the pristine virtues of leadership, which are truthfulness, justice, selflessness, sacrifice, service, accountability and compassion. To a large extent, many Nigerian politicians have a distorted view of leadership. Very often, candidates vying for political positions are only interested in what they can accumulate for themselves, rather than the service that should be rendered to the people. Some people see opportunities of leadership as a time to loot and to settle godfathers and cronies. For Plateau to move forward, leadership must be about service and

---

[12] Ibid

the uplift of the people. Speaking about who should hold public office, Gerald E. Cave said:

> ...they should be the most righteous and wisest; persons of character and distinction, of honour and integrity; they should be dependable. These worthy people should set an example and insist on the highest standards of performance. Their task is to advance the public interest, maintain peace, promote the general welfare, and deal kindly with people. They are to administer public affairs with wisdom, compassion, justice and sensitivity. They are to protect and safeguard public property as a sacred trust and to account for their actions to the public. They are to proclaim just laws and see they are carried out honestly and fairly. They are to be judged by their good deeds and remembered for their good works.[13]

Good governance therefore "implies a high level of organizational effectiveness in relation to policy-formulation and the policies actually pursued, especially in the conduct of economic policy and its contribution to growth, stability and the overall well-being of the citizens".[14] Plateau State needs courageous leaders who will be able to stop the culture of patronage to so-called loyalists, and articulate policies that are fair and just while ensuring an even distribution of development across the state.

2) Civil Service. For Plateau to move forward, the plight of civil servants, who are the engine room of state functions, must be adequately addressed. We very often think of violence only in terms of armed conflicts. Another dimension of violence against people that is not easily noticeable is the denial of their rights and

---

[13] Rev. Fr. Innocent Jooji, *Mending the Cracked Pot: Perspectives on Conflict, Non-violence, Social Justice and Reconciliation in Nigeria.* (Ibadan: Daily Graphics Nigeria Ltd, 2003) p.121
[14] Ibid., p.119

privileges. The delay or total denial of salaries, benefits and entitlements due to civil servants, as is the current situation in the state, is violence against them because it generates tension and even violent reactions. There is no way Plateau State can grow if the workforce is dissatisfied. To my mind, the prompt payment of workers' salaries should be placed first before any structural development. We cannot afford to build fiscal structures while the population is hungry.

3) Inclusive politics. Our state is presently going through serious political turmoil. Politicians are sharply divided and bitterly opposed to each other. We appeal to politicians to stop the fighting. Since the elections are over, any well-meaning Plateau politician should begin to explore avenues of contributing to the growth of the State. The hallmark of a vibrant democracy is gallantry in accepting defeat and magnanimity in victory. While a particular party has to form the central government, it is important that the opposition parties are not treated like lepers in the State. This is because the prevalent 'winner-takes-all' syndrome fosters a sense of frustration for those excluded from the political system. The new government should learn from the example of our President-elect, Alhaji Umar Yar'Adua, who has extended a hand of friendship to his fellow contestants from other parties. I see this as a very wise step because Yar'Adua does not underestimate the distractions, troubles and subversions the opposition are capable of causing him if they continue to oppose his government. The opposition are capable of distracting the government by protracted legal suits, incitements and sabotage. However, I am glad about recent happenings among our political class in Plateau State. The "Healing Point" programme, as I said, is a positive sign of Government's desire to reconcile the State. I heard there is presently a joint transition committee comprised of delegates from the State Government and delegates from the Governor-elect to organize a smooth transition in the state. We are also aware that Governor Joshua Dariye visited the new Governor-elect to congratulate him on his recent victory at the polls. I hope these are sincere moves to get us out of our present political predicament. While the government is enjoined to tolerate and carry along the opposition, the opposition, on their part, should be just, fair and constructive in their opposition.

4) Infrastructural Development. We earlier established the close-knit relationship between peace-building and infrastructural development. Where there is no peace, there cannot be development. Likewise, when there is no development there is bound to be frustration leading to violence. Development is, therefore, a roadmap to peace. Development engages the populace, reduces poverty and minimizes tension in the system. During the last Jos Catholic Archdiocesan Synod in July 2006, I asked the over four hundred delegates coming from every part of the State to list the most urgent needs of Plateau State, and their responses can be summarized thus: education (more funding for education in the State), health (more hospitals especially in rural areas), agriculture (subsidize agricultural input and implements), security (take security reports seriously), commerce (rebuild Jos Main Market and attract investors), employment (engage idle youths), and infrastructure. Infrastructure includes basic amenities like potable water, electricity, especially in rural areas, good roads in both townships and villages, and bridges to connect the villages to the city. If these needs are met and evenly distributed across the State, more will have been done in the area of peace-building than spending money on workshops and the payment of police and the Army to enforce calm.

Conclusion
We cannot conclude this reflection on moving Plateau forward without challenging the various stakeholders on their roles in the Plateau project.

A) Politicians. Plateau State has suffered enough of political tussles. As such, politicians who claim to be patriotic must forget about personal interests, forgive the past and work towards a better

Plateau. May I state that all the past crises in the State had underlying political motivations. They only appeared on the surface to be ethnic or religious but they had serious political undertones. Very often, they started off as political struggles and later assumed other dimensions. Peace in Plateau State largely depends on the sincerity of politicians to work towards achieving it. Our politicians must stop playing politics with the well-being of our people. Our people are tired of the bickering among the political class, and that explains the general lack of interest from the masses about political happenings in the State, because they have lost confidence in the political class. The attitude of most people is to sit down and look. After all, the masses have nothing to gain. Impeachment or no impeachment, they are not bothered because they are not even sure of the next government. Let our politicians give peace a chance, so that we can also benefit from the much-talked-about dividends of democracy. What is politics, after all, if not the development and security of the people?

B) Religious Leaders. Religious leaders are supposed to be agents of peace. None of the three major religions practised in this state preaches violence. Christianity is about love, Islam is about peace, and African traditional religion values communal life. There is this famous 'Ubuntu' philosophy which reflects a typical African worldview. It says, "I am, because we are". Where then is the place of violence in religion? All religious leaders are challenged to be advocates of, and educators in peace. Besides, religion needs peace to thrive. Religious leaders should not be found making inflammatory remarks or preaching inciting sermons, and should not allow religion to be manipulated for political goals. Our people are quite religious and they trust their religious leaders so much. Religious leaders should see this trust as a unique privilege for promoting peace.

C) Youths. The youth is the most active group in the society. Unfortunately, Nigerian youths are often used to perpetrate violence. I want to challenge our young people to realize that they must be responsible for the protection of, and investment in their future. If they are used to destroy the present heritage, what hope do they have in life? Youths should not allow themselves to be deceived by mischief-makers, because most of the trouble-makers have their children living comfortably and securely in other places, yet they want other people's children to die for them. Youthful energy is not meant to be dissipated in fighting but to be invested in worthwhile ventures. My question to young people is: "If you destroy your heritage today, what will you inherit tomorrow?"

D) Women. Women must realize that they and children are the most vulnerable in conflict situations. While we appreciate the role women have so far played in calming nerves in Plateau State, we still urge them to do more in the homes by conscientizing their husbands and children on the dangers of violence.

D) Media. It is often said that the media are the spine of democracy. A free press is necessary for democracy to flourish. As such, the media should be constructive rather than destructive in their reporting. It is also unfortunate that the 'brown envelope' syndrome is penetrating newsrooms, and news items are being influenced. Media men and women are challenged to be investigative, truthful, factual and balanced in their reporting. In conflict situations, the media have a duty to report in a manner that mitigates conflict rather than exacerbating it

Finally, my dear friends, mine has been a frank contribution on what it takes to entrench peace so that Plateau State can move forward. During this sharing, I established the connection between peace and key areas of our social life. We started by stating that the average Plateau person is a lover of peace and that the dream of our founding fathers for the future of the state was very lofty. The late J.D. Gomwalk laid a solid foundation for a vibrant state but something went amiss with the passage of time. Suddenly, peace and hospitality became very scarce commodities in the supposed 'Home of Peace and Tourism'. Our convergence in this auditorium is a reflection of our desire to regain the lost glory. Peace is not utopian for us. It is achievable, but we must be ready to pay the price. I therefore invite all citizens of Plateau State: politicians, civil servants, religious leaders, youths, women, the media and the private sector to join hands in healing Plateau State. We must be ready to humbly accept our mistakes, forgive one another and sincerely seek to work together for the common good of Plateau State. As we step into another dispensation, we look forward to more peaceful days so that we can attain the greatness we have always dreamt of for Plateau State.

A WORD WITH CHAIRMAN OF THE
PLATEAU STATE TRADITIONAL COUNCIL
Courtesy Visit to the late Gbong Gwom Jos,
His Royal Majesty, Da Dr. Victor Pam Bot, DIG RTD., December 16, 2005

Your Royal Majesty,

Peace be with you.

We come here as a delegation from the Catholic Archdiocese of Jos on behalf of all the Catholics in Plateau State. We desired to pay you this visit immediately after your coronation in 2003, but circumstances could not permit us. Today is the day the Lord has allowed us to come to see you and to bring our greetings of friendship, peace and love to you, your family and the entire kingdom you represent. Even though belatedly, permit us to congratulate you on your appointment to the prestigious stool of the Gbong Gwom. We accompany this greeting with prayers that the Lord will bless you with the wisdom of Solomon and the strength and shepherd skills of David, so that you can successfully lead your people on the path of peace, righteousness and progress. Your background as a former senior police officer will no doubt be a great asset to you as you search for ways to promote peace and to tackle insecurity and social vices, among which is the consumption of **goskolo,** an illicit gin with destructive potential for the body system.

You and I are members of the recently constituted Plateau State Inter-Religious Council for Peace and Harmony. I hope that we shall, together with the other distinguished members of the Council, join hands of fellowship to see that no stone is left unturned for peace and harmony to become the state anthem of the Plateau people. Your being a member of the Plateau State Security Council and the Chairman of the Plateau State Traditional Council is of great advantage. In those capacities you can easily convey to Government and the security agents the feelings and problems of the masses.

From some higher institutions we hear of cultic practices that result in the deaths of innocent students. From some urban dwellers we hear of incessant robbery attacks. From some youths we hear disgruntled voices because of unemployment and the difficulty of getting admission into higher institutions unless they know somebody who knows somebody. From the countryside we hear of some conflicts leading to the destruction of lives and property. Yet we know that such conflicts could ea sily be avoided if dialogue is used as a tool for social engagement. These are issues of great concern. We therefore have individual and collective responsibility to see that we create a conducive environment for peace and harmony to reign now and in the future.

I always use the analogy of a tripod to show how we all have to collaborate to bring out the best in our society. A woman needs three stones on which she can balance her pot to cook *tuwon acha.* Remove a stone and the pot collapses. The three stones are Government, traditional rulers and religious leaders. These three arms must not only work consistently, honestly and selflessly together, but must be seen to be doing so. Dia logue, consultation, and proactive measures can go along way in eradicating or minimizing the situations of conflict that may arise from time to time.

My last and very big concern is the way our politicians in Plateau State carry on. The actions and inactions of politicians to a large extent contributed to the imposition of the State of Emergency in May 2004. That singular action cast aspersions on Plateau State, regarded as "the home of peace and tourism." Having emerged from the State of Emergency I thought our politicians would put their act together and work concertedly for the socio-political and economic progress of Plateau State, keeping in mind that they owe the younger generation a prosperous and peaceful future.

What I see now is the 'survival-of-the-fittest' politicians.

What I see now is a clash of personalities that cripples good governance and creates an atmosphere of fear and insecurity.

What I see now are individual politicians who, as long as they satisfy their political aspirations or interests, are unconcerned even if the whole of Plateau State should be forced into extinction – they play the fiddle while Plateau State burns.

What I see now is an unwillingness on the part of the Plateau elders to come together and say "enough is enough – we may have different political opinions and aspirations but our greatest concern should be the present and future welfare of the Plateau children, youth, women, physically challenged and other social groups."

Where does that lead us to? 2007 is still far away but the indicators are such that if we do not put our act together, overcome our narrow personal interests and concentrate on the common good of Plateau State, the story will not be a good one to tell.

I see a situation of social disorder arising out of political confusion.

I see us consuming ourselves in inter-and intra-partisan political crises.

I see Plateau State retrogressing in terms of social development instead of taking the lead among the States of the Federation.

The feverish preparations for 2007 on the national and state levels are pointers that there is more than meets the eye.

I am no prophet of doom. If I speak so negatively, it is to urge us to avoid what will lead to instability.

I pray together with all men and women of good will for peace and progress in Plateau State and in Nigeria. We must pray fervently against the ill-motivated designs of individuals or groups who wish to plunge Plateau State into crisis. We should remember that prayers work, and work powerfully too. Selfish politicians, beware! Those in or out of Government who only pursue personal interests instead of the common good of Plateau State, beware! Greedy and corrupt people, beware!

Your Majesty, I am sorry to bother you with my litany of agonizing concerns. Having spoken to you I feel more at ease, knowing that you, the Government, our elders, politicians and, indeed, all of us concerned citizens of Plateau State will do only those things that are just, right and fair so that peace may flow like a river in Plateau State and beyond.

Let me conclude by wishing you a spirit-filled Christmas and a New Year of peace and multiple blessings.

Thank you for your kind attention.

STAKEHOLDERS IN PLATEAU PEACE PROJECT
A meeting with some political, government, traditional and opinion leaders, at the Pastoral Centre, Jos, January 27, 2006

I prefer to address you as brothers and sisters.

I wish to thank you immensely for coming to this gathering requested by me. As indicated in the invitation, I was eager to kill two birds with one stone. The first invitation was to the presentation of my booklet **The Dialogue of Life: An Urgent Necessity for Nigerian Muslims and Christians.** I strongly believe that genuine dialogue which goes beyond mere lip-service on the part of the adherents of the Islamic and the Christian religions will go a long way in healing the wounds of our nation and in providing the ingredients for not only spiritual but also social, economic and political progress. This second invitation is to enable us to reflect together on some issues of social concern in Plateau State. You and I want to see the progress, security and unity of the Plateau people. Plateau State is blessed with very favourable climatic conditions, a highly enlightened and friendly people and very great potential. Those who visit Plateau State always want to come again and again. Some even opt to settle here permanently. Little wonder that the state has earned the title, "Home of peace and tourism". This peace is what we all are eager to cherish, sustain and propagate. We are blessed with a variety of cultural and ethnic groups, vibrant Christian, Islamic and African traditional religious faiths. With government and political structures in place, our people expect the best from the practice of democracy. Nigerians are unanimous in the belief and conviction that military rule was an abnormality and therefore undesirable; democracy is the way forward. Having chosen the democratic option, we need to be guided by the ethics of democratic governance. We are to ensure that the end result of our democratic practice is the improvement of the life of our people, lifting them from poverty to economic well-being, from poor health conditions to healthy living, from ignorance to enlightenment and from division to unity.

I am privileged to travel to different parts of Plateau State on a regular basis, in the course of my pastoral duties. I usually spend many weekends with the people, encouraging them in their religious practice and also finding time to interact with those especially at the grassroots. My frequent encounters with the people give me an idea of what they enjoy and also what they suffer in terms of social amenities. I am able to appreciate the cultural diversity and richness of this great State. I always hear the people say what they consider to be their basic needs: good schools, good roads, available and affordable health care, good and early supply of fertilizer/tractors, good drinking water, security, distributive justice, etc. If our political, traditional and religious leaders collaborate well, the people's desire for social progress, economic viability and political harmony will certainly be a reality. If leaders from the National Assembly, the Presidency, the States and the Local Governments also collaborate sincerely, the results will be positive development and change. Failure on their part to provide what is now popularly tagged the "dividends of democracy" can only result in social tension and general discontent. The need to work for and ensure peace and social order is of supreme importance.

We the spiritual leaders assure you, the political, traditional, opinion leaders and security agents, of our support. Religious leaders cannot be religious leaders and at the same time be partisan politicians. Our duty is to provide a clear moral roadmap or guide. We should not allow ourselves to be dragged into political controversies or indeed be used for selfish political motives. The society needs healthy politicking: politics without hatred, politics without revenge and politics without bitterness. We need a political class that aspires to serve the common people. Even if politicians belong to different political parties or the same party, they must have unity of purpose and a focused strategy that ensures that politics is played with dignity, respect and decency. Politicians will always have differing political opinions and interests, but these opinions and interests should be subordinated to what is good for the people they claim they are in politics to serve. Once the political actors start throwing verbal missiles at each other, or try to make political opponents as uncomfortable as possible, we are no longer talking of principled politics aimed at serving humanity. Once the print or electronic media become the theatre of crude, uncomplimentary and hostile political allegations and confrontations, we are in for unhealthy political rivalry which leads to fear, tension and insecurity. When energy is dissipated in political wrangling, the poor people, the supposed-to-be beneficiaries of the so-called "dividends of democracy", are the first casualties. It is true that when the elephants fight, it is the grass that suffers.

It is my pastoral responsibility to pray for those in leadership at the local, state or national levels. It is also my pastoral and prophetic responsibility to point out what is objectively considered to be right or wrong. I hear the voice of some of our people crying in the wilderness of poverty, insecurity, disease and hunger. I hear cries from the people that some of our politicians are busy fighting one another instead of delivering the dividends of democracy. People cry out that some of our politicians are involved in the struggle for political supremacy or the political survival of the fittest and have forgotten their covenant with the people, namely, to make life better. It is said that Plateau State has been politically polarized and people are identified as either belonging to one group or the other. It is claimed that some indigenes of Plateau State do not feel safe in the home of their birth because of political differences. Even religious leaders who are supposed to be objective arbitrators are said to have used their spiritual positions of vintage in a mundane manner in the on-going political game.

How long can we wallow in political confusion, suspicion, anxiety and tension? If we continue in this way we can only get the crumbs instead of the real benefits of democracy.

Today we assemble here as brothers and sisters. Let us ask ourselves mind-probing questions. Do we really have the interest of the economic and political advancement of Plateau State at heart? What are some politicians fighting for? Where are the elders who should help the process of healing and reconciliation? Are we fighting for the good of the people or for our individual advantages? What sacrifices are we all prepared to make if we claim we have the interest of Plateau State and her people at heart? What do we benefit from character assassination, bitterness, and washing our dirty linen in public, i.e. in the media? Ask yourself: how is it that, either by omission or commission, you are responsible for the political tension in Plateau State? (*Laifi tudu ne sai ka hau naka kafin ka ga na wani*, you need to climb the heap of your faults in order to notice your neighbour's). As the 2007 election year approaches, what are your strategies as politicians? Is it following due political process, or is it a matter of engaging in character assassination, instigating violence, manipulating or rigging one's way to victory?

The future of our children is at stake. If the political leaders and the elders do not strive to narrow the communication gap and declare a cessation of political hostility, I am afraid we shall infect the younger ones with the virus of political disorder, thus creating a very bleak future. We need to remember that in about thirty years' time many of us here will either be too weak or too old. The Bible says, "… when you were young, you used to get ready and go anywhere you wanted to; but when you are old, you will stretch out your hands and someone else will bind you and take you where you don't want to go" (Jn 21:18). If mere political power or economic gains are our motivating factors let us remember what the holy books say, "Vanity of vanity, all is vanity ". We should be asking ourselves what we can do for Plateau State, rather than what we hope to get from Plateau State only for our personal economic or political benefits. I call on all of us, especially the politicians, to bury the hatchet once and for all. Somebody says he can bury the hatchet all right but he will always mark the spot. Let us bury the hatchet and not worry about marking the spot where it is buried because we shall not need it again. We need to give each other the right hand of fellowship, transcending our ethnic, religious and political differences so that in our old age we can say that we are handing over to the younger generation a culture of peace, dialogue, progress and the common good and not a culture of confrontation and violence.

Thank you for you kind attention. I now invite us all to a fraternal dialogue and interaction.

DIALOGUE OF LIFE: AN URGENT NECESSITY FOR NIGERIAN MUSLIMS AND CHRISTIANS

The Presentation of A Booklet, "Dialogue of Life: An Urgent Necessity for Nigerian Muslims and Christians", Jos, January 27, 2006

It is my singular privilege and honour to welcome you and to acknowledge your personal attendance at this ceremony of the presentation of my booklet entitled **Dialogue of Life: An Urgent Necessity for Nigerian Muslims and Christians.** It is my humble effort to encourage greater harmony and peace between the adherents of the Christian and Islamic religions in Nigeria. I was very conscious of your time constraints and very busy schedules, but since the urge to invite you was very strong, and knowing that the issue of religious harmony is dear to your heart, I just had to write to invite you. As traditional, political, religious and opinion leaders, we know that where peace and harmony are lacking due to tension generated by religious or indeed ethnic or political reasons, the conducive atmosphere needed for progress will be lacking. I am confident in asserting that you do not wish to see a situation where religion and politics are used to cause anarchy or social disorder. Religion is for peace. Politics is for social progress and good governance. This must be kept constantly in mind so that the conduct and special engagements of Christians and Muslims will testify that we are all promoters of inter-religious, inter-ethnic and political harmony. Parents and elders must talk to their children and inculcate in them the strong desire for peaceful coexistence so that they do not take violent measures at the slightest provocation. Dialogue is more civilized than the resort to violent behaviour in the name of defending one's religion.

The bloodshed witnessed in different parts of our country in the name of religious struggle is a sin before God. Neither Islam nor Christianity encourages killing in the name of God. We always blame the devil - poor devil - when we engage ourselves in mindless and needless crises. If the devil is the culprit, the engineer tele-guiding these unfortunate conflicts, I wish to call on Nigerians to wage a decisive war against this monster called the devil; to confront, challenge, attack, cripple, frustrate and disorganize him/her with our spiritual weapons to render his/her diabolic strategies impotent.

The word 'dialogue' comes from the Greek word *dialogos* which means conversation, a discussion or exchange of ideas and opinions, especially between two groups, with a view to resolving conflict or achieving agreement. 'Monologue' on the other hand is used derogatorily for any long uninterrupted piece of speech, by one person, especially a tedious or opinionated speech which prevents conversation. Perhaps we of the different religious traditions have been engaging largely in a monologue, where each group extols the beauty, the values of its religion, and proffers convincing arguments why its religion is the best. We often lack the humility to accept the positive elements of the others' religion or even to commend some good initiative of theirs. We are so inward-looking that we refuse to be open to new ideas or methods, believing that we can learn nothing from each other. Condemnation of each other, hatred, suspicion and the competitive spirit to outdo or eliminate each other seem to characterize our relationship. This attitude tends to replicate itself in the political and ethnic spheres. We move in parallel lines, with very little hope of convergence.

In my booklet, I advocate a dialogue of life which means a "cross fertilization" of our lives, an interaction in concrete daily life in a genuine and sincere manner between Christians and Muslims, a dialogue which opens us to accept each other and to share together at a deeper level. Muslims must open their hearts to Christians and Christians must open their hearts to Muslims in sincere love. I can associate with a Muslim freely and share intimately, but that does not make me a Muslim. Likewise, a Muslim can fraternize freely with Christians and still go back to his or her religious practices and traditions. That we worship differently does not mean we should be at each others' throats or create an atmosphere of distrust and suspicion around us. Genuine dialogue among us can improve politics, governance, family life and community spirit. The sharp dichotomy between Christians and Muslims is regrettable. The unhealthy polarization which pitches Muslims and Christians against one another is retrogressive. Some countries even within the West African sub-region with sizeable Muslim and Christian populations behave differently from the way we do in Nigeria. They hardly fight and destroy lives and property in the name of religion. There is a respectful coexistence. Why must ours be different? Why do we take up arms just because somebody says something about our religion that we do not like? We must not kill or destroy people's means of livelihood in the name of showing zeal for our religion. It is necessary for us preachers to watch our utterances so that we do not play on people's religious sentiments to ignite violence. Religion should help us become holier human beings, not violent people. Religious and traditional leaders must have the courage to tell the youths to "stop it" when a religious crisis or any other crisis begins. Youths in Nigeria generally listen to their elders. Indoctrinating our children to hate others because of their religious identity is un-Christian and un-Islamic. Let us open our hearts to each other. When we meet in the privacy of our churches and mosques, what we pray for and discuss should be how to become holier in the sight of God so that we can make it to heaven. Social issues that threaten peaceful coexistence are to be looked at and ways to stop them explored.

Once we urge ourselves to holiness, corruption and many other social vices will be drastically reduced. If a Christian or Muslim functionary is given money to provide good drinking water, build a clinic, renovate a school, he or she needs to be honest and transparent in the use of such funds. Let us use religion to wipe away social vices, not use it as a weapon against the other person considered to be an enemy simply because he or she chooses to worship differently. We need to learn to attend each other's social functions. The customary mutual exchange of greetings and gifts which some Muslims and Christians practise at Sallah and Christmas is to be commended and recommended. During the recent Sallah celebration, I called some of my Muslim friends to wish them well, among whom were the Grand Khadi of Plateau

State, the Deputy Chairman of Jama'atu Nasril Islam (JNI), and the Galadima of Wase. I received goodwill greetings from a Fulani Muslim in Kaduna who wanted to share the joy of Sallah with me. The Emir of Wase, Dr Haruna Abdullahi, who was on the Islamic pilgrimage, called from Medina to wish me well and to assure me of his prayers. This is a dialogue of life.

That I am a Christian and you are a Muslim is an accident of history that has God's permission and providential supervision. If I had been born in a predominantly Muslim area, perhaps I would have been an Imam or Sheik. If the Emir had been born in a Christian-dominated area, who knows, today he would have been either a bishop or a cardinal. God knows better why he allowed us to be who we are and to be placed in the geographical territory we come from. He requires us to practise our faith in love and to be sensitive to each others' needs. Never in the name of God should we spill a neighbour's blood. Religion, i.e. true religion, binds us together. We are to use it positively to improve humanity. Let us each light a candle of peaceful coexistence, because we are all God's children made in his own image and likeness. Thank you for joining me here today and for demonstrating your love for harmony and peace among Christians and Muslims in Nigeria. God bless us and bless Nigeria.

THE CHALLENGES OF POLITICAL AND RELIGIOUS CONFLICTS TO THE CHURCH IN PLATEAU STATE

A Keynote Address at the 8th General Assembly of the Catholic Archdiocese of Jos, August 17, 2010.

With deep gratitude to God we gather for our 8th Annual General Assembly with the theme: "The Challenges of Political and

Religious Conflicts to the Church in Plateau State." You may recall that the theme of our last Assembly was: "The Church in Africa in Service of Reconciliation, Justice and Peace". At the last assembly we dwelt on the prophetic role of the Church in promoting the cardinal issues of justice and peace in society and being in the vanguard of reconciliation. Our theme for this year was inspired by the incessant crises faced by our dear State since 2001. These have polarized people along religious and ethnic lines, bred social discontent and dented the image of a State that was famed for its very peaceful disposition. We must do all in our power, with God helping, to restore the glory of Plateau State and to detoxicate it by removing its abhorrent association with violence. Politics and religion are gifts from God. While politics must create a harmonious social order through good governance, the maintenance of law and order and the protection of the common good, religion seeks internal spiritual purification and transformation. It directs our attention to issues of righteousness, social cohesion and good inter-personal relationships. These are two gifts which, if used well, will foster comprehensive development. The misuse of these gifts creates a situation of chaos. There is no doubt that these gifts have been misused for selfish reasons, as a result of which violence became inevitable. A culture of political and religious intolerance is being developed to the extent that rather than using politics and religion for social and spiritual development, we are turning them into weapons of mutual destruction.

During this gathering, we hope to find veritable ways of promoting all that is good, noble and patriotic and contributes to healthy social growth and peaceful coexistence. As members of the Church which has Christ the Prince of Peace as its foundation, we must seek to reverse the negative and dangerous trend that has brought us to the present situation. No doubt during the crisis sanity took leave of absence, and what followed was irrational actions dictated by intolerance.

As is the practice during this Assembly, we shall pray, work, interact and listen to God speaking to us just as we speak and listen to one another. Talks will be delivered by persons who are professionals in their fields. As usual, our different Commissions will present their annual reports, providing us with a panoramic view of their activities and initiatives in the past year, thus allowing us to ask questions and make an input where necessary. There will be interactive sessions and group discussions with a view to helping us to measure the spiritual, pastoral, political, ethnic and social temperature in order to foster peace and harmony in our society.

Our nation is turning fifty in October. It will be a jubilee of grace celebrated by Nigerians to thank God for keeping us together as a nation, even when sometimes our actions have brought us dangerously to the brink of collapse. Blessed with immense human and natural resources, and well-positioned for positive growth, we prefer to squander our opportunities by always emphasizing what divides us rather than what unites us, thus retarding our social development. While we have happily (I hope) done away with the monster of military rule, we are still panting in the throes of democratic governance. Our democracy is yet to bring the much-needed relief from hunger, insecurity, illiteracy, and unemployment, and the problematic issues of health and housing. While a few wallow in unbelievable wealth, many go to and wake up from bed deprived of the joy of the basic things of life. The cost of Nigerian democracy is so high that a lot of resources are spent on elected or appointed senior government officials who enjoy mouth-watering pay while the common workers can hardly make both ends meet. Our population continues to grow, yet there is no corresponding improvement in our social infrastructure. Rural and urban dwellers can only hope to "manage life". The rich mineral deposits and agricultural potentials are neglected even as the oil revenue is a great distraction to us. There is a struggle for the soul of Nigeria either by Northerners, Southerners, Westerners or Easterners. Everyone is crying aloud of marginalization, and this boils over in one form of violence or the other. If it is not the Niger-Delta youth militants fighting against underdevelopment, environmental degradation and the unfair distribution of the oil wealth, it is the Movement for the Actualization of the Sovereign State of Biafra (MASSOB) claiming political marginalization, or the Oodua People's Congress (OPC) also alleging marginalization, or more recently the fundamentalist activities of Boko Haram with destructive social consequences. The contentious issue of whether our President should come from the North or the South is a symptom of the absence of a national spirit. Energy is concentrated on narrow political, ethnic or religious interests rather than the common good. Are we surprised that we continue to wallow in one crisis after another?

The numerous conflicts since the 1980s said to be of a religious nature are a sign that not all is well. We are said to be a religious nation but we must ask whether our religiosity is limited to the building of expansive places of worship in strategic positions and wearing flamboyant religious dress, or is about the transformation of the heart. Obviously our religiosity betrays mere externalism, or else why do we go about our religious activities with such intolerance and insensitivity? Why is religious pluralism an obstacle to national growth and peaceful social relationships? We continue to multiply fanciful religious titles and claim visionary, healing and prophetic gifts, and yet our nation witnesses vicious hostility between ethnic, political and religious groups, with the news of unbridled corruption, kidnapping, women trafficking and youth hooliganism capturing newspaper headlines. All these desecrate the spiritual space in our land.

The January 2010 crisis witnessed in Jos, whose effects are still lingering, has been diagnosed by many as a religious crisis. I have consistently argued at different fora that the crisis cannot be simply said to be a religious war. I maintain that the underlying causes of this crisis are many, but the religious element has been unduly emphasized to the extent that the other factors tend to be swept under the carpet. While many have reduced the crisis to simply Muslims fighting Christians or Christians fighting Muslims, many have tried to discern the causes as political, ethnic, and economic, as youth unemployment and land matters. During an interview with the CNN in the USA, the then Acting President

Goodluck Jonathan was asked: "What about Jos, where we just saw an explosion of violence between Muslims and Christians? What can you do about that? The then Acting President responded, "No, no, no. It's not a problem between Muslims and Christians. That is quite wrong actually...." (cf. *Saturday Sun*, April 17, 2010, p.44). It was declared on the floor of the Senate that the problem of Jos was not caused by religion. Some prominent sons and daughters of Plateau State also agree that religion is not the only cause. Honourable Bitrus Kaze, a Member of the House of Representatives representing Jos South/East Federal Constituency said in an interview that: "the root cause of Jos crisis has always been on who owns the land and not on religion, politics or ethnicity...." (cf. *Daily Sun*, Tuesday, March 2, 2010, p. 22). Traditional leaders from Nasarawa, Benue, Taraba and Plateau States met and unanimously agreed that 'the root cause of the disturbances was politics and not religion" (cf. *The Guardian*, Saturday, February 13 2010, p. 49).

At a meeting in the Aso Villa President Goodluck Jonathan (then Vice President) called many elders and stakeholders from Plateau State and asked why violence continued to erupt in Plateau State. Those who spoke did so frankly. The reasons adduced were many, ranging from the indigene/settler issue, land matters, perceived injustice, the quest for political domination, youth unemployment, to a superiority complex. Hardly anyone said that religion was the major cause of the conflicts. When the President allowed me to speak, I observed that as regards the cause of the crisis, "Today religion has been discharged but not acquitted". I stressed that the causes of the crisis are multidimensional, and must be found and comprehensively addressed rather than being narrowed down to religion alone, which allows those unattended social/political issues to fester and boil over each time. To limit the crisis to religion is either a strategy to avoid social/political responsibility, or the desire to attract sympathy and even financial support from fellow religious bigots.

The crisis has generated so much distrust that it will take a lot of work to rebuild Muslim-Christian trust and relationship. The lack of clear understanding of the origin of the crisis has generated problems even among Christians. While some see nothing in the crisis other than the attempt by Muslims to encroach on the sacred space of what is considered to be a very Christian State, others think that the root causes of the crisis are social/political, and that therefore political solutions must be found. The gains we have made in Muslim-Christian dialogue have suffered a great setback. Any attempt to initiate a meeting or dialogue between Muslims and Christians is viewed with suspicion and seen as a weakness or a compromise of one's religious integrity. Surprisingly, in the wake of the crisis, many NGOs were in the forefront of the struggle to re-establish peace. While some religious preachers spat fire and preached so as to inflame religious passion, I was pleasantly surprised to notice, at a recent religious gathering, the representatives of the Police and the State Security Services (SSS) urging peaceful coexistence and mutual acceptance. While some religious leaders are advocating a militant approach to the crisis, many non-religious organizations are working for peace and talking about peace. What an irony! It is heartening to note that even in the midst of all this, groups interested in dialogue and interreligious harmony continue to work. The Emir of Wase, Alhaji Dr. Haruna Abdullahi and I have not relented in our efforts at bridge-building between Christians and Muslims, even though some people want us to stop. Such groups as the Damietta Peace Initiative being facilitated in Jos by the FMDM Sisters, the Centre for Conflict Management and Peace Studies of the University of Jos headed by Prof. Shedrach Best, the Institute of Governance and Social Research under its president, Prof.Isawa Elaigwu, the Women of Faith Network (both Muslim and Christian women) under the umbrella of World Religions for Peace, Young Ambassadors for Peace, the Dynamic Women and Youth Interfaith Association, the Plateau Partnership for Reconciliation, Peace and Development, and of course our Archdiocesan Justice, Peace, Development and Caritas Commission, have been actively engaged in efforts to break barriers in order to restore what was once a beautiful spirit of coexistence between Muslims and

Christians in Plateau State. The message of love must override the message of fire-for-fire. The culture of life must overthrow the culture of death and the spirit of violence must be eliminated by the culture of dialogue.

The forthcoming 2011 elections give us reasons to worry. There are already feverish preparations and one can say paranoid political calculations. We hope all these will translate into peaceful political developments. There are however signals that the politics of do-or-die is set to continue. The heightened controversy about zoning is unnecessary. Zoning or no zoning, all we want is a good leader who will promote peace and social harmony. We as a Church must be careful so that we do not add tension to the already delicate political atmosphere. We must use the sacred pulpits to build the faith of the people rather than incite them to political hatred and violence. Just as we must condemn politicians who use the youths to cause confusion, we must also ensure that our churches and mosques, pastors and imams are not influenced by selfish politicians to cause tension and instability. We must contribute our quota towards good elections, by enlightening and mobilizing our people to register and vote, urging the Independent National Electoral Commission (INEC) and the relevant security agents to ensure a free, fair and credible election in which everybody's vote will count. We must pray for the success of the elections. Beyond this, we should allow the politicians to do what they are experts at, namely, politicking, but hoping they will to do so in the fear of God and in love of our people. Denominational antagonism caused by politicians who want to appeal to denominational sentiments may surface. Let me say that from now on, one politician or another is likely to pay a visit to my office asking for prayers or initiate a private conversation with me, but will announce to others that he has won over the Archbishop who is supporting his political ambition. I urge all Catholics to be careful, to be wise and discerning. Catholic Bishops, priests and religious do not dabble in partisan politics. We implore our politicians to avoid mischievous political calculations and utterances that will cause bad blood.

I wish to conclude by calling on the adherents of Christianity and Islam in Plateau State to stop seeing each other as enemies and tearing one another apart in the name of religious and political differences. The Lord is ready to spread peace and prosperity over Jos and indeed Plateau State (cf. Isaiah 66: 10-14), but we must repent, forgive and overcome evil with good. We must have realized that the crisis has done no person and no community any good. It has rather caused pain, tension and losses. All crises in whatever name must stop. I challenge this Assembly to come up with a "Prayer for Political, Ethnic and Religious Peace in Plateau State". This will be said in churches and during family prayers. May the weeks, months and years ahead bring positive social and political change and peace in our land. I wish us very fruitful deliberations. Welcome to our 8th General Assembly, which is now declared open.

God bless.

JANUARY 17, 2010 JOS CRISIS:
IS RELIGION THE CAUSE?

Message to the Solomon Lar-led Presidential Advisory Committee on Peace and Reconciliation in Plateau State

WRONG NOMENCLATURE

The real cause or identity of the crisis of 17 January 2010 remains hidden. Many choose to call it a religious crisis, meaning a crisis between Muslims and Christians. I have consistently maintained that the real causes of the crisis are multidimensional and therefore no single factor can be said to be the isolated cause. The crisis was triggered by the interplay of political, ethnic, socio-economic and cultural factors, and like previous crises it took on a religious dimension. Certain conflicts may appear religious but may after all be a façade for pursuing narrow political, ethnic or economic objectives.

BEYOND RELIGION

There is a need to go beyond the surface, or transcend the so-called religious causes, in order to dig out the underlying nagging and festering issues; for if we do not identify them, we shall continue to witness a circle of violence and needless destruction of life and property, which God forbid. The convenient manner in which we tend to hang everything on religion and blame all the violence on religion smacks of escapism. While religion cannot be excluded as a contributory factor to the crises we have so far witnessed, the fact of the matter is that there is a struggle for territorial control, political power, ethnic identity and relevance. These are issues which go beyond religion and which we religious leaders cannot claim to have the capacity to tackle.

THE CASE OF NORTHERN IRELAND

Those familiar with the history of Northern Ireland will know that, while its conflict was largely seen to be a religious war between Protestants and Catholics, the facts on the ground show that the troubles began when the British granted independence to twenty-six of the thirty-two counties in 1920 and partitioned the island, dividing the Irish people and imposing a British identity on the North. The political leaders exploited and discriminated against the Irish minority, denying them basic rights. In 1998, after thirty years of war and several thousand deaths, voters accepted the Good Friday Peace Agreement. The agreement called for a cease-fire and weapons decommissioning, and established a power-sharing government. Under the agreement, Ireland abandoned its territorial claim to the six Northern counties, while England agreed that Northern Ireland citizens would have the right of self-determination. It also established an elected Assembly. Other provisions set up an all-Ireland North-South body, enshrined human rights, equality, and justice and promoted the Irish language and culture. What appeared for a long time to be a "religious war" was settled on the altar of politics!

SOME FACTORS RESPONSIBLE FOR JOS CRISES

At the meeting of Plateau State stakeholders with Dr. Goodluck Jonathan (then Vice-President, now Acting President of Nigeria) at the Aso Rock Villa on 1st February 2010, speeches were made that were frank, honest and passionate and revealed the true underlying causes of the crises in the State. Some of the issues that came up were: the motive behind the creation of Jos North Local Government, indigeneship certificates, the creation of electoral wards, indigenes versus settlers, the superiority complex of this or that group, expansionist tactics, non-integration, bad governance, the policy of exclusion, the denial of rights, the Federal Government not liking Plateau people, media bias, failure to respect host communities, the non-pursuit of perpetrators of violence, the partisanship of security officials, etc.

From all this, one can see how issues other than religion are the real factors behind the crises. They can be reduced to: land matters; political power; and ethnic interests. These are often clothed in a religious garb because Nigerians love and respect religion and religion is a convenient tool for all purposes. The burning of places of worship at the slightest provocation, and sometimes with no provocation at all, is an expression of social discontent directed where it is believed it will hurt the most.

REPERCUSSIONS
It should be noted that each time there is a crisis and we call it a religious crisis, it causes more damage to life and property. Religion is a very sensitive issue. This explains why in the last national census religion was excluded from the questionnaire. When we appeal to religious sentiments, many of our people easily become victims of manipulation. They easily lose the power of reasoning and can do anything in the name of protecting or defending their religion. The more we focus on our crisis as a religious one, the more we shall prolong the problem. Once a crisis is said to be religious, we arouse the sentiment of outsiders (outside the State and even the country) who feel they must identify with their co-religionists to fight for their faith. They feel they have to express religious solidarity. Little wonder that even those in leadership positions, business, academia, security, and the media (national and international) begin to see the issues not from an objective point of view but through the lens of religion and efforts are made to support their co-religionists, thus attracting attention to the crisis and prolonging the violence. If we do not call the crises by their names but insist on saying they are all about religion, Jos will become a market for religious zealots who will import dangerous ideologies and embark on negative propaganda

that will continue to create one crisis after another. It is better that we identify this crisis with its name and tackle it. The quest for religious dominance and the struggle for numerical growth are no doubt among the causes, but they are not the exclusive factors. There must be a multidimensional approach to a multidimensional problem.

ENSURING IT DOES NOT HAPPEN AGAIN
As a religious leader and Chairman of the Plateau State CAN, I have never planned or encouraged Christians to fight in the name of religion. If Christians and Muslims were fighting each other on account of religious values or doctrines one could say they were motivated by religious issues; but as soon as people are discontented with issues that have nothing to do with religion the first places they attack are places of worship, just to give the impression that it is a religious conflict. I am sure that if no places of worship were destroyed, it would be hard to sell the idea that a religious war was going on in Plateau State.

We should focus on the real issues such as proactive security measures, rather than adopting the fire brigade approach. We should ensure that flashpoints are properly monitored, the youths are well tutored at home and enjoy social security from government as well as being meaningfully engaged, the elders and political leaders engage in constant dialogue (rather than personality clashes), and victims of crises are assisted so that they do not have to abandon their homes or business premises; if not, we shall have a polarized city, with Muslims living in and controlling certain parts and Christians living in and controlling some other parts, which is retrogressive and anti-social.

Some religious leaders and preachers, we must admit, are happy fanning the embers of religious hatred and encouraging followers to fight in defence of their faith. This presupposes that the God they serve is too weak to fight his cause. We are in danger of passing on our religious traditions that are characterized by hate messages, negative propaganda, mutual suspicion and bitter opposition to the other person who holds different religious views and beliefs. Muslims fighting Christians or Christians fighting Muslims will never solve our social problems. It is only through concerted efforts and using the values of our two religions that we can bring peace, prosperity and progress to our State and nation. The recurring crises are an expression of something that is wrong in the society. Religion is being used as a tool for individual or collective bargaining. The solution, however, lies in political, ethnic and religious accommodation rather than the exploitative use of religion.

Archbishop Kaigama with former Plateau State Commissioner of Police, Mr. Gregory Anyating, during a courtesy call by the latter

Talking peace

Section Three
THE CRISES:
COUNTING OUR LOSSES

IN THE BEGINNING…. SEPTEMBER 7, 2001 JOS CRISIS

A perspective of the Archbishop released September 13, 2001

Plateau State, the "home of peace and tourism" was thrown into great confusion on Friday 7th September, 2001 as the city of Jos became a battle ground between Muslims and Christians. This totally unexpected confrontation was a very rude interruption of the peace and harmony enjoyed by the people on the "Plateau of tranquillity" Many mosques, churches, vehicles, houses, shops, etc, belonging to both Muslims and Christians went up in flames as Christian and Muslim youth engaged in senseless and wanton destruction of lives and property. Corpses of human beings and the remains of burnt vehicles littered the streets – all in the name of religion. Could this be religion? It cannot be religion. Religion binds, but when Muslims and Christians engage in wanton destruction such as this the underlying reasons are certainly far from religious. They could be politics or ethnicity coated with religious sentiments. Any civilized religion teaches its adherents the sacredness of life and respect for others and their property.

Friday September 7 started on a bright note. Consultors of the Archdiocese of Jos had assembled in my office to discuss crucial Archdiocesan matters, among which was the need for the whole Archdiocese to take up a special collection for the victims of ethnic and religious conflicts in Benue, Nasarawa and Bauchi states. Rising at about 2.00pm, we looked forward to the priestly ordination of five deacons the next day, Saturday, September 8. At about 4.00 pm after I gave the deacons my message before their ordination and was preparing to go to the Cathedral with them for a rehearsal, the Cathedral Administrator, Fr. David Ajang, rang to inform me that it was not safe to move outside. He said alarm was being raised that some "Muslim youths"[15] were advancing to some strategic Christian churches and establishments with sticks, knives, spears, cutlasses, guns, etc. The "Christian youths" soon rallied around to defend the parish houses and churches in the Jos metropolis. Throughout Friday evening the youths stood in stout defence of the churches. What we thought was a minor skirmish was developing into a full-blown conflict. I had telephoned the Deputy Governor, who was Acting Governor as the State Governor had gone on a two-week break. I also telephoned the General Officer Commanding (G.O.C.) of the 3rd Armoured Brigade. The Deputy Governor and the G.O.C. are both Catholics. The Deputy Governor promised me and the parishes some armed policemen. The G.O.C. said there was no cause for alarm, as soldiers were being sent out to mount guard in strategic places. I repeatedly expressed concern about the safety of the Cathedral, the Seminary, the Pastoral Centre, the O.L.A. Hospital, convents and schools. By Saturday morning the tension was very palpable. Some churches and mosques were burnt. It is hard to identify the actual cause of this crisis. No official explanation has been given.

---

[15] The term "Muslim" or "Christian" youth is used in a very loose sense, as there is no clearly established proof that those mentioned as "Christian" or "Muslim" youths are genuine representatives of their respective religions. Since these two religions are the predominant religions in Plateau State and indeed Nigeria it is for this reason that people often easily divide groups or activities into Christian or Muslim.

But it is being said that the crisis originated as a result of the appointment of a non-Plateau Muslim as head of the Poverty Eradication Programme in Plateau State, a thing some Plateau State indigenes believe is an insult to the majority of well-qualified Plateau State Christians.

The priestly ordination of five deacons was to be at 10 am at the Cathedral. We allowed preparations to go ahead since we believed that the minor conflict would soon be over. The people from parishes had started arriving and some priests were already at the Pastoral Centre when we had to announce a cancellation of the ordination as it was no longer safe to venture out. Children and women including Muslims started to troop to the Pastoral Centre to take refuge as they had done the night before. War was here. Jos was in a state of pandemonium. My telephones rang ceaselessly as people wanted to know if all was okay and if the priestly ordination would still go on. Others, among whom were sisters, were asking for protection. I was literally on the phone every minute either receiving or making calls. Stories - real or imaginary were now spreading like wildfire. A caller wanted to know if it was true that a priest had been killed and "the Cathedral burnt". It was difficult to ascertain this at first but eventually we found out that it was not true. However, in only a matter of time some Christian youths were injured, and Fr. Ajang the Cathedral administrator had to rush them to hospital. The Assistant Cathedral Administrator, Fr. Anthony Kangyep, in a phone call told me that big trouble was coming.

He kept me informed of developments, but at a certain point no call came from him and no one answered my calls to him. I knew something was wrong. It was at that time that it was alleged that some Muslim youths were advancing. The Christian youths ran for their life along with some visiting priests who had come for the ordination. The six policemen on duty were said to have run also. The Cathedral parish house was set ablaze along with four cars. When the Christian youths saw the flames they braved a return to the Cathedral premises. At this time the Christian youths were able to put out the fire that had started burning the right side, the sacristy, of the Cathedral. The altar boys' clothes and the sacristy floor carpets were burnt, and the ceiling was already on fire when the youths put it out. The house of a Catholic woman living opposite the Cathedral was completely burnt. Fortunately the woman had been able to earlier evacuate her over twenty dependents to safety.

The parish church in Angwan Rogo, situated in a predominantly Muslim area, was burnt. Other Protestant churches and houses were burnt too. The Christian youths set some mosques, Muslim houses and vehicles ablaze. The areas that suffered much fighting and burning of houses, mosques and churches were in the Nasarawa Gwom, Ali Kazaure, Sarkin Mangu, Bauchi Road, and University areas. Several attempts were made by some youths to burn the O.L.A. hospital. My house was in danger of being attacked by some youths. One of my houseboys noticed this development at the hilly back part of my house and alerted the youths who were in the Pastoral Centre. The youths soon took up position on the hill and in no time the other youths were driven away.

One may ask where were the security agents? On Friday night I telephoned the relevant police, military and civil authorities informing them of the impending danger. I was told that the situation was under control and that soon security agents would be made available to our churches and institutions. Throughout Friday night, apart from the policemen sent to the Cathedral, no security agent came to any of our other establishments. I made repeated telephone calls to both the Acting Governor and the G.O.C. The Cathedral parish house was already burnt before they sent four soldiers to my house and four to the Cathedral. Apart from the Cathedral, which enjoyed protection from the six policemen (who on Saturday had to run in the face of advancing violent youths), none of our churches or institutions enjoyed any security presence, while we learnt that the main mosque in Jos (Masalacin Juma'a) enjoyed full military and police protection right from the beginning of the crisis. Was it a case of deliberate oversight or selective discrimination? My attempts on Saturday and Sunday to contact the Commissioner of Police, the Acting Governor and the G.O.C. proved abortive as either their lines were too busy or there was no one to answer the phone. It must be mentioned that Christian youths, among whom were Protestants and Catholics, did a lot to protect the property of the Catholic Church. They kept vigil at night and during the day remained very close in the vicinity. From the little food we had in the house, plus the eight rams donated to me during pastoral visits and the two cows slaughtered in preparation for the ordination, we could feed both the youths and the refugees who had taken shelter in the pastoral Centre and other centres. A Muslim family of six were among the people who had taken shelter and were fed for three days, before they asked to be reunited with their children in the Air Force barracks. Two priests conducted them to their families. The senseless destruction and killing continued on Sunday. Catholics who were brave enough to attend Sunday Mass in the Cathedral and in the Novitiate Chapel in Tudun Wada were attacked on their way to or from the churches. In most churches the youth maintained a strong presence. The Federal Government sent more soldiers down to Jos, which brought great relief. On Monday, people could be seen moving about on foot. As the situation was calming in the Jos area we heard that Bukuru, Kuru, Heipang, Pankshin had their own share of the crisis with consequent destruction of lives and property.

Throughout the period of the crisis my two telephone lines were working. I was like a telephone operator as every minute the phones kept ringing - messages from sympathizers or priests and sisters who needed one help or another. Telephone calls from the Nuncio, Archbishop Osbalado Padilla, and the Archbishop of Abuja, Most Rev. John Onaiyekan, were a moral booster to me. The Minister of State in the Ministry of Science and Technology, Mrs.Pauline Tallen, was very helpful as she called me again and again and then contacted the President, the Inspector-General of Police, and the G.O.C. to tell them how serious the problems were in Jos and the need to take firm action. Col. John Madaki, having been told by Archbishop Onaiyekan that I was trapped in my house with no food, asked a military officer to bring a few measures of rice and packets of spaghetti to me. This I donated to the cathedral priests since they had lost all their clothes, food, money, etc.

On Tuesday, the tension was much less. Many of the people trapped in the Pastoral Centre including priests, deacons and seminarians were able to leave. We all thought peace was gradually returning but unfortunately on Wednesday 12th in the morning gunshots were heard all over and once again people ran for cover and the Pastoral Centre was again full to capacity with children and women. Relief came from Abuja Archdiocese on Tuesday. I visited refugee camps at the Airforce base, police barracks, NDLEA Headquarters and parishes, to greet the refugees and distribute some food stuffs. On Wednesday food brought from Abuja was cooked by sisters and served to refugees in the Pastoral Centre and the police barracks. There were more people in the refugee centers on account of the happening on Wednesday morning. The Wednesday disturbance was said to have been caused by a group of people who went looting on Dilimi Street and the soldiers had to deal with them. This resulted in an exchange of gunshots. In the evening I got a phone call from the Governor, Joshua Dariye, asking me and other religious and opinion leaders to give a message of peace on both radio and Television. The Deputy Governor, Michael Botmang, came to my house at about 8 pm with the Commissioner of Information with a TV and radio crew, and we recorded my message appealing for peace (I had earlier done an interview for NTA). The Secretary to the State Government rang a few minutes later to thank me for the message.

Today, Thursday 13th, there is relative peace but it is the peace of the graveyard. There is a high degree of suspicion and mistrust between Muslims and Christians. Anything can still happen. But with the military presence, any ugly situation is likely to be brought under firm control.

There was writing on the wall that trouble was brewing but nobody gave it a serious thought.

There was no coordinated security network, which explains why big churches and institutions were not given police protection. This crisis could have been averted.

As the crisis was said to be a religious one it is surprising that very little security was provided for religious leaders.

Is it only when things have failed that religious leaders are summoned to meet, pray and appeal for peace? A meeting of elders and religious leaders was called for Wednesday 11th at 10 a.m. I was informed by a permanent Secretary only fifteen minutes to the time of meeting! Is it standard procedure?

Up to Wednesday, no government official asked the Catholic Church how they had been able to deal with the refugee situation, not to talk of making any relief provisions available. From the relief sent by the Federal Government the following was allocated to the Catholic Church on Thursday afternoon: ten blankets, ten mats, five bags of garri, three bags of guinea corn, three bags of rice and two bags of maize.

The great needs for the refugees and those who have lost houses and property are food, medicine, clothing, shelter, blankets, mats, cooking utensils, water, etc.

SHARING THE PAINS OF VICTIMS

A Homily at the Mass for Victims of the September 7 Jos Crisis and the Jos Main Market Fire Disaster held at Our Lady of Fatima Cathedral, Jos, March 16, 2002.

We in Plateau State have been confronted since September 2001 with two trying events: the first was the ethno-religious crisis which resulted in the wanton destruction of lives and property, displacing many people and robbing them of their means of livelihood. When we were almost putting the incident behind us and vowing that it should never happen again, another tragedy of great proportion took place: the ultra-modern Jos Main Market, the commercial centre and pride of Plateau State, considered to be one of the largest, finest and functional in Africa, was gutted by a mysterious fire. Many ordinary people depended on this market for buying and selling. This tragedy dispossessed them of their means of livelihood and plunged them into severe poverty.

Our Lord taught us in the "Lord's prayer" to pray for deliverance from evil. It is in this spirit that we turn to our God to implore him to heal our state and to ask him also to provide in his own way for those who are rendered homeless and jobless and to grant eternal peace to those who lost their lives during the events.

Despite the losses and set-backs our God is still a good God. He is our shepherd and by his grace we shall not want. Perhaps he wants to see how solid our faith or trust in him is by testing us on what prophet Isaiah calls the furnace of distress (cf.: Is.48:10).

Our God is a God of love. Some may ask, but why does he allow evil such as this to befall his children? Why would fundamentalists destroy the magnificent World Trade Centre in New York, leaving thousands dead? Why would the Lagos bomb blast claim so many lives? Why would promising young girls perish in the Bwalbong Secondary School fire disaster? Why would harmless 5 year olds have their hands and legs cut off in the war in Sierra Leone? Does God allow evil? Why did he not create a world so perfect that no evil could exist in it? Why? Why? Why? The answer to these cannot be found until we see God face to face after this life. Prophet Isaiah rightly says that we cannot comprehend the ways of God because his ways are not our ways and his thoughts are not our thoughts. The lesson we learn from the parable of the weeds is that good and bad exist together until at the end of time when the bad will be destroyed and good will triumph forever.

Is God responsible for evil in the world? No. Ezekiel 18:23 is clear that God does not take pleasure in the death of a wicked person, rather he prefers to see him renounce his wickedness and live. God created our first parents and wanted them to be happy forever. They disobeyed him by eating the forbidden fruit. Sin and evil entered the world as a result of their disobedience. God in his love gave human beings the gift of intellect and will - we have freedom to choose good or to choose evil. Freedom is however misunderstood by some today as a license to do what we want.

Many times when a tragedy occurs we say it is an "act of God". Yes, God is in charge of everything but he has also given us freedom to choose to do good or to choose to do evil. When we use our freedom wrongly we invite sin and evil upon ourselves. When a drunken driver knocks down and kills a boy we say it is an act of God. When the Ministry of Health does not pay nurses and doctors well and they go on strike and sick children and pregnant mothers die in their thousands we say it is an act of God. When a police man shoots at a driver at a roadblock and calls it an accidental discharge because the driver failed to produce his "particulars" we say it is an act of God. We tend to attribute to God those things that happen as a result of our carelessness or wrong use of our freedom. We do not want to take responsibility for our actions. It was not God who burnt the cathedral house here during the crisis! Many of the evils that happen to us are man-made and are preventable even though disasters such as earthquakes, floods, droughts are not our making. If for instance there is adequate security for people, with the police having good communication equipment, better weapons and transport, armed robbers or criminals cannot torment people. If there is enough water in the fire fighting vehicles, fire disasters can be greatly minimized or prevented. If a contractor building a school does not collude with government officials to inflate the contract and yet use inferior materials, the school building will not collapse on the children. If education is well funded at primary and secondary schools a period most important in the development of children, we will not be producing undisciplined and semi-illiterate children. If universities are duly treated as the fertile ground for training future leaders with a good study environment, with professors' and students' needs adequately met, there will be no cultism or indiscipline, immorality and violent behaviour among students. If youths are gainfully employed, they will not be idle and therefore there will be fewer crimes and violence. A lot of what happens to us human beings are as a result of wickedness, negligence, deliberate omission, insensitivity and not taking our duties or personal responsibilities seriously. I believe that if every person takes his or her duties seriously, honestly, and we play our part well, God will deliver us from the many evils that befall us. After all, it is said that heaven helps those who help themselves.

God's will is that all his children should be saved in Jesus Christ (1 Tim 2:4). He wishes us to be happy now and thereafter. Sometimes when evil befalls us some good can come from the evil. We therefore urge all those affected by the recent sad events to have greater faith and trust in God. Like it happened to Job, we pray the Lord to restore to them their fortunes a hundred fold. We should all do our parts in helping them to alleviate their suffering. We however warn any person, or groups of persons who may rejoice in the misfortune of the Plateau people or those who may directly or indirectly create confusion in Plateau State using religion, ethnic sentiments or politics to beware. God will soon lay bare their evil plans. They should repent and resolve to build rather than destroy. May the Lord deliver us from all evil, now and in the future. Amen.

2004 YELWA CRISIS: FEBRUARY 22 -24, 2004
An account of the crises in parts of Southern Plateau released in March, 2004.

The Parish Priest of Yelwa Parish, Fr. Paul Dajen briefed me on the 27 February 2004 on the recent crises that had engulfed the Yelwa- Yamini, Shimankar and Ajikamai areas of Lantang South and Shendam Local Government areas in Plateau State between the 22 and 24 February, 2004.

By his account, the crisis seems to have an economic motive.

It would appear that following the ethno-religious crises of 2001 in the same area, in which many were killed and property destroyed, the Fulanis who are cattle rearers, were aggrieved because they had lost many cattle, claiming that their cattle had been either stolen or killed. In an attempt to forestall the loss of their cattle to thieves and to revenge the past misfortunes they had suffered during the 2001 crises, the nomads were said to have invited a group of "mercenaries" some of whom were said to come from Chad, Niger and some parts of Taraba State and were quartered around Kukah.

The Parish Priest reported that the violence that ensued saw the destruction of houses in Yelwa with many killed, while many fled Yelwa, Shinmankar, Ajikamai and Yamini villages. In previous crises mosques were destroyed in Yelwa. In this crisis, churches within Yelwa were destroyed. The Catholic Parish Church which was destroyed during the 2001 crisis had just been re-roofed and renovated but it was destroyed again. The Parish Priest's residence which was not destroyed during the previous crisis was burnt. Hospitals, clinics and schools were also destroyed. Some women hospitalized in a clinic in Yelwa were said to have been burnt to death along with the clinic, and over 30 primary school pupils were said to have also been killed in their school. The Parish Chairman of St. Stephen's Catholic Parish, who was a Knight of St. Mulumba, was killed in the crisis, as well as the driver of the Parish Priest of Shendam who was in Yelwa to rescue his mother.

Tension was building up in the surrounding Shendam, Garkawa and Mikang towns. The Chief of Garkawa asked the parish priest, Fr. Dajen, who since 2001 had been living in Garkawa because of fear of attack in Yelwa, to come over to Jos to inform me the Archbishop so that I would put pressure on the Government to do something urgently. As soon as I was briefed by Fr Dajen I called the Speaker of the Plateau State House of Assembly, Mr. Simon Lalong, who comes from Ajikamai, one of the villages destroyed. I asked what they were doing as a Government and he told me that the Governor had visited the area the day before (Thursday 26th) and had secured approval to get soldiers involved in controlling the situation. He said there were enough policemen and soldiers to contain the situation, to make sure it would not spread from the Yelwa area. He told me that the Governor was leaving for Abuja (Friday 27th) to discuss with Mr. President about the crisis and to ask for helicopters to enable the security agents to track down the whereabouts and movements of the mercenary fighters in the bush. I also called the Deputy Governor Mr. Michael Botmang, who assured me that the situation was under control and, in fact, a meeting of the Inter-Religious Committee had been summoned in Jos to douse tension.

As of today (Friday 27th) the priests in that area are reported to be okay. Fr Paul Dajen has been advised by me to stay away from that area for now. The Parish Priest of Shendam, Fr. Patrick Tali and his two assistants leave their parish residence at night to stay in the military barracks and return home during the day until they are sure that the threatened assault on Shendam is no more. I understand from Fr. Dajen that Fr. George Gorap and his assistant of Kukah parish are okay, even though I have not heard directly from them.

The reccurrence of the so-called mercenary attacks is largely because the Government authorities care little about security, becoming very complacent as soon as a tensed situation eases off. With knowledge of the previous crises in Plateau State, one would have thought that the government would by now have an elaborate security system in place in the area, and ensure that intelligence reports are gathered on a daily basis and forwarded to the appropriate quarters. It would be difficult for the crisis to degenerate to such a level if some effective security was maintained. It becomes even more baffling to think there is a military barrack just a few kilometers away in Shendam, and the police posts are located in the villages attacked, and nobody had foreknowledge of the planned attacks. It is also perplexing that modern weapons such as the attackers used could be brought in from outside without being detected by security forces on our roads. Something must be seriously wrong.

We are, however, convinced that the crises will not spread out to other places as is being rumoured. It is very sad that many lives have been wasted and property destroyed with the various tribes, Muslim and Christian, already terribly affected.

RENEWED HOSTILITIES IN YELWA: MAY 2, 2004
An account of the crises in parts of Southern Plateau released in May, 2004.

Again, the crisis in Yelwa has reared its ugly head resulting in human and material casualties. This time around, it is said that the crisis appears to be a revenge attack by the local Tarok ethnic group in coalition with other tribes against the Hausa-Fulani ethnic group. In the previous crisis, it would seem that the Hausa-Fulani inflicted a lot of casualties and drove out of Yelwa all those who were not of Hausa-Fulani origin or of the Islamic faith and had their houses and property demolished. When the residents of Garkawa heard that many of their kith and kin had been attacked and killed and their houses completely destroyed, they too are said to have decided to attack the Hausa-Fulani community in Garkawa. Many were killed and their property destroyed. The Hausa-Fulani survivors ran away from Garkawa. This means that the Hausa-Fulani living in Garkawa were driven out, just as the Hausa-Fulani living in Yelwa had earlier sent away all the other ethnic groups from Yelwa. By this, it meant that Yelwa was now exclusively for Hausa-Fulani or those of the Muslim faith, while Garkawa was for the other local tribes who are mostly Christians. Since the attacks of February 21 to 24 ended, there have been isolated attacks from both sides. Attacks have been carried out in Bakin Ciyawa and some communities of Demshin and Mabudi areas.

The event of Sunday 2 May is said to have been provoked by an incident in Kawo village near Yelwa. My source of information, Fr Paul Dajen, the parish priest of Yelwa who still lives in Garkawa town (as his house and church in Yelwa have been burnt), told me that on the fateful day, the church bell rang at 7 a.m. Some Christians went out to the church premises but were attacked by persons suspected to be Hausas. People were soon mobilized to repel the persons who had come with the intention of attacking the inhabitants of Kawo. Word spread very fast and a group soon advanced on Yelwa, bent on ridding it of the Hausa-Fulani. They wanted to regain control of Yelwa because they believe that Yelwa area was given out to the Hausa settlers by the Goemai or Tarok to settle for farming purposes, but now the Hausas want to control it and even give it an Islamic status. Many Hausa-Fulani people were attacked and killed in Yelwa and most of their houses were burnt. The survivors ran for their lives, taking refuge in safer areas. In fighting the Hausas, the attackers also suffered casualties as some of them were killed. It is claimed that when soldiers arrived on the scene, they fired into a crowd killing or wounding some people. In all, about 60-70 persons are said to have died on both sides during the fighting, with the Hausa-Fulani suffering greater casualties this time around.

There is no doubt that several lives have been lost and many people displaced on both sides. Some ran away out of fear of the poor security situation. Some people have however tried to interpret the crisis as a religious one. Nothing could be further from the truth. If it was indeed a religious crisis our priests would not continue to remain at their duty posts, helping where possible, preaching peaceful coexistence and appealing for calm. They take great personal risks for the sake of peace in the area. To the best of my knowledge, there has never been a meeting of Christian religious leaders in Plateau State in order to plan attacks on Muslims or to wipe out any ethnic group. Rather, both Muslim and Christian religious leaders have consistently appealed for an end to the crises and have encouraged dialogue instead of hostile confrontation. What is happening is an expression of frustration, of discontent over economic, social, and political issues in the Yelwa area. Unless something is done drastically the crisis will continue to fester. It happens that when these crises occur, people call them religious, perhaps because most of those who are involved belong to the two main religions in the area: Islam and Christianity. Yes, religion may play a role, but I believe it is not the major cause of the crises. Religion is often used as a weapon, because it is easier to appeal to religious sentiments to foster one's economic or political agenda.

Those who have alleged genocide in the on-going crisis have certainly misinterpreted the situation and are making a hasty generalization. In the absence of a carefully worked out formula for peaceful coexistence among the ethnic groups, crises of this nature are inevitable. At the slightest provocation, people are prepared to take up arms in order to make their point. Sophisticated arms have found their way to the two fighting groups. The two sides involved in this crisis have been at one time the aggressors and at another time the victims of aggression. Both groups have lost lives and property. The crisis is more of guerilla attacks than a deliberate and coordinated attempt by any tribe to exterminate the other. It is therefore a misnomer to refer to this crisis as being of a genocidal nature. A number of people have certainly been killed. Most of the people have run away in fear and hopefully will soon be located. The news reports of 500 killed are an exaggeration. Sources of information during such crises must be credible and devoid of sentiments.

The fact is that the Ankwai, Tarok, Garkawa ethnic groups living in the Yelwa area have had an uneasy relationship with the Hausa-Fulani through the years. Major disagreements over land, cattle and traditional rulership have been at the roots of the disaffection, precipitating serious crises. The issues at stake have never been really addressed by the traditional rulers or the State authorities. The vicious circle of attacks and counter-attacks will continue if the issues are not settled at the root. The Tarok and Goemai claim that the Hausa-Fulani migrated to Yelwa area for farming purposes. Having been accommodated and given the freedom to conduct their businesses, they woke up to find that the Hausa-Fulani newcomers seemed to be doing better economically. The local residents claim that the Hausa-Fulani do not pay proper allegiance to the traditional chiefs of both Tarok and Goemai Lands, and seem to have made Yelwa an Islamic enclave. Signboards which refer to Yelwa as Zamfara, after the first state to introduce the new Sharia in Nigeria, are very provocative to the non-Hausa Muslims. One can guess that the fear of Hausa-Fulani economic and social domination, as well as the fear of a strong Islamic influence in an area that practises the African traditional religion alongside Christianity, is what gives rise to the recurring social tension.

The response of the civil authorities to crises is always belated. Curfews are imposed or military men deployed to the crisis areas only after the damage has been done. Since 2001, it should have been clear to the authorities that certain parts of Plateau State are very prone to violence and all available resources should have been mobilized to forestall this. Unfortunately, as soon as one crisis finishes, the civil authorities seem to go to sleep until another one erupts before panic measures are hurriedly put in place. Most of the time, the measures are only cosmetic and superficial. It must be pointed out that the security agents, especially the soldiers sent to restore peace are said to be sometimes divided according to their religious or ethnic affiliations. It has been claimed that Muslim soldiers try to help the Muslims and Christian soldiers help the Christians, giving the impression that the crisis has a religious undertone.

The Archdiocese of Jos on its part continues to use all available means to appeal for calm and peaceful coexistence. Our relationship with the Muslim community is very cordial. There has been a mutual exchange of visits recently and we are in touch with some Muslim leaders in Jos. A visit from the powerful Muslim Emir of Wase to my house in January this year is a confirmation of such cordial relationship. Christians and Muslims whom I have spoken to all condemn in no uncertain terms the wanton and reckless destruction of lives and property in this and previous crises. The crises regrettably have given Plateau State a negative image, both nationally and internationally, thus making nonsense of the famed "home of peace and tourism". Because of security implications, I as the Archbishop have not been able to travel out to visit the displaced persons. It is too risky to move around in the Yelwa area without police or military protection. Our priests cautiously remain in their parishes only making essential movements. Pastoral visitations cannot be carried out in this atmosphere of fear and suspicion. Those who ascribe religious motives to this crisis should see that it is not the case. If it were, our priests who continue to remain in their areas of postings would have been the direct object of attack. We continue to work, to pray and to hope that peace and calm will return permanently to the southern part of Plateau State. It must be said that the rest of Plateau State is enjoying great peace and tranquillity. I have a meeting next week with two Muslim leaders and the President of the Church of Christ in Nations (COCIN), being part of my initiative of keeping dialogue alive.

Many people have been displaced. Five of our parishes have been destabilized: Yelwa, Kuka, Turaki, Demshin and Bakin Ciyawa. Displaced people have fled to Jos, Quan Pan, Pankshin, Taraba State, Bauchi State and other safer areas. They are without houses or means of livelihood. They need economic assistance. Most of the gifts I received during the Easter period have been sent to assist some of them, but the mouths to feed are too many. Many of our catechists and their families have neither houses nor food. We are taking up collections and donations and doing what is within our means to provide for the distressed people. The Church will continue to give the moral encouragement and assurance of hope to the people that by God's grace all will be well. The Presidential Peace Committee is meeting in Jos over the crisis. They have met before! Whether anything good will come out of this meeting, only time will tell.

OUR PEACE MISSION TO YELWA

A Peace and Reconciliation Rally in Yelwa on Friday, August 6, 2004

1. On the 27th of July, 2004, I requested the Administrator of Plateau State, Gen. Chris Alli, (Rtd.) after he had addressed the opening of the General Assembly of the Catholic Archdiocese of Jos, to kindly allow and facilitate a peace mission which I wanted to undertake to Yelwa. I suggested that I would like to do so in the company of the Emir of Wase Alh. Dr. Haruna Abdullahi, who is the Jama'atu Nasril Islam (JNI) President in Plateau State and with whom I have a friendly relationship, and the Long Goemai Hubert Shaldas II, the traditional ruler under whose jurisdiction Yelwa falls.

2. After due consultations, the visit was fixed. The Emir of Wase, the Long Goemai and I agreed to meet in Shendam at the Long Goemai's palace at 9.30 am on Friday the 6th of August. After prayers and a few remarks, we all set out in a convoy of cars for Yelwa with the Long Goemai and the Emir of Wase driving in the Long Goemai's car - a very symbolic gesture.

3. The venue for the meeting with the Yelwa community was the primary school. When we arrived at around 10 am we saw a number of Muslim leaders and a good number of Christians who had come from the neighbouring towns and villages where they have been residing since the crises. Some members of the Muslim community thought we would address them separately at a designated place. I however thought that it would be more meaningful and a gesture of trust and confidence-building to address both the Muslims and Christians together, in the spirit of reconciliation. With the encouragement of the Emir of Wase, the Muslim community who had gathered elsewhere joined the other people at the primary school, where we addressed them jointly, the first joint meeting since the crisis began in 2002. There would have been over 4,000 people at the meeting including Muslim youths, women and elders and many Christians who had been mobilized by the Catholic priests of Shendam, Langtang, Turaki, Garkawa, Baking Ciyawa, Namu, Kurgwi, Chip,

Kwande, Kwa, Kwalla and Demshin to come to the gathering. Some Christian residents of Yelwa who had deserted the place also came back as soon as they heard that the Catholic Archbishop was coming to visit them in Yelwa.

4. The Deputy Chairman of Shendam, Mr. John Nanduet, welcomed us to Yelwa. The opening prayer by me was followed by my speech, which largely expressed sympathy and condolences on the unfortunate occurrences in Yelwa and environs and prayed God to have mercy on the victims of the crises and to beg forgiveness for the atrocities committed by human beings against fellow human beings. I encouraged all to ask forgiveness from each other because we have all sinned by allowing such atrocities to be committed. Innocent blood had been shed, properties and means of livelihood destroyed and the peace shattered. Apart from repenting and promising never to allow such things to happen again, we must engage in constructive dialogue with each other rather than resort to hostility at the slightest provocation. I told them that if we needed soldiers and policemen to stand over us to supervise peace among us, then the peace would be a mere artificial construction. The proof that peace had returned would be when the soldiers and policemen had moved back to the barracks with their armoured tanks and guns and we all embraced each other and resolved to co-exist peacefully no matter our ethnic, political or religious affiliations. I asked if we were interested in peaceful co-existence and all answered in the affirmative; so I requested that we shake hands as a gesture of forgiveness and good neighbourliness. This was done in an animated way - Christians shaking hands with Muslims and Muslims shaking hands with Christians - a very moving gesture indeed. Adults and children alike were seen shedding tears as they once again beheld the eyes of those they had known and loved before the crisis.

Having expressed appreciation of the role of the State Administrator and his peace initiatives, and of the support of the traditional and religious leaders in preaching the gospel of peace, I prayed and requested that some prominent elders of Plateau State who were also politicians must not only be heard but must be seen to be working towards total peace and harmony among the Plateau people. I called out the names of elders such as Deputy Senate President Senator Ibrahim Mantu, Chief Solomon Lar, Da D. B. Zang, Gen. Jeremiah Useni (Rtd.), Air Commodore Jonah Jang (Rtd.). Alh. Yahaya Kwande, Alh. Shuaibu Alhassan, Senator Cosmas Niagwan, Alh. Saleh Hassan, Ambassador Fidelis Tapgun, Hon. Habu Shindai, Hon. Damishi Sango, Chief Joshua Dariye, etc. and hoped they would convene a meeting transcending their political or ethnic or religious affiliations and truthfully talk of ways to bail Plateau State out of its present political predicament, devoid of partisan interests. This would no doubt complement the various peace efforts.

5. The Emir of Wase, while thanking the State Administrator for allowing his participation in the Peace Forum, spoke passionately and extensively on the need for peaceful co-existence and mutual forgiveness, warning that to take another person's life is a great sin before God. In a symbolic gesture, he greeted the Long Goemai and asked all the Muslim and Christian residents of Yelwa to show their loyalty to the Long Goemai their traditional ruler. Men, women, youths and elders all filed out to greet the Long Goemai - a very positive gesture. I believe by this gesture, they were accepting his authority over Yelwa. This will greatly help in the search for a lasting peace in Yelwa.

6. The Long Goemai thanked the State Administrator for his various peace moves and expressed appreciation for the initiative of the Catholic Archbishop in convening such a peace meeting. He spoke on the need for patience, tolerance and forgiveness.

7. Short speeches were given by the JNI Chairman of Shendam and the CAN Chairman of Langtang South, who spoke on behalf of the CAN Chairman of Shendam Local Government, urging all to co-exist peacefully and to forgive the past.

8. I concluded by asking all those who were obstacles to the return of displaced people to reconsider their stance and to remove the barriers; and I told them that if any man, woman, or child was being detained against their will, they should be

released so that they could return to Yelwa.

On behalf of the Catholic Archdiocese of Jos, I presented some gift items: a total of 432 bags of guinea corn, maize, millet, beans; 540 blankets, 540 mats, 18 cartons of bar soap, 270 buckets, 540 plastic plates, 540 plastic cups, all brought to Yelwa in three lorry loads.

These gifts were sponsored by the Catholic Relief services Abuja, a charity arm of the US Catholic Bishops' Conference in collaboration with the Archdiocese of Jos. The gifts were handed over to the JNI and the Red Cross for distribution to all without discrimination. The members of the Justice and Peace Department of the Archdiocese were left behind to monitor the effective distribution of the items.

A total of over 3,000 bags of assorted grains, thousands of blankets, mats, cartons of bar soap, plastic buckets, plates and cups had earlier on been distributed according to numbers and needs of the displaced people in Shendam, Turaki, Kukah, Langtang, Garkawa, Namu, Kwande, Bakin Ciyawa, Kurgwi, Kwalla, Kwa, Demshin, Amper and Chip with specific instructions that they should be distributed only on Saturday 7th August at 8.00 am on the same day and time as relief materials would be distributed in Yelwa, so as to prevent people taking double rations or moving from one village to another for more rations.

9. After the closing prayers by the JNI chairman of Shendam Local Government Area, the Muslims left while the Catholics present proceeded to the Catholic Church premises for the Holy Mass. A few canopies were erected. Most people however stayed under trees, since the parish church had been destroyed twice and the father's house had been razed to the ground. The Mass was attended by priests of nearby parishes, catechists, the Long Goemai and about 2,000 worshippers. The central message was forgiveness and reconciliation. All ended peacefully. The next Mass to be said in the same premises will be on 22nd August, when the people dispersed will be expected to attend. They cannot stay in Yelwa now because they have no houses.

Recommendations

- The authority of the Long Goemai as the traditional ruler under whose jurisdiction Yelwa falls must be upheld and he should exercise his powers to inspire unity and reconciliation among all the people of Yelwa. He needs to be supported by the State Government in this regard through the provision of communication gadgets and security for his person. The last time the Long Goemai visited his subjects in Yelwa was over one year ago and he and the suspended Governor were stoned by some Yelwa residents.

- Intelligence gathering must be intensified not only in Yelwa but also in all the villages of Plateau State.

- Thuraya mobile phones could be purchased and distributed to traditional rulers, village heads and prominent religious leaders. These facilities are to be maintained at Government expense and to be used only for security matters. Police Stations and military barracks need to be fully equipped with these too, so that they can be easily alerted in case of any tension. Local Government chairmen and councillors should have theirs.

- The exchange of visits by traditional rulers needs to be encouraged and funded by Government. The logistics are very important: security, publicity, transport etc.

- Those whose houses were destroyed in Yelwa and environs are to be helped to reconstruct them. The mosques and churches are to be reconstructed with no delay and the residences of religious leaders or traditional leaders destroyed should receive priority attention before the others. As opinion leaders, the Government's gesture of goodwill to these leaders in reconstructing their houses will have a greater impact on the people whom they lead.

- For now, no Christian is comfortable residing in Yelwa because they have no shelter, and secondly they are not sure of security. Efforts must be made to guarantee both security and shelter to both displaced Muslims and Christians. This must be done in a transparent, honest and just manner.

- The media presence in the rural parts of Plateau is either very minimal or non-existent. The State Radio and Television and the NTA should reach all the nooks and crannies of Plateau State. At present this is not the case. The absence of regular and objective information opens the door for unfounded rumours, sometimes leading to needless hostilities.

- The distribution of relief materials if done haphazardly will be another source of tension. Relief must be distributed openly, fairly and truthfully without discrimination.
- There should be more patrol vehicles for the police and the military in villages, especially during market days. The aim is to generate security confidence in the people, not to extort money from helpless villagers or motorists.
- An inter-faith skills acquisition centre could be established in Yelwa and Wase to give the idle youth s some functional education to stop them from being used by the elites for ethnic, political or religious mischief.
- In God we trust. He desires peace for us not war or violence.

NAMU CRISIS: AN OVERVIEW
An account of the crisis released April 21, 2004.

The Government of Plateau State recently set up a Judicial Commission of Inquiry to look into the Namu crisis in Qua'an Pan Local Government Area in the Southern Senatorial Zone of the State. The crisis revolves around the ownership of Namu contested between the Goemai and Pan people. Although the findings of the Panel of inquiry have been submitted to Government, these have not yet been made public.

On Monday, April 10, 2006 a wave of killings erupted in the area leaving so many dead and wounded. While it is hard to say with precision the number of deaths, many sources have quoted figure of between 25 and 100 and even 200 lives. The parish priest, Rev. Fr. Albert Endat, however, opines that the majority of those killed were the alleged mercenaries who were mostly Muslims.

It is conjectured that the cause of the fracas was the leakage of the result of the Judicial Commission even if the immediate cause was associated with a disagreement over the fetching of sand from a land of which a Pan man claimed ownership. It became an excuse for a clash where the erstwhile neighbours inflicted causalities on each other. Even here, with the deaths registered, it is hard to say what exactly the real cause is.

In the effort to help the victims of the fracas the Parish Priest of Namu, who chose to remain with his people, was roughhandled by the security agents.

The situation is now calm and negotiations are still on to ensure continued peace and dialogue.

Reports from the Parish Priest of Namu and the sisters in the clinic confirmed that a group of armed men who had been imported into Angwan Yashi were killed. Quite a number of casualties were also recorded on both the Goemai and Pan sides.

While the fracas lasted, the Catholic Clinic in Namu provided shelter and medical facilities to the victims irrespective of their tribe or religion.

On hearing about the conflict, I immediately held discussions with the Police Commissioner and the State Governor, asking them to ensure that the crisis was controlled. I called a meeting of some prominent Catholic sons and daughters of the area with my Vicars-General and some Deans to seek for peace and dialogue. Though tempers were very high the sacrificial message of Christ on Good Friday and the brainstorming session convinced the members to see the reason to pursue peace. An elder from each side of the divide addressed the people at home on the local TV asking for a ceasefire from both sides and the embrace of dialogue.

On our side too, a meeting of all the priests from the area or working in the affected area has been summoned to ensure that we remain on course as brokers of peace and forgiveness.

Masses have been scheduled in Shendam and Kwa as a way of bringing all the people together.

The Members of the Laity Council, the Knights, the Women Organizations, and the Youth in the area are being mobilized to be sensitized on the importance of peaceful co-existence.

The two Vicars-General are on a mission to the affected areas to reconcile and encourage the people to bury the hatchet and cooperate in building a peaceful society.

While it is important to note that the crises in the area and indeed in the State as a whole have been symptomatic of poverty, unemployment, and bad governance, one is optimistic that the various steps being taken by the different interest groups will bring about the desired peace and harmony in the area.

UNITING GOEMAI AND PAN NATIONS
A homily of the pastoral visit to Kwa and Shendam parishes on May 12 & 13, 2006 for the unity of Goemai and Pan people.

At Mass we always read the word of God, as an invitation to us to allow God's word to be the guiding principle in all we do or say. The 1st reading from Colossians 3:1-17 is a practical instruction of St. Paul to the Christian community in Colossae but also very relevant for the Christians of Kwa and the Christians of Shendam. It is a message of fraternal love and of good Christian conduct addressed to all of us. Let us all go back home and read this passage over and over again. Christ's agenda for good Christian conduct is summarized in the beatitudes in St. Matthew's Gospel we have just read: Blessed are the pure of heart, blessed are the peacemakers, blessed are the humble. If we desire to be good Christians and to make it to heaven, the road map is there for us:

be pure, be humble, be peace loving, be merciful, be able to endure persecution.

The Holy Mass for us Catholics is a meal of love and unity. Those who participate in it benefit from it if they have the love of their neighbour and love of God in their hearts. If we come to the Mass with hatred in our hearts it is like coming to a useless jamboree. The Eucharist is the centre of the Christian life. In it we share the body and blood of Christ with one another as members of the same family- God's family. We begin our Mass by confessing our sins, asking God to forgive us for the sins we commit in words, thoughts and actions. We also ask our brothers and sisters to pray for us. God requires harmony, purity of heart and unity of purpose among Christians for a worthy and fruitful celebration of the Eucharist.

Ever since I arrived in the Archdiocese of Jos as its chief pastor, I have not failed to emphasize in each of my pastoral visits that we should all live in peace and harmony with one another because we are all God's children and therefore belong to one family. The pastoral staff you see me hold is an indication of my paramount duty of promoting unity and peace among the faithful. It is an expression of desire that we in the Archdiocese of Jos must be united in heart and mind just like the early Christian community (cf. Acts 2:45). Before Christ left his followers to return to his Father he said a prayer for unity: "that they may all may be one" (cf. Jn 17:21). Christ's wish is that all those who believe in him are to be bonded to one another in such a manner that no room for division is allowed. Despite social status or ethnic affiliation, baptized Christians are one in Christ. St. Paul tells us that there is no longer any difference between Jews and Gentiles, slave or free, men or women. "You are all one in union with Christ Jesus" (cf. Gal 3:27-28).

A Christian is one who is uncompromising in following Christ. He lives in Christ, walks in Christ and proclaims him as Saviour and Lord without fear or shame. Jesus is the light because he leads us out of darkness. He is the Way because if you follow him faithfully you end up in heaven. He is the Truth, because he never lies or fails. When we are baptized we put on Christ as we put on our clothes. At baptism we are signed with the cross, meaning that we belong to him the good shepherd; we listen to his voice and faithfully keep his words. It means we shall put into practice his teachings on love, peace and forgiveness.

A true Christian is known in moments of difficulty. God tests our faith in different ways. A woman may fail to conceive after many years of marriage. A man may become sick for years and despite going to many doctors the sickness will not go away. A father loses his wife and four children in a car accident in one day! In such moments, if one is not strong in faith he or she may think that God has forsaken him or her and may begin to look for other solutions. Some soon forget that Jesus is Lord. We have such accounts in the Bible. After Jesus told his followers that he would give them his body and blood to drink, Jn 6:66 tells us that many of his followers turned back and would not go with him any longer. When a young man was told to sell and distribute his goods to the poor he went away very sad because he was very rich (cf. Lk 18:18-23). Mk 14:51 tells of a man who was following Jesus but ran away naked when the soldiers tried to arrest him. He left his clothes behind! Peter denied Jesus three times when the going became tough. Judas once a good follower of Jesus sold him for thirty silver coins. Think of ways you have betrayed Jesus. Where or who do we turn to when we run into difficulties? Do we abandon Jesus and his ways believing that his ways are not effective for us?

The crisis in the Namu and Shendam areas surprised us a great deal. Many lives were lost and people's homes, farms and property were destroyed. What surprised us the more is the fact that those involved in the crisis were mostly Christians. Why should a Christian spill the blood of another Christian or any human being for that matter? Why should a Christian deliberately set fire to another person's home or property? We are sad, ashamed and scandalized that those who answer the name Christian can do this. Where is our faith in the Risen Lord? How can we proclaim the good news of salvation to non-believers when some of us are the architects and perpetrators of violence? There is no doubt that there are issues of social justice that need to be handled properly by Government, but should failure to handle these as expected make us resort to violence to the extent that we destroy ourselves in the process? If we are not happy with a certain decision or policy there must be a better way of expressing our discontent: dialogue, or legal means. What baffles me is that we in Nigeria in the name of ethnic or religious interest always destroy what has taken us many years to build. After the senseless destruction we are left with regretting the loss of lives, means of livelihood, homes and non-public infrastructure, yet none of the issues we have fought for is resolved.

When I was the Bishop of Jalingo, I was a living witness to the crises between the Jukun/Kuteb (with the same cultural roots), Tiv and Jukun, Tiv and Fulani. Hospitals, schools, houses, shops, farms were destroyed and many lives were lost. The question is, have all their problems been solved? NO. The resources Government should have used for new projects are used in rebuilding the destroyed public facilities or providing relief for the displaced. The lives lost cannot be brought back. One would have thought that their fighting would bring progress, but far from it. The people still live in even worse poverty. Would it not have been better to dialogue?

No matter what has happened here, you are still members of our Archdiocesan family. We have come here today to assure you that we are together. We remind you to see God in your neighbour. Whatever you do to the least of your brothers you do to Christ. Beyond this world there is no issue of tribe, religion or land. This world is not our home we are just passing through. Our true home is in heaven. Why fight for the gains of this world and lose eternal life? Beware of false stories and rumours which fuel violence. We must remind you that the blood of tribe should not be thicker than the waters of baptism. What has happened shows that our tribal affiliations are far above our Christian values.

I condole with those who lost family members and sympathize with those who lost property. I commend the effort of some

Christians who showed love to their neighbours by offering food and shelter to displaced persons. I commend those youths who refused to take part in this violence. I commend the Laity Council who on behalf of the lay men and women of our Archdiocese issued a strong message emphasizing the sacredness of life and the need to use dialogue as a way of resolving differences. The priests and the reverend sisters have been unanimous in expressing concern over the sad developments in the Namu and Shendam areas. Now the attention of the whole world is on us as we prepare to celebrate one hundred years of Catholicism in our land. Instead of showing the world our strength of faith we are showing hatred and violence. While we are aware that some social issues need to be addressed properly, we the priests and the religious are truly unhappy that despite our consistent preaching of peace and harmony some of us will take up arms against each other. I wish to commend the special effort of the parish priest of Namu, Fr. Albert Endat, and the sisters working in the Namu Catholic Clinic, Sr. Martin de Porres, OLF and Sr. Pauline Moorkwap, OLF. At the height of the crisis they stood by their people, helping the wounded, feeding the hungry and giving assurance to the frightened women and children who ran to them for safety. Fr Endat in trying to help protect those in the parish compound was manhandled and humiliated by soldiers. In spite of this he remained strong and caring to all the people who ran to the parish for protection. Those who have told negative stories about him are unfair and uncharitable to the man who literally risked his life to save others. Sr Pauline, a Goemai reverend sister and an eye-witness to the events in Namu, testified to me that Fr Endat played a commendable role and helped everyone. Sr Pauline confirms that as a parish priest Fr Endat has never discriminated against anyone on the basis of tribe. In fact, when the gunshots became very disturbing to her, it was Fr Endat, a Pan man, who at great risk took her, a Goemai woman, on a motor cycle to Dabat to get transport to Shendam. Fr Endat a Pan man, Sr Pauline a Goemai woman, and Sr Martin De Porres from Doemak have all shown us how to practise Christian love by going beyond our tribal affiliations even in difficult times. The love of our neighbor is rule number one for us Christians.

Let us hope that this will be the last time that we will allow this to happen to us. Let us all pray for inner healing. We must not hand over to the younger generation the kind of hatred we have exhibited in this crisis. Let us all repent. The Bible teaches us that if your brother or sister offends you, go to him/her privately and show him/her his/her fault and if he/she does not listen, take one or two other persons with you and if he/she will not listen to them, then tell the whole Church... (Mt 18:15-17).

BRIEF ON THE 2008 JOS CRISIS
A perspective of the Archbishop released November 30, 2008

On November 27, 2008 elections were held into political offices at the local government level across Plateau State. The day of the election was generally quiet and calm. Elections were held without any civil disturbances particularly in Jos North Local Government Area.

In the early hours of November 28, 2008 as the election results were being brought to the collation centre at RCM Primary School Kabong, it was said that some youths had started mounting road blocks at the Bauchi Road area of Jos, alleging that the election into the Chairmanship seat of Jos North Local Government had been rigged. The priest in charge of Sacred Heart Catholic Church, Kabong, where the Primary School which served as the collation centre is located, said that there was commotion all through the night as residents of Kabong did not sleep that night. Meanwhile, some supporters of the opposition political parties were roaming around the venue threatening that they would not accept the result of the election. Shortly after, there were reports that there was a confrontation between the youths of Kabong and the supporters of the opposition parties. The supporters of the opposition parties were said to have been chased away.

The Assistant Cathedral Administrator of Our Lady of Fatima Cathedral, Jos, Fr John Gyang, said that while the Cathedral Administrator was celebrating morning Mass, a group of youths started stoning the Cathedral rectory and burning surrounding houses. The violence soon spread to Osumenyi Street and Angwan Dalyop where residents were sacked attacked, and killed and houses burnt. It was then that we saw smoke rising simultaneously from different parts of the city. It is important to note that this violence started even before the results of the local government elections were announced.

As the violence spread, security agents were not forthcoming to rescue the situation. A lot of our parishes kept calling for help as they were under serious threat. By noon time, however, security agents started coming into the city to help check the situation. Unfortunately, they were not sufficient in number to contain the conflagration as it spread rapidly to different parts of the city:

In the afternoon, the State Governor, Jonah Jang, made a state-wide broadcast in which he called for calm and also gave the security agents an order to shoot on sight anybody found perpetrating the violence. He also imposed a dusk-to-dawn curfew on the city of Jos and environs.

The situation remained tense on November 29, 2008 even though the violence had reduced because of the presence of security agents. On Sunday November 30, 2008, some parishes in Christian-dominated areas held Masses for the faithful amidst fear. A lot of Protestant churches and property were destroyed and some Protestant clergy were killed. We in the Archdiocese of Jos recorded losses in terms of the killing of some of our parishioners, the destruction of homes and property and the destruction of some our churches.

A WORD OF CAUTION TO THE MEDIA

Released December 2, 2008 as Chairman of Christian Association of Nigeria, CAN, Plateau State

Some foreign electronic and print media often contribute in aggravating situations of crises in Nigeria. In reporting ethnic, political or religious crises, they have often depended on individuals or organizations with a noticeable bias who dish out false, exaggerated, confusing and sometimes malicious figures of casualties to promote their selfish or parochial interests.

When effects of crises are badly or incorrectly reported, they contribute to the escalation of the crises, which often spread to otherwise peaceful towns and villages. The biased reporting of crises in Nigeria by some foreign media often tends to demonize one of the parties in the conflict. Some of the international media houses have Hausa programmes and reporters who during crises tend to interview only one of the parties or ask questions that whip up sentiments and then proceed to tell the story as if it is the gospel truth. We wish to ask the management of these media organizations to ensure that stories or news items gathered, especially during crises, are not influenced by half truths, innuendoes and falsehood.

The recent crisis in Plateau State started allegedly as a reaction to the local government elections, but to our utter dismay and shock, it progressed to the destruction of churches or church-related property. Deaths recorded were from the mutual attacks by Christian and Muslim youths as well as those resulting from the encounters with security agents. The whole event of November 28, 2008 seems not to have been just casual, but planned and orchestrated by the initial aggressors. The State Commissioner for Justice in a press briefing at the State Police headquarters on November 30, 2008 confirmed that it was a pre-meditated act; that was why some of the perpetrators apprehended had military and police uniforms as well as arms.

We worry when numbers are bandied by media houses in the

heat of crises even when figures of casualties have not been confirmed by security agents to ascertain the authenticity or otherwise of the facts. To avoid misinformed opinions and exaggerated statements, we urge the international media and their local counterparts to always ascertain from genuine sources and cross-check their facts thoroughly before feeding the world with information that could do incalculable damage to the society. While we cannot claim to know the genesis and the reason for this crisis, we are aware of the government position through the broadcast by the State Governor that the crisis originated on November 28, 2008 from Ali Kazaure (which is a Muslim-dominated area).

We are tired of crises aggravated by mindless reporting by foreign media whose sources are often biased persons or groups with a hidden agenda. For example, on November 29, 2008 at 9.00pm local time, BBC World (TV) reported that three hundred persons had been massacred and buried in mass graves. On November 30, 2008, the same BBC (TV) at 2.00 pm local time reported that three hundred & sixty corpses had been deposited in the Jos Central Mosque. Similar unsubstantiated reports and exaggerated figures of casualties were given by CNN, Al Jazeera, etc. and even some Nigerian media such as the *Sunday Trust* of November 30, 2008 and the *Daily Trust* of December 1, 2008. These reports are highly suggestive. Similarly, the Yelwa crises of 2004 were reported by some foreign media in a biased manner, neglecting the initial huge loss of lives incurred in February but overemphasizing the one of May, thus creating the impression that Christians were the aggressors. The casualty figures of the Yelwa crises were highly exaggerated for political and religious reasons to depict Plateau State our cherished home of peace and tourism negatively.

We are writing this not to cause disaffection or rift between Muslims and Christians in Plateau State, but to underscore the fact that this negative reporting has been the trend for a long time. Continuing in this biased reporting will lead to anarchy, chaos and more loss of lives and property. Foreign media should always cross-check facts and be aware that rumours and malicious information are not lacking in crisis situations. There was nothing wrong in crosschecking the information of the killings with the Interreligious Council for Peace and Harmony or the Jama'atu Nasril Islam (JNI) and the Christian Association Nigeria (CAN). These bodies have been making concerted efforts to ensure permanent peace on the Plateau. The media should not only be interested in crises, but should cover peace initiatives undertaken before and during crisis periods such as the meeting between JNI and CAN in the Jos Central Mosque on November 20, 2008, as well as the unyielding efforts of the Interreligious Council for Peace and Harmony towards peaceful co-existence between Muslims and Christians in Plateau State.

Thank you. We hope for a better relationship with the media. We believe that positive and objective reportage devoid of sentimental outbursts will help create a healthier and more peaceful society.

SALLAH GREETINGS AFTER
THE NOVEMBER 28, 2008 JOS CRISIS
Exchange of solidarity messages with the Muslim Ummah. December 7, 2008.

In the aftermath of the Jos crisis, triggered by Local Government elections but culminating in the destruction of churches and mosques as well as lives and other properties. I sent the following sallah messages to some Muslims on 07.12.08.

May Merciful God grant us the spirit to continue to love and live together despite the sad and tragic events that have happened. I join you to pray during this Sallah for those who died, were injured or lost property. May our work for peace and good relationship between Muslims and Christians go on. Allah bless you and your family.

To the Emir of Wase Alhaji Dr. Haruna Abdullahi I wrote:
Your Royal Highness, May Merciful God grant us PEACE and understanding despite the sad and tragic events that have happened. I join you to pray during this Sallah for those who died, were injured or lost property. May our work for peace and good relationship between Muslims and Christians speed on. God bless you and your family.

I received some of the following replies

Sheik Badamasi Abdulazeez: *What again does one need in this world when friends from far and near remember one and his family members at periods of disasters and joys. I very much treasure your love and concern. My humble prayer is jazakallah khairan i.e. that may Allah reward you abundantly here on earth and in the hereafter, amin. Thanks.*

Sani Ibn Salihu: *Happy Sallah. May we imbibe the lessons of the Abrahamic Sacrifice and continue to work for peace. I feel highly encouraged by your energizing words. I therefore pledge to continue to work with you for our society's common good.*

Abdullahi Maidawa Kurgui: *Thank you sir. Wish you success in peace building.*

Ustaz Khalid Abubakar: *Amen Bishop! May God the Almighty ensure this supplication. I appreciate. As religious people, we must work harder in our partnership to achieve peace.*

Emir of Wase: *We spoke on the phone and he said, "We shall continue our work. We shall not be discouraged or frustrated, God willing".*

<u>Isah Alhassan Aljasawi</u>:
Thanks. I live to remember your concern for me always.

<u>Alhaji Inuwa Ali</u>: He is a man over 75 years old. I am sure that he wanted to tell me something positive as he has always done, but I believe he has problems with sending text messages. I got two empty texts from him.

There is good will. The work of inter-religious dialogue will make even greater progress than before.

MEMO TO THE NUNCIATURE, ABUJA
Released January 18, 2010 on the attacks in Nassarawa Gwong Area of Jos North LGA

There is a crisis in Jos again, specifically in the Nassarawa Gwong area of the city. As usual, there are all kinds of stories and biased reporting. At our inter-religious council meeting yesterday, it was clear that there is no real authentic and verified cause of the conflict. Muslims in Jos tell the story to suit their interests and Christians do the same. The dimensions of the crisis have been increased by careless comments, utterances and biased media news stories. There is gross exaggeration and misrepresentation of facts. It became clear to us at the meeting of the Inter-Religious Council yesterday, 18.01.10 (at which was present the Director of the State Security Services and the Secretary to the Plateau State Government) that even the official information given out as the reason for the crisis was defective. Emotions are high. The youths are restive, both Muslims and Christians. A twenty-four hour curfew has been imposed today by the Governor. Sporadic gunshots are heard in the Nasarawa Gwong area and are gradually expanding to other areas. The Secretary of the Christian Association of Nigeria (CAN) just called me now to say that the area where he resides in Bukuru (some ten kilometres from Jos) near the Christian Theological College is under serious threat and some house burning is going on. The police seem to be helpless in the face of it.

It appears there is deliberate propaganda in tracing the origin of the crisis, and we shall end up not knowing the real cause of it. The story which said that the parishioners of St. Michael's Catholic Church Nasarawa Gwong were attacked at worship, the parish priest killed, and the church burnt is not true. They had peaceful Sunday worship until towards the end, when the upsurge of the crisis was reported to them and some parishioners from the vicinity went home while others from far away had to stay back in the parish until late evening before they were helped to return home by some security agents. There are certainly conflicting reports. One which the Muslims tell is that a Hausa Muslim man who hired some Muslim youths to rebuild his house burnt during the November 2008 crisis was attacked along with the hired youths by Christians, and the Christians tell their story that a Christian was pursued by Muslim youths into a church and the church was attacked and burnt by Muslims, thus triggering the crisis. The stories are as diverse as they are ridiculous.

My telephone line has been inundated with calls from Christians from different quarters in Jos claiming they were surrounded and were under imminent attack and that from the sound of guns they were hearing, the guns in use were sophisticated ones. The Catholic Cathedral Church bell kept ringing all morning today alerting Christians and security agents that there could be an attack. Since yesterday, we Muslim and Christian leaders have been having a series of meetings aimed at calming the situation in the city. I woke up today very early and my telephone line has not stopped ringing. In my capacity as the Chairman of the Christian Association of Nigeria in Plateau State and the Co-Chairman of the Plateau State Inter-Religious Council for Peace and Harmony, I have made efforts to talk with government and security officials. I have sent text messages to them and talked with the Governor today (two times) and the Director of the State Security Services. I was assured that efforts were being made to return the situation to normal and that a state Security Council meeting was already in session.

Even though the crisis appears to be a religious one, the real reason I believe is the struggle for ethnic and political supremacy between the Hausa tribe and the local Jos ethnic groups as well as the hangover of who is an indigene and who is a settler. The sudden eruption of the crisis, I believe, is a result of pent-up anger from the last crisis of November 2008. It is perhaps an attempt to accomplish unfinished business by those concerned.

SOLIDARITY MASS/HEALING FOR VICTIMS OF PLATEAU CRISIS

A narrative report of the Solidarity Mass for victims of the January 17 and March 7 Jos ethno-religious crises in Plateau State held at St. Jarlath's Catholic Church, Bukuru on March 19, 2010.

On the 19th of March, 2010, Catholics and non-Catholics within Jos City and its environs turned out in their thousands at St Jarlath's Catholic Church, Bukuru, some fifteen kilometers from Jos to pray in a Mass of Solidarity organized by the Archdiocese of Jos for victims of the recent ethno-religious crises. The Mass was graced by a large number of priests, religious, the lay faithful, government dignitaries including the State Deputy Governor, the Hon Pauline Tallen, past governors and many others. The Mass was presided over by Peter Cardinal Turkson, the President of the Pontifical Council for Justice and Peace, Rome, who brought the message of solidarity from the Universal Church with the assurances of prayers for peace from the Holy Father, Pope Benedict XVI.

The Mass was the Christian response to the attacks that saw

hundreds killed in cold blood in a crisis that is often said to be religious, although we know that it was generated by a mixture of political, economic, ethnic and religious factors. Men, women, children were very visible as they expressed deep compassion and empathy to the affected persons. Prayers were said for a cessation of the cycle of violence, peace in the land, the eternal repose of departed souls and for social harmony between Christians and Muslims. In the homily, I acknowledged the painful and difficult moment we all face with loss of lives and property, a community traumatized and no justice in sight, yet our Lord and Master has asked us to forgive injury. The call by Libyan leader Gaddafi that our country Nigeria be divided into two along religious lines, namely the Muslim North and the Christian South, was condemned. This could be a pointer to the possibility that some of the crises in our state are orchestrated by forces outside the State.

Goodwill messages and assurances of prayers were received from His Holiness, Pope Benedict XVI, Cardinal Ivan Dias, Prefect of the Congregation for the Evangelization of Peoples, Cardinal Peter Turkson, and other dioceses in Europe, America and Africa.

Relief materials were distributed to the affected victims whose homes and means of livelihood had been destroyed through the assistance of the British Catholic Agency for Overseas Development distributed to them. The materials so distributed included clothing, blankets, mats, assorted grains and many others. The Mass was well attended, as it witnessed a large turn-out of worshippers. The villagers came from Dogo Nahawa itself, Zot Foran and Rasat.

It was really very pathetic to see men and women who had lost their entire families and having no place they could call home because the attackers had burnt all they had. The presence of many faithful was a great source of comfort, just as the prayers consoled them too. They look forward in hope.

The Catholic Archdiocese of Jos continues to solicit prayers for the people as well as material assistance to help with their eventual rehabilitation.

DOGON NAHAWA MASS OF SOLIDARITY

A Narrative report of Solidarity Mass for victims of the March 7 crisis at Dogon Nahawa on March 21, 2010 at St. Fedelis Catholic Church, Dogon Nahawa.

A Mass was said at St Fidelis Catholic Church, Dogon Nahawa (About 20 kilometers south of the city of Jos) where persons said to be Fulani cattle-rearers visited fatal attacks on the residents killing women and children, possibly in reaction to the loss of their cows and loved ones in a previous crisis. In my homily, I thanked Almighty God for the gift of life and peace, even in the midst of the present situation, encouraging all to lift up body, soul and spirit to cry to God in one voice and to surrender the situation to God. I called on all to surrender to God, the One who controls the whole universe even if all things seem to be getting out of hand. I also stressed the need for Christians to look up to God in seemingly hopeless situations like this, by putting their hope and trust in God who alone can take care of their welfare. I therefore admonished them to be steadfast in the midst of this challenge to their faith and trust in God. I also urged all of them to forgive the murderers and destroyers, and leave vengeance for God alone who would fight their cause. I prayed God to heal both the physical and spiritual wounds of the victims, for the repose of the souls of all those slain, and for an end to such wickedness.

Earlier on in his welcome speech, Rev Fr Philip Jamang, the Priest in whose jurisdiction the area falls, was full of thanks for the Mass saying that it would go a long way to uplift the people. He also thanked all those who had come to pray with them as they mourned their dead.

In a goodwill message, the Parish Council Chairman, Hon Victor Gyang, expressed warm sentiments of appreciation to the Archbishop, priests, the religious, the knights and their ladies, catechists, traditional rulers and all who graced the occasion, saying that their presence had lifted them from their sorrows. In their separate remarks, the Dagwom Rwei of Du, Da Phillip Kim, the representative of Jos South Local Government Council Chairman, Hon Pam Chuwang, the Afizere Women group and the Chairman of RCC Church, Foron, Rev Luka Dogo, stressed the need for Christians to be united in love and to be there for one another at all times, particularly in moments such as this.

Meanwhile in the course of the Mass, special prayers were offered and some of the villagers representing the families of the victims were prayed for and blessed while relief materials from Catholic Agency for Overseas Development, UK (CAFOD), Catholic Relief Services, USA, Missio Aachen and dioceses in Nigeria and parishes in Jos Archdiocese were distributed. Of the 25,000 displaced persons, over 5000 are Catholics with nearly all of them still facing lack of accommodation and the immediate needs of life. The two Catholic churches in Ubiel and Chwelnyap are still in ruins and need to be rebuilt. The faithful were encouraged to reinforce family prayer and seek the face of God, who has promised to be with his people no matter how trying the moments seem to be.

2010 CHRISTMAS EVE BOMBINGS

A perspective of the Archbishop released December 30, 2010

The January 17 2010 crisis brought untold hardships to many residents of Jos and its environs. The hopes, aspirations and dreams for a happy, fruitful and peaceful New Year were soon dashed as barely two weeks into the New Year, a crisis triggered by a little incident in the Nasarawa Gwong area soon spread to other parts, resulting in tragic killings and needless destruction. From that period to now, a few attacks have been witnessed in villages neighbouring Jos city and recently, guerrilla attacks have also taken place with unpleasant consequences. Despite the crisis-prone year, which many lived through in anger, shock, pain, tears, agony, confusion and frustration, we were all optimistic and upbeat about a hitch-free and peaceful 2010 Christmas celebration. This is against the background of our inability to celebrate the previous Easter Vigil and other Holy Week ceremonies with tranquillity on account of the curfew in place at the time and the near peace of the graveyard that prevailed. Parishes had to celebrate the Easter Vigil in broad daylight to beat the curfew time, thus deprived of the luxury of the usual solemn ceremonies. However, with some relative peace experienced, we looked forward to a wonderful Christmas celebration, having enjoyed a successful, beautiful, well-attended and inspiring Christ the King procession only a few weeks before. It was not to be.

As I was having my supper around 7.00pm on the 24th of December and getting ready for the 2010 Christmas "midnight" Mass at Our Lady of Fatima Cathedral, to begin at 10.pm, I heard explosions, but did not give it a second thought as I believed that it was the usual fire works by the youth on such festive occasions. The sounds however were louder than the usual fire crackers. I soon got to know from Fr. Blaise Agwom, the parish priest of Sacred Heart Parish, Kabong (Gada Biyu) in Jos that there had been several bomb explosions in their zone with some casualties. About the same time, Fr. Gabriel Gowok, the parish priest of St. Michael's Parish, Nasarawa Gwong rang to inform me of several bomb blasts at the Angwan Rukuba area of his parish leaving some people dead. These blasts had taken place almost simultaneously and appeared to be targeted at places where people were gathered for recreation or commercial purposes.

I asked the two parish priests to provide for me an eye-witness account of the incident. Below is what they sent to me:

Report of the Bomb Blasts Which Occurred on the 24 December, 2010 at Kabong (Gada Biyu) Village, Jos

I am Rev Fr Blaise Agwom, the Pastor in charge of the Sacred Heart Catholic Church Kabong (Gada Biyu) Jos, and this is my eye-witness account of the ugly incident that occurred about five minutes past 7 pm on the night of the 24 December (Christmas Eve).

I was in my room very close to the Church preparing for the Christmas Vigil Mass which we had earlier announced to the parishioners the previous Sunday would be at 9 pm, when I heard an unusually loud explosion some 100 metres from my house. However, considering the season we are in, I quickly waved it aside as a display of fireworks which is a universal and common phenomenon during the Christmas season. It was later that we got to know that it was a bomb blast which occurred by the main road close to the "Goodluck Jonathan over-head bridge" where marketers and their customers were doing their rush-hour shopping for the Christmas. About six people were killed there by the blast, including Mrs. Catherine Babale, who was the President of the Catholic Women Organization (CWO) of our Church, and who was also one of the pioneer Church wardens. She had left a pot of soup boiling on the fire and gone to buy additional foodstuffs in that local market when this disaster struck and sent her to her untimely death.

The second blast occurred about five minutes later right inside the village, about 200 metres from the church besides the house of one of our members, by name Mr Zi Tok. The "bomb" was placed between a restaurant and a beer parlour where people were socializing. That one killed two people and injured many.

The third blast occurred about three minutes after the second one just about 50 metres from our parish house, damaging two houses. The splinters and shrapnel also hit the parish house with negligible damage. Fortunately, nobody was killed but some people were injured including a mad man who was lying down close by.

The fourth "bomb" exploded on a busy pedestrian road that passes between our Church and the shops attached to the RCM Primary school. This particular bomb exploded around 7:20 pm, killing eight unsuspecting and harmless people who were walking on that road. It was the shrapnel from this particular blast that hit the Church in different spots destroying the glass of the main door of the Church and some windows. It also destroyed the windscreen and tyres of a Hennessey saloon car belonging to one Mr Lawrence Sindimma, which was parked beside the Church. It was also this very blast that hit an electricity transformer which is also close to the Church, thereby causing total darkness in the entire area. For this, we plead with the State Government, the authorities of Power Holding Company of Nigeria (PHCN) and Jos North Local Government to come to our rescue by fixing the transformer so as to restore electricity to the area.

We wish to state categorically that there was no bomb planted inside our church, neither was the bomb intended for the church since the church was empty and in darkness at that time. From the explanation above, it is clear that those who carried out this dastardly act knew exactly what they were doing and they had specific locations where they wanted the bombs to explode. They deliberately chose crowded spots. Thus, dropping it in the church at that time would have been a waste of their bomb since there was no single person in the church then.

Another bomb exploded between the main gate of the primary school and the main road, harming nobody. The final blast was on the small bridge before Tati Hotel. That too did not harm anybody. That was the blast that was erroneously thought by some people to have been planted or meant for the newly constructed overhead bridge named after President Goodluck Jonathan. Furthermore, to the best of my knowledge, there was no blast at the newly-constructed Satellite Market. The ones enumerated above are the only ones that occurred. This report represents the true happening in Gada Buyu (Kabong Village) as witnessed by, and it has been verified by our community elders including Prince Nyam Gwom , the acting Chief of Kabong and the catechist of our church Mr. Paul Gilong, who was also an eye-witness. Because of this inhuman and cold- blooded assault on innocent harmless and law abiding citizens, who were preparing to celebrate Christmas, we could neither celebrate our Vigil nor Christmas Masses. The Police came in around 4 am on 25 December and collected the corpses (brought in from different locations and deposited near the church), after taking pictures.

In the morning of the 25th (Christmas Day), the local youths tried to stage a demonstration and the soldiers drafted around to maintain law and order were shooting in the air. Three youths were mistakenly hit and one died instantly, while two were injured and are receiving treatment in the hospital.

To the best of my knowledge, this represents the true situation of things and we want the world to know that these acts were a deliberate attempt to disrupt the celebration of Christmas, the birthday of the Prince of Peace. We pray for the repose of the souls of all those who lost their lives and for peace in Plateau State and Nigeria.

Rev. Fr. Blaise Agwom, Parish Priest,
Sacred Heart Parish, Kabong (Gada Biyu).

Report on the December 2010 Crisis in the Angwan Rukuba Area of Our Parish, by Rev. Fr. Gabriel Gowok, Parish Priest, St. Michael's Catholic Church Nasarawa Gwong, Jos

It all began as a rumour that "Christians will not celebrate this Christmas in peace this year". It was taken as no serious talk, but with passage of time things started unveiling as seen below:

24 December 2010

1. At about 7:00 pm simultaneous bomb blasts at Angwan Rukuba, Sauki Hotel. Report say the number of the wounded taken to hospital was thirty, and dead bodies at the scene were twenty three.

2. The second blast happened at a beer parlour and all ten in the bar were killed and about twenty- five wounded.

25 December 2010

Silent killings, attacks on innocent persons in cars or trekking, on both sides.

26 December 2010

1. Some youths in the Nasarawa Gwong area, enraged by the attacks and killings, suspected to be targeted at Christian or non-Hausa residential areas, sought to revenge the killings. Some four persons are said to have been killed.

2. Sporadic shooting and burning of Christian and Muslim houses and places of business

Security intervention stopped the violence.

My Conclusions:

The December 24 attack was certainly a terrorist attack carefully planned and designed to destroy the holy period that means so much to Christians.

Whatever the motives (political or ethnic) behind the attack, it is seen by many as an assault on Christianity.

The attackers wanted to use the Christmas period to create maximum impact and generate more national and international interest in the affairs of Plateau State.

The incident must have the support and collaboration of outsiders. That suddenly those same youths who used only knives, arrows or locally made guns in previous crises are now using bombs shows external collusion to do evil in Plateau State, to bring her to her knees.

The attacks on Christians and Churches in Maiduguri, Borno State at about the same time as the attacks in Jos (which happened in mainly Christian-dominated areas) may not be a mere coincidence.

Some news media again seemed eager to say one of the bombs was aimed at the Catholic Church, as was the case when they tried unsuccessfully to suggest that the crisis of January 17, 2010 was triggered by the Muslim youth attack on St. Michael's Catholic Church in Nasarawa Gwong. That Church was never attacked. The accounts of the two parish priests in this present crisis show that the Catholic Church was not the object of attack; rather, it was generally aimed at bringing confusion during the period that is of utmost significance to Christians.

As for the number of casualties, figures vary, but the news from the State media say over 30 were killed and over 70 injured. Others put the estimate of the dead at over 80.

The security agents, the State and Federal Government need to identify the root causes of these attacks and persons behind them. Is this about politics, intimidation of Christians, or an expression of ethnic and political discontent using a very holy season of the Christians?

As of this evening, 27 December, the situation seems calm. It appears the security agents are more visible and effective. I am in regular contact with the military leader of the Joint Task Force, Brigadier General Hassan Umaru, a Muslim, who facilitated our Christ the King procession even when the Christian Police Commissioner feared to approve it initially.

Jos and indeed Plateau State needs prayers for permanent peace. The writing on the wall as regards the 2011 elections is not too good. We pray and hope for violence free electoral campaigns, peaceful, free and fair elections.

SOLIDARITY MASS FOR BOMB BLAST VICTIMS: COURAGE! RISE UP AND WALK

A homily at the Mass for Victims of Christmas Eve bomb blast and other sporadic attacks on villages around Jos, held at Our Lady of Fatima Cathedral, April 1, 2011

My dear brothers and sisters in Christ, we have gathered here to reflect and pray about the sad dimension the Jos crisis has taken since 24 December 2010. We remember how bomb blasts occurred in different parts of Jos resulting in multiple deaths, injuries and loss of property. We cannot bring back the dead to life but we can pray for the eternal repose of their souls. May they find eternal peace and happiness with the Lord. We cannot fast-track the healing of those still lying ill due to the effects of the bombings or the sporadic attacks on the villages around Jos, but we can pray for their healing of mind and body and a speedy recovery. We cannot restore the houses and means of livelihood lost by many but we can pray to God to give these people the spiritual strength and courage to cope with their situations of need and to provide for them according to his ways and means. Our presence here is a moral, psychological and spiritual support to the surviving victims and families of the deceased victims. We say to them "Courage! Rise up and walk". A Latin adage says, "*Dum spiro spero*" –"Once there is life there is hope". The Eucharist which we are celebrating for your intentions today is for us Catholics the highest prayer that brings healing of mind and body, and addresses the needs of both the living and the dead. It is our firm conviction that God does not abandon us in terrible situations. He is a rock, a refuge and a shepherd. We pray the Lord to bring the crisis to a permanent end so that we can all enjoy the gift of Plateau State and Jos and that those who want to come here will find a conducive environment to live or do business in.

We are awfully sad that sentiments of fear of one another, distrust, and insecurity are dominating our inter-personal relationships. Where we once saw ourselves as brothers and sisters, Muslims participating in the celebration of Christmas and Christians joining in the celebration of Eid El Fitr, we are now so polarized that we are afraid to see each other, visit each other or attend each other's celebrations because we are not sure when we can be attacked. It is very sad that to go to one part of Jos one has to travel in a roundabout way to avoid entering a neighbourhood that is considered hostile to one ethnic or religious group. It is sad that even some food items sold in the market are suspected to be poisoned and so people are advised not to buy from certain people or certain quarters. It is sadder that even those who should stand up and say, "Enough is enough" or tell the perpetrators of violence to stop are the ones secretly encouraging revenge. It is sad that we see each other in terms of "we and them", or "they and us", with each group referring to the other as the enemy group. It is a tragedy that our children and youths have been indoctrinated in such a manner that they see other persons who practise a different religion as enemies who must be dealt with. It is very sad that some youths have lost the culture of respect for life. They attack and kill at the slightest provocation and their mentors hail them as brave people. We forget that with the skills acquired in these acts of violence they will download them to our homes and ethnic communities, and that whenever we have a misunderstanding they will use these same skills and weapons effectively to our detriment.

What should the adherents of the Christian and Islamic religions do now, since it is from the followers of these two religions that the violence seems to emanate, while the so called "pagans" are living peacefully with one another? We should all repent and seek better ways of resolving differences, through dialogue. We must restore the meaning and dignity of life. Life is not a cheap commodity that can be taken at will. We must re-orientate our youths for a life of meaningful existence. We must identify those religious or political or ethnic leaders who whip up religious, ethnic or political sentiments and manipulate the youths to cause trouble.

We must intensify our prayers and never give up praying and working for peace. Despair is the devil's greatest weapon. It will be tragic if we all say that the Jos crisis is beyond us and it will be more tragic to believe that this crisis is only about Muslim and Christian differences. It is also about some social/economic/political issues that those in authority must identify and resolve quickly. They know this. The reports of panels/commissions/committees of inquiry have the panacea to stop these crises. There must however be a political will to implement the reports. Asking religious leaders to pray, or hanging the blame on the neck of religion, will not solve the problems. Prayers must go along with good works and concerted efforts to eliminate violence. The passion, energy and dedication exhibited during recent political campaigns and the comprehensive manner political office seekers traversed the length and breadth the nation, the states, local governments and even districts was very amazing. If they could campaign in a similar manner for peace, youth employment or socio/economic development, we will build a first-class Nigeria or Plateau State, and many foreigners will be crowding our embassies abroad looking for visas to come to Nigeria. If we begin to think and behave as Nigerians, not as isolated religious, ethnic or political groups, if we think of the common good and adopt a patriotic spirit, we can revolutionize our economy and hasten infrastructural development right now and not wait for the utopian 2020.

We have suffered enough through these crises. We pray and hope that the elections beginning tomorrow will spare us the agony of another type of violence. Let us give peace a chance. Political parties and their leaders must ask their followers to respect people's lives and property and to be orderly and reasonable in electoral victory or loss.

The Word of God in the first reading calls us to repentance for all the acts of shame committed on our land (cf. Dan 9:4-10), while the second reading encourages us to overcome evil with good, as vengeance belongs to the Lord (cf. Rom 12: 5-16). And the Gospel tasks us to remain in God's love (cf. Jn 15:9-11), as love conquers all.

We encourage those affected by this crisis to take heart. I urge us all, especially during this season of Lent, to show practical love and support them in whatever way we can. We appreciate those who have helped the victims of the crises and the parishes that have organized solidarity Masses and identified with them. Today at this Mass we are remembering in a very special way those affected who belong to our Catholic family. Our Justice and Peace Department throughout all the past crises has been helping everybody, Christians and Muslims, but today the prayers we are offering are for about 260 Catholics, some robbed of their lives or their means of livelihood, and some injured. In past crises I sent a card to each victim with a small token gift. We are doing the same today, thanks to some dioceses who have been very supportive of us in many ways. All the victims of the crisis or their families, whose parishes sent us their names, will get a letter of consolation from me and a small token monetary gift. The money has been blessed and is meant to be used by you as a small seed. May the Lord multiply it for you. Please let us sustain the spirit of caring for one another. In a circular I sent some time ago, I asked every parish to constitute a visitation committee to visit families struck by tragedy to encourage them in the name of the Church. True, pure and blameless religion, St. James says, is to reach out to orphans, widows and all those in need (cf. James 1:27). We task all Christians and Muslims who worship the one true God to practise true religion by only doing those things that promote and protect the neighbor, rather than taking the neighbour's life or property or injuring him or her in the name of religious zeal. May the Lord protect us from future violence and may our elections which begin tomorrow be the most peaceful ever. Amen.

CIVIL DISTURBANCES IN JOS NORTH LGA
- AUGUST 29-30, 2011
A narrative report by the Justice, Development, Peace/Caritas for the Archbishop
released September 1, 2011

Introduction
The outbreak of violence in Jos on Monday August 29 and 30, 2011 with heavy casualties and loss of property reminded the world again of the deep-rooted nature of the Jos conflict, and the consequences of not addressing its root causes. Prior to the events of these two days, Jos had experienced almost five months of relative calm in spite of pockets of skirmishes around Masallacin Juma'a, Bauchi Road, Filin Ball, Duala Junction and parts of Nasarawa Gwong areas of Jos North LGA. The violence of August 29 and 30 which erupted in Gada Biyu and Rukuba Road in the Jos

North Local Government Area (LGA) once again assumed religious dimensions with deadly clashes between Christian and Muslim youth when the Izala Muslim sect decided to perform the Eid al-Fitri (end of Ramadan Fast celebration) prayers at their old grounds and mosque located on Rukuba Road. Until Monday August 29, this venue had been abandoned by the sect since 2001 as a result of being burnt on several occasion during the 2001 and subsequent crises.

The Violence
According to reports from Justice Development and Peace/Caritas (JDPC) Peace Agents and Emergency Preparedness and Response Teams (EPRT) in the affected communities, members of the Izala sect in Jos North went to the Rukuba Road grounds on Sunday, August 28, 2011 to clean it for the upcoming Eid celebration, but the community did not allow them, due to the perception that the 2010 Christmas eve bomb blast that affected the community was allegedly committed by Islamic fundamentalists, and to other security challenges they foresaw. The sect however insisted on using the place for this year's Eid prayers.

It is reported that on the morning of Monday August 29, 2011, some members of the sect again went to the ground to have the place cleaned up before the official time slated for the Eid prayers. This time they were initially allowed in until some misunderstanding broke out over alleged provocative utterances by the sect members on loudspeakers, resulting in the community youth asking them to vacate the place. At this point, security personnel arrived on the scene.

The youth of the community engaged the security personnel in some arguments until the situation got out of hand with the blockade of some parts of Goodluck Jonathan Road, from Gada Biyu to the Polo Roundabout and to the Rukuba Road/Utan Lane by irate youths. It is reported that, the situation deteriorated until soldiers opened fire on the youths, resulting in some casualties. A house was subsequently set on fire with violent clashes between the Rukuba Road youth and the Izala sect worshippers. The youths then reportedly charged into the prayer grounds leading to loss of life and burning of vehicles and motor cycles belonging to the worshippers.

It took the joint efforts of the military, a special anti-terrorist force and police personnel to bring the situation under control; they used the few vehicles/motor cycles of the worshippers and their trucks to evacuate members of the sect out of the area to safety.

As news of the violence spread, there were sporadic gunshots in other areas in Jos including Anglo-Jos and Gangare opposite the University of Jos Centre for Continuing Education. There was also a serious gun battle between some youths and soldiers at Katako Junction and Shagari Corner/Angwan Rimi areas of Jos North.

The conveying of the dead bodies by the Izala sect members back to their communities further fuelled the violence as it was alleged to have inflamed passions and led to the burning of some Churches at Haliru Street (Christ Apostolic Church) and the killing of a pastor and members of his family.

Observation/Recommendations

We commend the role of the security agencies in bringing the situation under control and keeping the peace in Jos, while observing with dismay that, despite the fragile security, situation and polarisation of settlements within Jos and environs, and the early warning indicators pointing to possible violence during the Eid celebrations, proactive steps were not taken to avert the unfortunate events of August 29 and 30.

Prior to the violence, JDPC Peace Agents and EPRTs reported the likelihood of violence during the Eid celebrations in retaliation for the 2010 Christmas Eve bombings in some parts of Jos. These reports were channelled to some security agencies who gave assurances of being on top of the situation.

The conduct of some security personnel during the violence left more questions than answers in the minds of the public as to their role during violent conflict. Some JDPC Monitors and staff observed security personnel shooting indiscriminately, thus incensing the youths and escalating the violence. The excessive tooting of horns and blaring of sirens by security vehicles on the roads of Jos also heightened tension and created fear and panic.

It will be insightful to learn of the measures that were put in place by security agencies either to dissuade the Izala sect from using their old prayer grounds in view of security challenges, or to ensure their (the Izala sect) security given the fragile security situation.

We recommend that security organs be more proactive in response to early warning indicators to help prevent future violent incidents.

We recommend a regular and active security engagement with religious leaders and the prior issuance of official warnings based on mutually agreed commitments for peaceful celebrations of religious festivals.

We also recommend a close collaboration between security agencies and civil society, to synchronize peace efforts and crisis management measures.

We recommend an investigation into the August 29 and 30 violence, and urge that culpable persons are brought to book to help stamp out impunity.

In view of some public perceptions of partisanship of the military, we recommend a serious re-orientation on the part of security personnel to engender public confidence.

The use of sophisticated weapons by civilians during violent conflicts must be given serious attention.

Conclusion

The latest violence brings to the fore the high levels of suspicion and mistrust among communities, as well as the volatile and unpredictable security situation in Jos.

In view of the early warning reports in the public domain prior to the violence, a functional and properly coordinated early response mechanism by security agencies and civil society could have prevented or mitigated the violence of August 29 and 30.

The need for proactive intervention in the Jos conflict at all times can therefore not be underestimated.

Peace-building efforts must be intensified by peace practitioners to create safe spaces for genuine dialogue among religious leaders in particular and all major stakeholders in general.

Most importantly, to enable durable peace, the root causes of the Jos crisis, which are in the public domain and have been analysed and documented on several occasions, must be addressed dispassionately at all levels by all stakeholders, especially the Government.

JDPC will not relent in its inter-faith peace-building and inter-communal peace and harmony programmes. We will continue advocate dialogue and support community peace structures until durable peace returns to Jos.

WHAT MANNER OF CRISES IN JOS?

Reflection by the Archbishop released 2010

Introduction

The core Northern Nigerian States are generally known to have a predominantly Islamic population, but of course with a vibrant presence of Christian communities. In Southern Nigeria, it is admitted that Christians are in the majority, but with a significant Muslim population. For decades Christians and Muslims have coexisted peacefully in Nigeria. Even in the North, where there are more Muslims than Christians, there has been relative harmony and peaceful living together. Despite the fact that the Constitution of the Federal Republic of Nigeria says Nigeria is a secular State, Muslims in Northern Nigeria have for a long time enjoyed the existence of Islamic Sharia courts. The funding of Islamic schools with public funds has been without problems, just as are the annual pilgrimages to Saudi Arabia which are either highly subsidized or very well facilitated with public funds. Christians too enjoy similar patronage in Christian dominated States. This goes to show that there is some degree of general understanding between Muslims and Christians. The rise of a fanatical (puritanical) Islamic group in the 1980s known as *Maitatsine* did not create any strain in relations between Muslims and Christians, even though the activities of the group resulted in the deaths of both Muslims and Christians.

The Sharia Impact

In my opinion, it was not until the launching of what is now referred to as 'political sharia' in 1999 that much religious heat started being felt in Northern Nigeria. As observed earlier, Sharia had already been in existence for decades without any problems, but its dramatic re-introduction not by Islamic scholars but by State governors of some Northern states following the example of the Zamfara State Governor, Alhaji Sani Ahmed Yerima, opened the floodgates of mutual distrust, suspicion, intolerance and a paranoid fear that have since characterized Muslim-Christian relations. While the Muslims saw the renewed attention to Sharia and its application as commendable Islamic piety, Christians saw it as an attempt to create an Islamic society. It was seen to be more of a political move than a religious one; hence it was referred to by many Christians as a "Political Sharia". Muslims were at pains to explain that the Sharia law such as the flogging of criminals or cutting off of the hands of thieves only applied to Muslims. Christians were unconvinced about it and insisted that the Sharia affected them in many ways. For instance, in some states, there was the alleged attempt to enforce a particular dress code. It was forbidden for men to travel in the same vehicle as women, even though there was no adequate provision for transport facilities. Cinema houses, beer parlours, etc were forced to close and the consumption of alcohol was either restricted to certain peripheral areas or totally banned. These were the issues of particular concern to Christians, and certainly in my view the precursor to serious inter religious-tension in the country. Some Christians living in core Northern Islamic States had to relocate to safer zones and had to close their businesses or limit their scope of operation. Jos, the capital of Plateau State, soon witnessed an influx of persons from the so-called Sharia states. New buildings sprang up very fast, the human and vehicular population increased, and a fast expanding metropolis became obvious.

Subtle Religious Discrimination in some Northern States

In my opinion, the sudden introduction of the Sharia Law in the form propagated by members of the political class who were neither clerics nor models of piety was to gain political capital and assert its political relevance. The fiery zeal with which it started soon diminished because there was a national and international outcry about some of Sharia's punitive measures such as the cutting-off of hands. Some of its ideals could hardly be implemented effectively. There were logistic problems of men and women traveling separately. Even the forbidden recreational spots such as beer parlours continued to be patronized secretly. The introduction of the Sharia police (Hisbah) did not make compliance any better. Today, many who relocated because they feared a very rigid application of the Sharia Law have gone back to the so-called Sharia States. Churches continue to grow and expand there; the main problem is that in some States churches are denied certificates of occupancy. Many of the churches located in these States were issued certificates of occupancy by the colonial authorities, and even then such churches were usually located in areas which were considered on the periphery of the towns. Today it is very difficult to obtain permission for new church buildings. Land is available for residential and commercial purposes but not easily for church purposes, as indicated in this *Takardar shaidar cinikin fili* from the *Ofishin dagaci* (evidence of purchase of land from the village head's office): "*Ba choci, Ba gidan giya, Ba login tare da duk wani abinda hukuma ta hana*" (No building of church, alcoholic parlour, hotel or any other thing forbidden by law). The teaching of Christian Religious Education is not allowed in primary, secondary, and tertiary institutions, while chaplaincy services are not provided for Christian students in State or Federal-owned tertiary institutions. Christian programmes on State-owned or Federal-controlled electronic and print media are disallowed, just as Christian pilgrimages are not facilitated in the same manner as the Muslim pilgrimages.

On the whole, it cannot be said that there is an outright persecution of Christians in Northern Nigeria, but it cannot be denied that there is a subtle unwritten policy to control the growth and expansion of Christianity in these core northern States, as is evident in the denial of certificates of occupancy and the non-broadcasting of Christian religious programmes in the State media.

Causes of Jos Crises –Myth or Reality?
When on the 17 January 2010 a serious crisis erupted in Jos, many concluded that because there was widespread burning of Churches and killing of Christians as there was burning of mosques and killing of Muslims, it was necessarily a religious crisis between Muslims and Christians. I tried unsuccessfully to convince many, including university professors, business men, lawyers, Protestant and Pentecostal leaders and even some Catholic priests and laity, that the reason for the crisis was not religious even though it manifested itself as religious. As religion appeals more to human emotions, it was easier to employ it to express social discontent. Its use would attract sympathy and generate more national and international attention. Usually people use the effects of the crises to determine the causes instead of looking for the causes before seeing the effects. A crisis is said to be religious simply because it involves members of the two predominant religions in the area: Christianity and Islam.

The media were awash with the news that the crisis was triggered by religious motives. It was said that the gathering of Muslim youths to rebuild a house early on a Sunday morning, was a pretext to launch an attack on Sunday worshippers, and that it triggered the crisis. Does a crisis in which scores of both

Christians and Muslims were killed and a number of businesses and houses burnt, mosques and churches destroyed, make it a religious crisis? My answer was and is an emphatic 'no'. I carefully analysed the trend of the 2001, 2004, 2008 crises as I witnessed them, and came to the conclusion that the aftermath of each crisis had a religious coloration but deep down the causes were multi-dimensional. There was a combination of economic, social, ethnic, political and, of course, religious factors. Unfortunately, after each crisis everybody is found shouting, depending on which side of the religious divide they belong to, that the members of the other religion want to destroy their religion. Yet the reasons are not to be found in religion but in social factors. That a Hausa man was appointed Director of the Poverty Alleviation programme instead of an indigene is not a religious issue, but it ended up in the destruction of places of worship and killings in 1994. That a woman passed by a group of Muslim worshippers in 2001 was no reason to begin killings and destruction of property. That a Muslim boy in 2004 in Yelwa wanted to befriend a Christian girl was not enough reason for the kind of massacres and destruction we witnessed of both Muslims and Christians and their property. The reason was deep-seated ethnic animosity and the bitter encounters between herdsmen and farmers. That people were discontented with the results of the local government elections in 2008 was no reason to burn churches and mosques and kill. Yet that was what happened and therefore the crisis was interpreted as religious. No matter how hard I tried to make even my close associates realize that the root causes, which are of a social nature, are the real causes of the crises in various parts of Plateau State, it was difficult to convince them. Many Christians reason that there is the religious motive of Islamic expansionism and the quest for more members in an area that is known to have resisted Islamic incursion since the Jihad of Usman Dan Fodio in 1804. I am, however, happily surprised that many are realizing that the crises are not about religion *per se*, but a struggle for social and political relevance in the midst of competition for scarce resources; yet because religion is such an emotive issue, it is easier to use it to maximum advantage than any other weapon.

During the visit of the then Acting Vice-President Goodluck Jonathan to the United States in April 2010, he was interviewed on CNN and asked, "What about Jos, where we just saw an explosion of violence between Muslims and Christians? What can you do about that?" He promptly responded, "No, no, no. It's not a problem between Muslims and Christians. That is quite wrong actually...." (Cf. *Saturday Sun*, April 17, 20101, p.44). It was declared on the floor of the Senate that the problem of Jos was not caused by religion. Some prominent sons and daughters of Plateau State also agree that religion was not the only cause. Among them is Hon. Bitrus Kaze, a member of the House of Representatives, representing Jos South/East Federal Constituency, who said in an interview that: "the root cause of Jos crisis has always been who owns the land and not religion, politics or ethnicity...." (*Daily Sun*, Tuesday, March 2, 2010, p.22). Traditional leaders from Nasarawa, Benue, Taraba and Plateau States met and unanimously agreed that, "the root cause of the disturbances was politics and not religion" (cf. *The Guardian*, Saturday, February 13, 2010, p.49). The Presidential Committee on Jos crisis in its findings mentioned a number of factors such as matters relating to long-standing communal suspicion and dispute over ownership/land matters in Jos, indigeneship, electoral malpractices, community insensitivity, imposition of candidates and politics of exclusion, economic factors, youth unemployment, non-implementation of past reports and White papers, farmer-grazer conflict, media propaganda, etc. The report says, "The Committee found that religion was not the main cause of the January 17th, 2010 crisis in Jos but it was rather exploited by some individuals and groups to gain political popularity and support. It also discovered that some religious preachers incite hatred and violence". On the ongoing crisis in Jos, a group of elders in Plateau State led by the former Secretary to the Plateau State Government, Mr. Ezekiel Gomos said, "The unending crises are traceable to deep-seated grievances that have economic, political, historical and social dimensions...left unattended for several decades and have transformed the once serene and peaceful city of Jos into a gunpowder keg, always ready to explode at the slightest provocation"(*Daily Trust*, Wednesday, January 12, 2011, p.4). With all these statements, I feel that religion deserves to be discharged and acquitted as the only cause of the Jos mayhem.

The Jos Christmas Eve Bombings

The Christmas Eve bombings in Jos were another dimension to the series of crises that had started in 1994. It was a carefully planned incident expected to disrupt a very important religious event that is at the heart of the Christian religion. I had thought this was the time for those who had been interpreting the crises on the Plateau as a religious crisis to stand firmly on their convictions and say that this particular attack was deliberately aimed at offending Christian spiritual sensitivities, but surprisingly the State Governor in a broadcast said it was politically motivated by his political opponents or detractors. I thought this was the time to tell the whole world that the Christian religion was being targeted and attacked, but political considerations made it convenient to shift the cause to politics. This is obviously because the 2011 elections are around the corner and nobody wants to offend either of the two main religions; so it was politically more expedient to find a scapegoat in politics rather than religion.

Acting the Ostrich

I however still maintain that the refusal to attend to the numerous issues at the root of the recurring crises is what is giving birth to new crises which are always interpreted as a war between Christians and Muslims. When the crises were wrongly called "religious" and I knew they were not, I kept warning that doing so would only trigger the interest of religious fundamentalists, here or elsewhere, who would feel that their fellow co-religionists were suffering in Plateau State and so would feel compelled, and as a mark of religious solidarity, to help their suffering members. This help could be of a moral, financial nature, or training in the art of religious war, or the supply of dangerous weapons to cause maximum destruction to the perceived enemies. As the then Chairman of the Christian Association of Nigeria, I was said not to be aggressive enough in my defence of the Christian religion. The fact is that because the religious aspect of the crisis was so overstressed, the attention and sympathy of many religious groups have been attracted to Plateau State. Apart from activities of the Boko Haram in neigbouring States, a fundamentalist organization going by the name *Jama'atu Ahlus-Sunnah Lidda' Awati Wal Jihad* has claimed responsibility for the multiple explosions/attacks in Jos, threatening to attack other parts of Nigeria. Who knows the huge resources invested in this enterprise by local and foreign interested parties? Who knows the many youths that have been trained in the art of bomb making and bomb attacks? Who knows when youths will graduate to suicide bomb attacks all in the name of religion, as demonstrated by the young Nigerian, Abdul Muttallab, who in 2009 on the eve of Christmas attempted to bring down the American passenger airline in the United States? The Christmas Eve attacks in Jos happened at the same time as attacks on churches in Maiduguri, Borno State and the killing of some Christians. Similar attacks and killings of Christians have been reported in Iraq and Egypt. Is there a grand international conspiracy to destabilize by force the Christian religion?

Conclusion

As far as I am concerned, the failure of authorities to consider critically the underlying social factors and to bring the architects of these crises to book is responsible for these repeated attacks. A new terrorist strategy has been born in Nigeria and we are now stuck with fanatical religious groups with links to the terrorist Al Qaeda organization. From the ordinary use of knives and arrows we have moved up a step higher to use bombs to blast people out of existence. This is a step away from suicide bombing. Perhaps the candidates to be used for this are still in training and we can only wait for their reign of terror to begin when they graduate. It is also rumoured that some youths are seriously considering resorting to fetish powers for protection and self-defence to withstand the constant attacks. If all the youths think about now is attacks and counter-attacks, what is the future for them? We inevitably end up in a vicious circle of violence.

This whole affair has gone beyond what religious leaders can handle. In previous crises religious leaders were summoned to preach to their people and to urge them to fast and pray. What is needed now is for the authorities to research the various factors that have come into play, masquerading as religion, and deal decisively with them. Culprits of crimes in the name of religion have gone unpunished. Acts of injustice have not been remedied. Distributive justice has been overlooked, giving rise to the many militant groups in the Northern and Southern parts of Nigeria. To reduce the present crisis to the mere machination of political enemies is to act the ostrich. It is mere escapism. What is needed is that the multi-dimensional root causes of what could destabilize Nigeria in the name of religion must be identified and tackled definitively, rather than the attempt to blame religion for what is obviously caused mainly by social factors. Religion should make better citizens and a holier nation, it should build a kingdom of justice, peace and righteousness, and it should not be used as a weapon of war and destruction.

WAITING FOR ANOTHER "RELIGIOUS RIOT"?
A perspective of the Archbishop released 2010

At a recent workshop on conflict management, a presenter pointed out that religion is a generator of conflicts, and gave instances of how at both the global and the local levels, religious wars have caused monumental destruction to lives and property. I asked him if he was aware also that at one time the Marxists posited that religion was the "opium" of the people, namely that religion induces a sleep-like behaviour. It gives a false satisfaction and encourages one to leave undone what should be done here and now in the utopian hope, for instance, that one's lack of struggle in the economic, social or political spheres will be compensated for with heavenly rewards. By showing a litany of crises that were said to be of a religious nature, the presenter wanted to tell the audience the harm that religion has done to humanity. There is no doubt that throughout history, precious lives have been lost on account of so-called religious crises, and a lot of strange and funny things have happened in the name of religion; but whether religion can be described as an opium or generator of conflicts is very debatable. If on the one hand religion is opium, how does one explain its positive global contributions to education, healthcare, human rights and a host of other social issues? If on the other hand, religion is a conflict generator , then it contradicts itself. The word religion comes from the Latin word, *ligare*, which means "to bind". The sincere practice of religion helps the adherents to develop a binding interpersonal relationship with the Supreme Being and harmony with fellow human beings. Religion unfortunately has come to be associated with conflict, either because it is being manipulated or because its practice is devoid of rationality.

Many violent crises have been experienced in Nigeria in the last twenty-five years. Even when facts indicate that these were ethnically or politically motivated, most of them, particularly in

Northern Nigeria, somehow ended up as a religious crisis. The question is whether there has really been a "religious crisis" in Nigeria when the riot happened as a result of a clash of genuine religious values. It is very convenient for what begins as a political or ethnic or student misunderstanding to be manipulated to wear a religious garb, because of the religious sensitivity of Nigerians and the deep respect accorded to religion in the country. It is said that Nigerians are very religious and they take their religion wherever they go. It is not surprising therefore that religion has been used and is being used as a tool for asserting individual or collective identity even as a political bargaining weapon.

The recent outbursts of riots to protest against the negative and blasphemous caricatures of the Prophet Mohammed in cartoons by the Danish paper, *Jyllanda Posten*, added unfortunately to the list of what are often termed religiously instigated crises that we have witnessed in this country. The expression of discontent associated with the cartoons assumed an ugly dimension in Nigeria , markedly different from the peaceful manner in which others in the Middle East and elsewhere demonstrated against the publications. The protests against the cartoons in Maiduguri erupted into a violent conflict, and within the space of four hours, many shops, houses, and churches were razed to the ground and, worst of all, a couple of dozen people were killed. Among those killed in the wake of this needless violent demonstration was a Catholic priest, Fr Michael Gajere, the Parish Priest of St Rita's Church, Buluntuku. Ironically, Fr Gajere was the Maiduguri diocesan Director of the Justice and Peace Programmes, but he succumbed to violent death at the hands of gangsters. According to the altar boys who were with the late priest, the armed gangsters entered Fr. Gajere's Church, cruelly hacked him to death and then dragged and set fire to him. It was as disgusting as it was beastly.

The violent protest in Maiduguri found echoes in Bauchi, Gombe and Kaduna even if for slightly different reasons. Before long, lives and property were lost. As corpses of victims were conveyed to Onitsha, a reprisal attack on Muslims of Northern origin resident in Onitsha enveloped the city and in no time the dead were counted in their dozens and property destroyed. Some Igbo protesters who believe that very often Igbos are the victims of religious or other crises in the North of Nigeria said "Enough is enough," and some of them embarked on a revenge mission at the end of which many Muslims were either killed or injured and mosques burnt. Tension was building in different parts of Nigeria, and but for the Grace of God we would have witnessed further monumental losses – no thanks to misplaced religious zeal.

The violence and carnage witnessed in the areas where riots took place impels one to ask why we in Nigeria always seem to be caught unawares. Is it because we lack proactive security sensitivity or we are happy that such crises create opportunities for looters, bloodthirsty hooligans or those who stand to benefit politically or economically from the ensuring chaos?

It is ironic that the Nigeria Government continues to spend huge resources and time in the name of convincing international investors to come and invest in our country. Let us honestly ask ourselves if we really have a favourable environment for foreign investors, tourists or visitors in our country. When we travel abroad, people tell us how insecure Nigeria is. Even as we patriotically struggle to convince them that Nigeria is among the safest places on earth, some believe that Nigeria is a country where crises easily erupt like a volcano with the capacity of consuming anybody in sight. The repeated abduction of foreign oil workers by militant youths of the Niger Delta seeking the entrenchment of their social and economic rights has not portrayed Nigeria to the international community as a safe place to do business. This is worsened by the frequent eruption of what is termed religious crises even when one least expects it. No matter what defences we put up to convince non–Nigerians that things are not as bad as the foreign media report them, some still believe that "the fear of Nigeria is the beginning of wisdom".

Our country Nigeria is a beautiful country. The crimes or murders committed in our major cities pale into insignificance compared to what happens in some cities of Europe, America and even in some African countries. We only have the bad luck of not being able to promptly correct false information and propaganda disseminated about our country through negative international media publicity.

All the same, one should wonder why in spite of the military, the State Security Service (SSS), and the police intelligence network, we are always handicapped in preventing crises or bringing them to an immediate halt as soon as they start. One may ask if it is a matter of criminal complicity, leadership negligence or security agents' indifference. When a crisis begins, no matter the reasons, it is expected that all efforts should be made to stop it from spreading. With an improved communication network, our security agents should have more security information and the public should be able to report without delay to them when there are invasions by armed robbers, assassins or hooligans. Requests for help to security agents are not always met with a prompt response, either because the security agents have no transport or equipment, or are afraid that the armed robbers or hooligans are better armed. If any help comes, it is often too late, and after untold harm has been done. It is sad that even where there is a military barracks a short distance away, senseless killings and destruction may be going on and the soldiers cannot put up a mere appearance even if to scare the rioters, the simple reason being that they have not received instructions to intervene from the "Headquarters".

In the case of the Maiduguri riots, it was reported that it took several hours before there was any decisive intervention by security agents. Likewise in Onitsha: it was not possible to arrest the breakdown of order until many were killed and property destroyed. One wonders why the police in Maiduguri granted the permit to demonstrate against the publication of the cartoon of Prophet Mohammed without anticipating a possible security breach. Similarly, a good situation analysis would have revealed that conveying the corpses of victims of the riots to Onitsha would trigger hostile reactions by their relations in Onitsha who would see the death of their loved ones in Northern Nigeria as act of unprovoked aggression. Why are we always caught off-guard?

Indices which in developed countries offer clues to unravel crime or to prevent crime are often overlooked here. This casual indifference must be checked by security agencies and government leaders.

It has almost become normal in Nigeria to expect a violent reaction once a religious group perceives that a non-complimentary utterance or action is targeted at their religion. Our authorities seem to be unduly self-complacent as they often believe that tension generated over religious issues will soon "fizzle out". It is almost becoming a habit that at the slightest provocation, hell is let loose and in the name of religion, lives and property are consumed and hard-earned means of livelihood are destroyed overnight, while social infrastructure are also recklessly destroyed. Where dialogue could solve the problem, we choose violence. Rather than being led by rationality, we are led by emotional outbursts when dealing with religious issues. If we could direct similar energy and passion to other areas of socio–economic endeavour, our country would rank among the greatest on earth. In traditional African society, conflicts and disputes are settled by elders at early morning or late evening community gatherings.

One would expect that with better education and contact with other civilizations, we would be able to handle our ethnic or religious differences better even when we feel that our ethnic, religious or political sensitivities have been assaulted. While many other societies are making rapid progress in scientific and technological discoveries, we seem by our attitude of killing and destroying at the slightest provocation to be retreating into the Stone Age.

It is really sad that instead of focusing on the things that unite us, we Nigerians prefer to dwell on matters that pitch us against each other. People put their ethnic group's interest before the national one or the common good and go out of their way to ensure that, dead or alive, their parochial interests should reign supreme. The patriotic spirit needed for the proper growth and development of a country is subordinated or subsumed under ethnic chauvinism or parochial interests in Nigeria. Adherents of the Christian and

Islamic faith fight tooth and nail to have their religious perspectives reflected in national policy matters and in appointments to strategic government positions. Where one person or a group feels edged out, religion is used to alarm those who care to listen that there is discrimination, marginalization, alienation, etc. The attempt by leaders to balance ethnic and religious issues in Nigeria, even though commendable, has brought about a situation where in appointments square pegs are put in round holes. In the name of federal character, merit is sacrificed on the altar of mediocrity.

The question must be asked if the frequent so-called religious crises which have occurred in Kano, Kaduna, Zaria, Kafanchan, Jos, Katsina, Bauchi, Lafia etc. truly originated to promote genuine religious ideals or to advocate improved holier lifestyles. Often crises start from very negligible incidents. If for instance there is a quarrel between a Christian and a Muslim over a motor–cycle accident or a sharp disagreement over debt repayments, the circle of events soon widens, and before long the whole matter is given a religious coloration. Since the matter is between a Muslim and a Christian, passers–by, who may not even know the full details of the incident, in the name of supporting their co–religionists can engage in blind attacks and irrational displays of brute force, so that a whole village community or town is soon engulfed in intolerable destruction of lives and property.

The 2001 crisis in Yelwa-Shendam, Plateau State which was said to be a crisis between Muslims and Christians was in fact more to do with cow theft, local leadership tussles, ethnic suspicions and antagonism than with anything religious. Churches, mosques, hospitals, schools, etc. were destroyed on the flimsy excuse that a Muslim boy wanted friendship with a Christian girl against the directive of the local Christian Association of Nigeria (CAN) that no Christian girl should befriend a Muslim boy and vice versa. Ridiculous as this seems, it is believed that this was said to be the cause of the crisis. We know however, that the real issues involved are property ownership, insecurity, unemployment and the competition for scarce economic resources which have to be shared between ethnic groups. Once social conditions improve and people are better empowered economically, there is going to be a drastic reduction in the cases of hooliganism masquerading as religious zeal.

The cartoon protests have been interpreted by some analysts to be a protest against the political third term agenda being vigorously campaigned for by some political acolytes of President Olusegun Obasanjo. The struggle for political relevance or supremacy is often enough reason in Nigeria to use religion as a lethal weapon. Its capacity to generate enormous emotional venom comes in as a convenient tool in the hands of selfish politicians and misguided or narrow minded religious leaders.

It is high time that we in Nigeria say 'no' to crimes committed in the name of religion. Religion does not encourage violence. Religion should bind us rather than divide us. We have had enough bloodshed and destruction under the false pretence of religious zeal. Parents of Christian and Muslim children must refrain from polluting the tender minds of their children with hate massages. Preachers must seek to deepen the knowledge of their religions by proper training, and refrain from preaching inciting or provocative sermons. Politicians who parade themselves as leaders championing religious causes only to exploit the advantages of religion for their ulterior political motives must repent. They must refrain from paying and instigating jobless youths to foment trouble in order to create the enabling environment for political confusion to flourish. The youths must desist from the culture of violence and embrace the culture of peace, non–violence and dialogue. No matter the circumstances or the degree of provocation, they must not spill the blood of another person in the name of fighting or defending religious and political interests.

The youths must remember that those who pay them a pittance to cause trouble, or those who promise them an eternal reward when they kill or are killed in the name of God, will not like the participation of their biological children or close relatives in the riots. In any case, their children may be abroad studying in prestigious institutions or may be gainfully employed. As we encourage the spirit of dialogue and enlightened reaction even in the face of provocative issues, our Government must be more proactive in stemming the tide of violence. During crises in Nigeria, too little in terms of security is done too late. Alert security agents should be able to frustrate orchestrated riots. The surest way, however, to stem the regular occurrences of riots which in most cases are motivated by factors other than religious, is to provide good governance, ensure distributive justice, and provide adequate jobs or enough farming, trading or skill acquisition incentives for the teeming population of our youth. Development is the other name for peace. Where there is peace there must have been justice and development, and where there is justice and development peace will flow like a river. Justice plus development and good governance minus ignorance and unemployment equals positive peace and social harmony.

Nigeria's leaders and security agents should not wait for another "religious" riot before embarking on the characteristic fire–brigade approach. Prevention is better than cure.

The Sultan of Sokoto, Alh. Dr. Sa'ad Abubakar III, and CAN President, Pastor Ayo Orisejafor

Peace meetings with religious groups, government, security agents, other stakeholders

The author with the US Ambassador during a courtesy call to the Muslim community in Jos

Stakeholders in peace building

Setting agenda for peace at a meeting of religious leaders and government officials

Peace meetings with religious groups, government, security agents, other stakeholders

The Archbishop's initiated-interfaith dialogue in session

Dialogue of life

The author playing host to former COCIN President, Rev. Prof. Pandam Yamsat

Peace meetings with religious groups, government, security agents, other stakeholders

The author receiving the former governor of Plateau State, Chief Joshua Dariye, at a peace forum in the Pastoral Centre

The Archbishop with Chief Solomon Lar and other stakeholders in peace building

Alhaji Abdullahi Adamu, former Nasarawa State governor being ushered in by the author at a peace forum at the Pastoral Centre, Jos

Peace meetings with religious groups, government, security agents, other stakeholders

Governor Jonah Jang welcoming Anthony Cardinal Okogie, Archbishop of Lagos, to Plateau State while the author (middle) looks on

Archbishop Kaigama being received by Long Goemai of Goemailand, Miskom Hubert Shaldas II, and Emir of Wase, late Dr. Haruna Abdullahi during a reconciliatory rally after the Yelwa crisis

Late Emir of Wase, Dr. Haruna Abdullahi, Chief Joshua Dariye, former governor of Plateau State, and Rt. Rev. Benjamin Kwashi, Anglican Archbishop of Jos (standing) at a peace workshop held at the Pastoral Centre, Jos

Peace meetings with religious groups, government, security agents, other stakeholders

Dialogue with the former governor of Nasarawa State, Alhaji Abdullahi Adamu

At a CAN Peace rally during which he delivered the message

Former Governor Joshua Dariye and his deputy, Michael Botmang, with the Archbishop at a workshop on peace building at the Pastoral Centre, Jos

Dialogue with Traditional Rulers

The author and the late Emir of Wase, Dr. Haruna Abdullahi, exchanging pleasantries

The late Gbong Gwom Jos, Da Dr. Fom Bot (middle), late Frank Tarddy, and the author during a visit at the Gbong Gwom's Palace

The Archbishop with some members of the Plateau State Traditional Council led by Da Jacob Gyang Buba, the Gbong Gwom Jos (second left), at the author's office

Dialogue with Traditional Rulers

The late Gbong Gwom Jos, Da Dr. Fom Bot with the Archbishop

The late Emir of Wase, Dr. Haruna Abdullahi with the Archbishop

International interventions

The author with the German Chancellor, Angela Merkel, the Sultan of Sokoto, Dr. Sa'ad Abubakar, Bishop Hassan Kukah of Sokoto and other delegates in Abuja during which he (Archbishop) spoke about the situation of crises in Northern Nigeria

The author (first left) with the German Chancellor, Angela Merkel, and other delegates at a peace programme in Berlin, Germany

International Interventions

Late Emir of Wase, Dr. Adbullahi Haruna with the author in Osnabruck, Germany to discuss peace and reconciliation in Nigeria

A warm welcome in a mosque in Osnabruck

Assumption Choir from Abuja Archdiocese entertaining delegates in Osnabruck

International Interventions

Muslim clerics demonstrating their mode of worship in a mosque in Osnabruck

The author with Rev. Sugmenda Teertha Swamiji (Hinduism) (middle), Abbot, Udipi Sri Puthige Math, from India and a senior Hindu priest (left)

On the author's left is His Eminence, Dr. Abdallah F. Al-Lihadan (Assistant Vice Minister for Islamic Affairs, Endowments, Dawah, Call and Guidance), Saudi Arabia. Fr. Joseph Shaba (a priest of the Syrian Orthodox Church of Antioch) and on the author's right is a senior cleric from Saudi Arabia

Solidarity with Muslim community

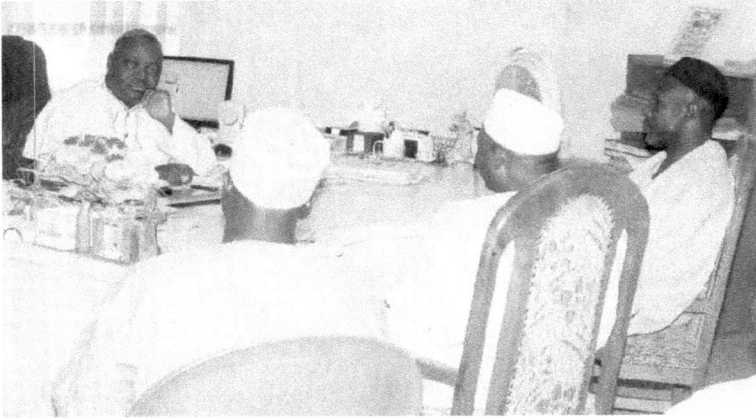
Meeting with a Muslim delegation

The Archbishop with representatives of the Wase Traditional Council and the Chief of Kona, Mr. Augustine Vengkani (2nd right) at his thanksgiving to mark his 25th priestly anniversary in Kona, Taraba State

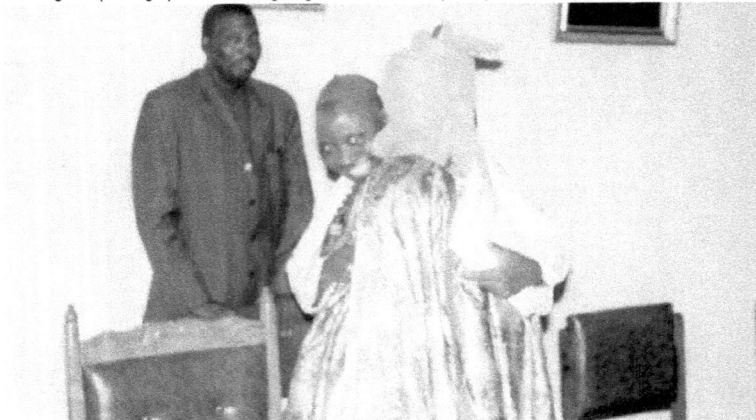
The author in a warm embrace with the late Emir of Wase, Dr. Haruna Abdullahi

Solidarity with Muslim community

Visit of the British High Commissioner, Bob Dewar, to the Jos Central Mosque during which the Archbishop delivered solidarity message

The Emir of Wase and the author signing a resolution on peace and reconciliation in Plateau State on behalf of the Muslim and Christian communities

The Archbishop with the Plateau State Grand Khadhi, Alhaji Adamu Kanam, on the occasion of Id El-Fitr 2002 during which the former presented a message for end of Ramadan from the Pontifical Council for Interreligious Dialogue in the Vatican

Solidarity with Muslim community

A visit to the Archbishop by the Dynamic Women and Youth Negotiation for Peace

Courtesy visit to the Archbishop by Imam Mohammad Ashafa and Pastor James Wuye, founders of Interfaith Centre, Kaduna, and coauthors of "The Pastor and the Imam"

Late Emir of Wase, the author and Bob Dewar, the British High Commissioner to Nigeria, at St. Michael's Church, Nassarawa Gwong in the aftermath of the 2008 crisis

Section Four
ATTEMPTS AT
INTER-RELIGIOUS HARMONY

OUR MISSION OF PEACE AND RECONCILIATION IN PLATEAU STATE

A Homily at the Prayer for Peace and Reconciliation held at the Rwang Pam Stadium, Jos, October 30, 2004

I welcome you all who have come from all the parts of the Archdiocese of Jos to pray in a very special way for Plateau State. May the Lord hear our prayers; amen. You and I know that since September 2001 to date we have experienced unpleasant happenings in the state - brothers taking up arms against brothers, brothers destroying valuable property of brothers. We became divided along tribal, religious and political lines. As we assemble here today we pray that all these will be reversed in Jesus' name. Peace is God's gift to us. If we have lost it temporarily and we ask God in faith, he will give it back to us. We therefore ask that true peace, genuine reconciliation and the healing of wounded hearts will become a reality for all of us. Sirach 35:17 says that "the humble man's prayer pierces the clouds ...until the Most High takes notice of him". We are confident that our cries to God for deliverance from the spirit of hatred, revenge and division will pierce the heavens and our Lord will be merciful to us.

Our first reading from Is. 57: 15-19 says that the contrite and humble person who seeks the face of God will find him. The Lord says, "From now on I will console, I will heal and fully comfort him. ... I will bring smiles to his [their] lips. Peace! Peace to him who is far and to him who is near". We ask the Lord to give his peace to the victims of the crises that started in Jos in 2001 and manifested in Wase, Yelwa and other places, with unfortunate loss of lives and property. We appeal to God to look from his throne of mercy to control the events in Plateau State; to heal our wounds and never to allow any crisis caused by politics, ethnicity or religion to happen again in this land. Both Islam and Christianity hold life as sacred and regard highly the virtues of love and peace. If the majority of people in Plateau State are Christians and Muslims how do we explain the fact that mosques and churches were destroyed, Christians and Muslims killed or displaced? Something must have gone wrong. The reading from the letter to the Colossians has a message for all of us in Plateau State: "Put on compassion, kindness, humility, meekness and patience; bear with one another and forgive one another... Take love as your belt and may the peace of Christ overflow in your hearts" (Col. 3:12).

The prayers we offer today are in accordance with Catholic traditions. We adore Jesus present in the Holy Eucharist. We believe he is our healer and comforter. In Mk. 5:24-33 we read the story of the woman who suffered the flow of blood for twelve years and had visited many doctors, spending everything she had only to get worse. When she found Jesus she touched the fringe of Jesus' cloak and was healed instantly. During the crises the blood of men, women and children flowed in Plateau State. By the special intervention of Jesus the bloodbath has stopped and we pray that blood will never be shed in our state again. In Numbers 21 we are told of the Israelites who complained against God and Moses in the desert. God was angry with them and sent serpents to bite them. Many died. They asked Moses to plead with God for they have sinned against him. Yahweh asked Moses to make a bronze serpent and set it on a standard. Whenever a person was bitten he looked towards the bronze serpent and he lived. The Blessed Sacrament in the monstrance is our New Testament bronze serpent. We believe that Jesus is present there and if we look up to him and ask he can heal us and our land. As we look up and recognize Jesus in the Blessed Sacrament what do we ask of him? I gave a formula during the National Eucharistic Congress in Ibadan in 2002. I said that our five fingers could represent our requests. The thumb is closest to the position of our heart. It represents those we love dearly such as our parents, brothers, sisters and friends. We pray for them. The index finger represents those who teach or are responsible for the training of others. What they teach can either build or destroy. They need our prayers. The tall finger represents the leaders – political, religious, traditional etc. They can make a big difference in people's lives if they lead their followers with the fear of God. We must pray for our president, Olusegun Obasanjo, our Sole Administrator Gen. Chris Alli (rtd), security agents and all those in sensitive political offices. Our prayer is that they will find the correct solutions to the political problems of Plateau State and Nigeria as a whole. We pray that the politicians in Plateau State will unite and act for the common good of the people rather than for their personal or selfish political ambitions. Religious and traditional leaders must intensify along with the politicians the search for harmony among the citizens of the state. The finger regarded as the weak finger represents the poor, the hungry, the displaced, and the helpless who have no one to fight their cause. It has almost become normal in Nigeria that before you get any good job, get admission to a good higher institution, get promoted or to receive your pension after retirement, if you do not know somebody who knows somebody who knows somebody you will suffer alone or die in silence. Let us remember the many helpless Nigerians in this situation. The last finger stands for "I". As I pray for others, including my enemies, I must pray for myself. It is only when I am good that I can offer something positive to the society. The climax of all our prayers today is that peace will flow like a river in all parts of Plateau State. Who can make this happen? God. Who can contribute to make this happen? You and I. The scripture says, "Blessed are the peacemakers..." Let us all work for peace and God shall richly bless us.

Our prayer for peace today cannot be in vain. Our God answers prayers. A priest visited a man and his wife whom he wedded after eight years. They had no child. He prayed with them and suggested that the man should go to Lourdes in France where the Blessed Virgin Mary appeared in 1858. People are known to have received a lot of miracles by visiting Lourdes to pray there. The man (Patrick) set off on a pilgrimage to Lourdes. There he lighted a candle before the Blessed Sacrament, prayed and returned home. Four years later the same priest went to visit the family and found four children playing in front of the house. He asked the oldest one who he was, the boy said he was the son of Patrick and the priest asked, "Who are the other three", the boy said, "this one is my brother after me, the other one is following him and the girl is our youngest sister". Then the priest asked, "Where is your mother?". The boy said, "Our mother has just been taken to the maternity hospital to deliver a child". The priest asked, "and where is your father?" The boy said, "our father has rushed back to Lourdes to put out the candle". God answered the prayers of Patrick and his wife beyond their expectations. That is how God will answer our prayer for peace today. His plan for Plateau State is peace not war.

We thank God that peace has returned to Plateau State. What we ask God for now is PERMANENT PEACE. November 18th is the designated date for the end of emergency rule in Plateau State. What next? *Quod Erat Demonstrandum*. We thank Gen. Chris Alli and his team for the good job done during this period of emergency rule and for initiating the peace conference. It was a huge success. The members of the Plateau State Peace Conference, comprising representatives of over 50 ethnic groups did what other parts of Nigeria should emulate. They sought solutions to problems of Plateau State not by confrontation but by peaceful dialogue. It has worked in Plateau State. It can work elsewhere.

Politicians in Plateau State must learn from the mistakes of the past. They should bury their political differences so that collectively they can shape the political, economic and social fortunes of Plateau State for posterity. As soon as democratic structures are re-instated, we beg those at the helm of political affairs to be sensitive to issues of social justice and to pay more attention to the needs of the people rather than accumulating personal fortunes.

The Plateau People should unite now more than ever. We are still "the Home of Peace and Tourism". May we continue to be so in Jesus' name. Amen.

IN THE SADDLE AS CHAIRMAN OF INTER-RELIGIOUS COUNCIL ON PEACE AND HARMONY

An inaugural speech as Chairman of the Plateau State Inter-Religious Council on Peace and Harmony, at the Government House, Jos, December 14, 2005.

His Excellency, Chief Joshua Dariye, Governor of Plateau State,
Members of the Plateau State Executive Council,
Distinguished members of the Plateau State Inter-Religious Council on Peace and Harmony,
Ladies and Gentlemen.

Peace is God's gift to humanity. His desire is peace for all, not war. Considering that there can be no option to peaceful and harmonious coexistence, the Plateau State Government has in its wisdom constituted the Inter-Religious Council and charged it with the responsibility of preaching peace, inspiring peace in all, seeking reconciliation and helping to heal the broken or wounded hearts as a result of the inevitable tension that arises in every human society.

I see this assignment as God-ordained, and it is my joy on behalf of the distinguished members of this body to congratulate and commend the Plateau State Governor for contemplating the composition of such a Council and for formally inaugurating it on 24th November, 2005.

I wish to believe that His Excellency has given a lot of thought to the composition of the Council and has taken time to choose men and women of integrity, whose antecedents demonstrate that they are lovers and promoters of peace. I call on all of us to be united in this venture to, in the words of the Governor, "intermediate on religious issues and forge understanding amongst adherents of our two dominant religions...also offer advisory services to Government on matters of religious importance so as to generate understanding, peace and harmony in the handling of such issues... to deliberate on reported cases of religious conflicts to find urgent solutions".

Wise people say that if one desires to change the world, he or she must start by changing himself or herself. Our collective desire is to promote religious peace and harmony and to help our people to use religion positively for not only spiritual progress but socio-economic positive transformation. All of us members of this Council must therefore pledge to begin our assignment with a personal resolve to work as a united group, transcending our religious and even political leanings and interests in order to arrive at the common good of Plateau State. This entails that we must be prepared to make personal sacrifices, and empty ourselves of prejudices about one another. The categorization of our people into Muslims, Protestants, Catholics, Pentecostals, etc often has negative consequences. Rather than view ourselves as made in God's image and likeness, we overemphasize our differences. God allowed differences not to destabilize humanity but as a variety which should enrich and build us. Those who kill or cause unnecessary harm to others for whatever reason violate God's plan for humanity, for life and for the future.

I foresee in this noble assignment three approaches: familiarizing ourselves with each other as a Council in the spirit of mutual trust, reaching out to the grassroots in our State and, when and where necessary, going beyond our State in search of peace. We shall need to work with villagers, urban dwellers, youths, women, students, security agents, traditional rulers, religious leaders, politicians, influential opinion leaders, etc.

Today people talk of what is termed "negative peace," that is the peace that springs from an absence of direct or systematic violence, but which does not mean that weapons are not easily available or social conditions of life have improved to the extent that hunger, ignorance and diseases have been drastically reduced. "Negative peace" to my mind is the sort of peace enjoyed by Nigerians today.

"Positive peace" however is what we yearn for and should work for. "Positive peace springs from the presence of justice throughout society with opportunities for all, a fair distribution of power and resources, protection from harm and impartial enforcement of the law. Positive peace means the elimination of the root causes of war, violence, and injustice, and the conscious effort to build a society that reflects these commitments." (CAFOD, "The rough guide to conflict and peace policy".)

It is said that "where there is justice there will be peace and where there is peace there must have been justice." Our search for permanent peace cannot be divorced from the issues of justice and truth. Pope Benedict XVI in his message for the 2006 World Day of Peace asserts that peace must not be seen as the "mere absence of war, but as a harmonious coexistence of individual citizens within a society governed by justice, one in which the good is also achieved, to the extent possible, for each of them. The truth of peace calls upon everyone to cultivate productive and sincere relationships; it encourages them to seek out and to follow the paths of forgiveness and reconciliation, to be transparent in their dealings with others, and to be faithful to their word".

As we put our heads together and rub minds to engineer "positive peace", let me remind us of what Gandhi, the late Indian Prime Minister referred to as the seven social sins against the society. These seven social sins, inscribed on the headstone of

Gandhi's tomb, are: 1) Politics without principle, 2) Wealth without work, 3) Pleasure without conscience, 4) Knowledge without character, 5) Commerce without morality, 6) Science without humanity, 7) Worship without sacrifice. We may need in the course of our work to identify where we are guilty or guiltless using the above list as a roadmap.

I wish to end my address by thanking you for accepting to serve on this Council. As we continue to perform the enormous task assigned to us with faith in God, our work will become a delightful duty, as we shall also share in the blessings of peace that God now gives and will give our people.

I pray that the observations or suggestions made by this body will help the State Government in its unquenchable desire to create a greater atmosphere of peace and harmony in Plateau State.

In God we trust, and we hereby entrust all our deliberations, plans, strategies, individual and collective struggles for peace and harmony in Plateau State to the Lord Almighty who alone can give peace and harmony.

I wish that each of us will associate with the prayer of the twelfth-century Friar, St. Francis of Assisi, and pray with him, Lord, "Make me a channel of your peace, where there is hatred let me bring your love, where there is injury your pardon, Lord, and where there is doubt, true faith in you... where there is despair in life let me bring hope, where there is darkness, only light, and where there is sadness, ever joy...."

I wish us all a happy and fruitful deliberation.

CHRISTIANITY AS A TOOL FOR CRISIS MANAGEMENT AND PEACE BUILDING

A paper presented at the 31ˢᵗ Supreme Council Convention of the Knights of St. Mulumba held in Jos, November 26, 2010

Preamble

It is with great pleasure and gratitude to God that I on behalf of the Archdiocese of Jos welcome and host you to the 31ˢᵗ Supreme Council Convention of the Knights of St. Mulumba in Nigeria. You are most warmly welcome to Jos city, the ever-peaceful city even despite the previous temporary disruption of peace. I thank God for journeying mercies granted to all of you who have come from far and near.

As we were growing up we saw neighbours in the neighbourhood disagreeing with each other, but differences were quickly settled. As little children, we argued and fought one another over very simple things. A couple of decades on, we heard of inter- and intra-ethnic squabbles that were almost tearing the brotherhood of years gone by. We saw elders of communities sit early in the morning or late in the evening under trees to resolve disputes in the village or between villages before they escalated. Our teachers told us of the civil crisis that was ravaging the land consuming uncountable human beings and properties. These conflicts were not limited to our land, as there was regular news of conflict between the Israelis and the Palestinians, and even today in the Middle the ill consequences of conflicts are felt daily. The recent attack in Iraq on Christians in a Cathedral Church, where dozens were killed and the Islamic militants made it clear that it was a legitimate attack on Christianity aimed at the destruction of its pillars in Iraq, is a pointer that we live in a very troubled world. The agitation in the Niger Delta has led to kidnapping and hostage taking (a lucrative economic venture today); terrorism now is becoming a way of expressing social discontent and peace is being threatened by the day. I see this presentation today on "Christianity as a Tool for Crisis Management and Peace Building" as an opportunity to share my experience with you Knights of the Church who are defenders of the faith and promoters of peace at all levels. I have in my own little way had a share of living through serious crises and I have made attempts towards peaceful resolution. With over 450 ethnic tribes in Nigeria and a diversity of religious opinions and creeds, some believe in gods that live in the forest, some rely on statues preserved in decorated shrines as gods, a good number turn to masquerades, diviners or soothsayers for spiritual salvation, but Christianity even despite denominational and doctrinal differences is predicated on Jesus who is the Way, the Truth and the Life. It has all it takes to foster peace at all levels.

Social Reality in Nigeria

Looking at our society today Nigeria is marked by a bewildering diversity of ethnicities and languages that gives it a multicultural outlook. One of the consequences is that Nigerian States continue to be divided along ethnic and cultural lines. There seems to be an obvious competition between regions as far as power and the control of resources goes. Nigeria is easily split between the North and the South, Christians and Muslims. Leaders in our country have sometimes instigated social tension using these divisions to rule a divided people. With over 450 languages, it cannot be wrong to say that three, Hausa, Igbo and Yoruba dominate the rest. Often these three claim to represent the interest of the minorities. But within them also there exists a suspicion that is not good for the country. The tussle between these three giants has definite socio-political consequences for the rest of the populace.

A World-Bank report has it that Nigeria presents a paradox. The country is rich but her people are poor. Her performance in terms of social indicators is increasingly and steadily among the worst in sub-Saharan Africa and throughout the developing world. This picture is bleak and capable of truncating peace in the land. It is a valid observation when people say that never has the level of corruption in Nigeria been so high, never has the welfare of many been so low and disorganized. Despite stupendous wealth of both human and natural resources, we are still lacking the coordination and cooperation to improve the lives of our citizenry. Selfishness and greed have been elevated to an art and egocentric tendencies predominate where public service should be the top priority. Increasingly government officials serve interests so different from those they swore to uphold, and some individuals and groups feed fat at the expense of the nation, oblivious of national objectives and projects.

Consider the cost of democracy in Nigeria. Imagine the sum total of emoluments of our National Assembly men and women. Think of the poor minimum wage of the common worker in a country like Nigeria, not to mention the hundreds of thousands of graduates that are churned out of our citadels of learning with little or nothing to lean on. Imagine the teeming numbers of youths who are denied education for constructive living, lacking problem solving orientation; they simply become restive and at the slightest provocation are ready to wreak havoc. Nigeria has had a history of politically motivated crises since the days of colonialism, but the last thirty years have seen an increase and worsening of violent communal conflicts, arising mainly from poverty, economic injustice, ignorance and religious fundamentalism.

In the past ten years, but especially within the last two, Plateau State, once known for peace and as a home and a host to diverse ethnic groups, suddenly turned into a conflict zone. These conflicts were triggered by multiple factors including historical, political, ethnic, economic, ones and in recent years a growing religious factor. Communities have been polarized; people who once lived together and shared life in common now live as enemies. Colleagues who have worked side by side for many years are now suspicious of one another. This has affected innocent children and youths who no longer trust each other. In the face of suspicion, distrust and resort to hostility at the slightest provocation, the Church must not only be heard, but be seen to be part of the effort to douse tension, encourage harmony and peaceful coexistence, and where conflicts have taken place explore practical avenues to resolve them.

The poor economic condition in the country that has occasioned food insecurity can trigger and sustain a crisis to unprecedented proportions. A hungry man, they say, is an angry man, any day any time. Note too that the dividends of democracy are only more eloquent on the pages of newspapers than in real-life situations of the masses. This necessarily results in low self-esteem and a lack of confidence. These are the lapses that must be filled by Christians, by Catholics whose orientation is unique. Blessed are peace makers and maintainers of peace for they shall be sons of God (Mt. 5:9). We are also advised to seek the peace and welfare of the city given by God. Pray for it, for in the welfare of the city in which you live you will have welfare (Jer. 29:7). And in Ps 34:14... seek, inquire for, crave for peace and pursue it.

The Church that reflects the Christian faith to the world must fashion ways and means to manage any ugly situation that arises and is inimical to the wellbeing of mankind. This is our saving mission, the heart of the work of Evangelization: to be a light to the world and the salt of the earth.

Crisis Management and Peace Building
Crisis presupposes the breakdown of the wellbeing of the human society. It is a process of dealing with situations which pose a major threat to the public. A crisis should be quickly contained so that it does not escalate, and so does not need a response mechanism. Perceived injustice, intolerance, ignorance, language barriers, a communication gap and selfishness are pivotal to conflict build-up. These crises come in different forms, cultural, ethnic, technological, political or social. Peace building is the effort of adopting proactive measures to stop crises and the attempt to neutralize the negative effects of crises where they have already taken place, and this is usually a gradual process. It is not a hasty affair like having a Passover meal, and neither is it rushed. Today many agencies are practically involved in peace negotiations, especially the United Nations, realizing that many ethnic or political groups and different religions are yet to find an enduring formula for peace.

Christianity and its Tools for Peace-Building and Crisis Management

In the past, power and might seemed to be the best ways of resolving problems. The most powerful won the day, the strongest exerted their weight over the weak; it was a matter of the survival of the fittest. The era of the Crusades saw the Church rise in battle against her opponents. There were wars between Christians and Muslims, Jews as well as pagans. Wars against heretics were spearheaded in the name of fighting a "just war" for the faith. The Church, having fought wars and executed heretics, today preaches non-violence to show the world that we have tasted both sides and that we are better off with peace than war. Today we see how countries wage war against each other and proliferate weapons of mass destruction, and so we hear of the "the axis of evil". It is surprising that many groups and even governments save for peace, but plan for war.

Christianity creates no room for violence, it gives no vacancy for a breakdown in inter-personal relationships, and seeks to employ all strategies to bring about peace. Pope John Paul II of blessed memory, known to be a great ambassador of peace, made the assertion that, 'violence and arms can never resolve the problems of man' (*A Plea for Peace*, March 17, 2003, para. 8). Pope Benedict XVI in his message for peace this year says, "The quest for peace by people of goodwill surely would become easier if all acknowledged the indivisible relationship between God, human being and the whole of creation" (p.14). No one should give up on peace. As a farmer has his tools for farming such as hoes, cutlasses, diggers, knives and other equipment, so also Christianity has its tools for building sustainable peace.

A. Reconciliation: Jesus advocates a method of reconciliation that is very practical: first of all, having a direct talk with the other party, then when it gets difficult get a witness involved, and when it gets more difficult involve the church (cf. Mt. 18). Christianity sets out to create avenues for negotiation even in the face of unprovoked hostility. One of the extraordinary legacies of the late Pope John Paul II was the reconciliation he sought and nurtured between Jews and Christians. Building on John XXIII's pioneering work, John Paul II was the first Pope to enter a Synagogue and again condemned anti-Semitism and insisted on the importance of dialogue with Judaism. He acknowledged that "the history of relations between Jews and Christians is a tormented one' ....and admitted that, 'erroneous and unjust interpretations of the New Testament regarding the Jewish people have circulated for too long, endangering feelings of hostility" (cf. *St. Patrick's Mission Africa*, vol 71, no.4 p.25). The document reminded Christians that Jesus was a Jew. In seeking reconciliation, we must acknowledge where we have erred, and be ready to look at issues from an objective perspective. Pope Benedict XVI in his memorable homily at his inauguration tried to reach out to the Jews welcoming them as his brothers and sisters, and said, "We are joined by a great shared spiritual heritage, one rooted in God's irrevocable promises" (*ibid.*). At the end of the Civil War in Nigeria, General Yakubu Gowon in his famous speech said there were "no victor and no vanquished". This kind of comment was needed at the time to pave the way for the peace process, reconstruction, rehabilitation and reconciliation. When the crisis in Ogoni land reared its ugly head, and Ken Saro Wiwa who led the Movement for the Survival of the Ogoni People (MOSSOP) was hanged, a peace process was initiated by President Olusegun Obasanjo. Today, the Federal Government is engaging the youths of the Movement for the Emancipation of the Niger Delta (MEND), who are fighting and protesting against environmental degradation and economic marginalization. This is being done in a constructive manner to minimize the damage done to the economic nerve (oil) of the nation and the projection of Nigeria's image as a violent nation. It is sad that after the Plateau crisis of 2010, some prominent Christians and church leaders would advocate war and violence; the message of the African Synod says, "The mission to serve peace will consist in building peace in each member of the body of Christ...capable of being engaged in the peace process in

Africa. It is primarily born from within, in the interior of individuals and communities" (*Synod for Africa. The Church in Africa in Service to Reconciliation, Justice and Peace*, Vatican City, 2009, no. 4).

Dialogue: At the 8ᵗʰ General Assembly of the Catholic Archdiocese of Jos, the delegates to the well-attended sessions agreed that we must all embrace unconditionally the message of dialogue. There is no problem that cannot be solved by dialogue. In stressing dialogue, Jesus asked, "What man among you going out for war will not send envoys to sue for peace before the army heads forward?" (Luke 14:31). In dialogue we enter into an appreciation of one another, and an understanding of our differences. Faced with terrorism, kidnapping and religious fanaticism, there is an ever-growing urgency to dialogue especially with people of other religions and ethnicity. This form of dialogue demands an attitude of honesty, mutual respect, esteem and acceptance. It requires prudence, forgiveness, truthfulness, meekness, openness on the part of those involved. Dialogue is not about conformity or uniformity. In dialogue we can disagree on issues but we resolve to keep together. We may differ in faith or culture but we give priority to our brotherhood/sisterhood. Pope Paul VI was quite correct when he said that whoever helps others to discover in everyone, beyond language, ethnic group, or race the existence of a human being equal to oneself, will transform the earth from an epicenter of division into a workshop of civil collaboration. When I tried to build bridges between the Catholic Church and some Islamic communities, as a result of which we developed a very cordial relationship with the late Emir of Wase, Alhaji Dr. Haruna Abdullahi, some people felt that I was encouraging submissiveness to Islam or comprising the Christian faith. They preferred sermons or messages of aggression, provocation and hostility. Jesus asked Peter to put back his sword, implying that violence was to give way to peace. Attempts must be made to promote dialogue between religions and also encourage ethnic, political or social groups to break down boundaries of division and erect pillars of unity.

Justice: In his encyclical *Pacem in Terris*, Pope John XXIII stressed the place for peace in a just society when he said this "demands that men be guided by justice, respect the rights of others and do their duty. It demands, too, that they be animated by such love as will make them feel the need of others as their own" (para. 35*).* Mother Theresa in her own case said that "being unwanted, unloved, uncared for or forgotten by everybody I think that is a much greater hunger, a much greater poverty than the person who has nothing to eat". The late Archbishop Oscar Romero of El Salvador asked by what right we have catalogued persons as first-class persons or second-class persons. In the theology of human nature there is only one class: children of God. Lack of fairness in any society results in the breakdown of law and order. The agitation by the militants in the Niger Delta is as a result of perceived economic injustice or imbalance which has resulted in kidnapping and other criminal activities. The Federal Government has resorted to dialogue and negotiations with the militants to minimize the harmful consequences of armed militancy in the oil-rich zone. An unjust society provokes tempers, rebellion and even bloody revolutions. Governments and political groups must stop violating the rights of people or communities. Only distributive justice can ensure progress, stability and peace. Justice for all is a categorical imperative, an inescapable duty for the whole of society.

Love: The sum total of what Christianity teaches is love, *Omnia vincit amor*, love conquers all. St Paul in I Corinthians 13:13 says the greatest of all gifts is love. In its highest degree love is the capacity to give and receive, to remember offences not with hurt, to appeal to reason rather than sentiments, to look at the face of a stranger and see the semblance of Jesus, to forgive without counting the cost, to move from 'me' to 'you' to love until it hurts. Love is both a method and content for peace. Pope Benedict XVI in his encyclical *Caritas in Veritate* says, "to love someone is to desire that person's good and to take effective steps to secure it" (para. 7). True love shapes a new way of living and relating to others; in everyday life love can create a culture that overcomes material inequality. Love should not be drowned by evil. Pope John Paul II, during the World Day for Peace in 2005, said, "No man or woman of a good will can renounce the struggle to overcome evil with good. This fight can be fought effectively only with the weapons of love. When good overcomes evil love prevails and where love prevails there is peace"[9] (para. 12). St Paul urges Christians in Romans 12:21 not to be overcome by evil but overcome evil with good. Love is able to open hearts, cement friendship, and put peace in circulation.

Conclusion

Christianity is based on and rooted not only in the teachings of Christ but in the person of Christ. For some today Christianity has come to mean a mere identification with a church or sheer external religious symbols and practices with undue attention to prosperity, miracles and extraordinary phenomena. Many today have a Christian vocabulary but not Christian experience. The world requires that we Christians should continue to be Christian even in very troubled times; to carry the cross without wavering. Recent statistics show that Nigeria ranks sixth in the world, with the greatest member of Christians after USA, Brazil, Mexico, Russia, and the Philippines. The question must be asked if our Christianity actually translates into a life of love, good moral conduct, honesty, peaceful disposition and genuine witness. Does the fact that Islam and Christianity are the two predominant religions and that we have evidence of religious piety all over the place make us "the most religious nation on earth"? Is there a deliberate attempt to understand and relate our two religions to concrete daily life or is there instead an unhealthy claim to superiority and mutual antagonism? Why should anybody kill in the name of religion? When can we deploy the rich religious values of Christianity and Islam to fight social vices such as corruption and violence, which seem to defy solution in our contemporary Nigeria? Endless questions, no answers. Perhaps your gathering here is part of the answer. We must however insist that those occupying public offices must seek the common good of the people they lead and nothing other than selfless service should be their priority. Unfortunately once in power people get intoxicated and even paranoid, seeing enemies everywhere and wasting precious energy and resources to deal with these imaginary enemies while the populace languishes in abject poverty. In such a case, violence in the name of politics, ethnicity or religion becomes inevitable. When we think of common interests and apply resources to them, we will discover that life can be better than it really is.

It is your duty as Knights to promote the culture of non-violence and above all to promote the Gospel way of resolving crises. You must not neglect our African traditional mechanism for conflict resolution either. We therefore charge you to be in the forefront of a just and peaceful society. Even in the midst of today's social evils, violence and immorality, like your patron saint, St. Mulumba, be courageous; speak the truth and let your lives shine (cf. Mt 5:16). Christianity is not a mere tool but a way of life based on Jesus. Base your lives on Jesus and you will make a very significant difference to our troubled society. Allow me to conclude with the words of St. Paul in Ephesians 5:14-15: "So stand ready, with truth as a belt tight round your waist, with righteousness as your breastplate, and as your shoes the readiness to announce the Good News of peace".

OVERCOMING EVIL WITH GOOD
Released in the aftermath of the Jos ethno-religious crisis, 2010

Background

Undoubtedly Jos city has been one of the most peaceful in Nigeria, favoured with a serene climate and natural beauty. The warmth and generosity of its people endears many. In the past decades, due to the tin-mining business, there has been a blend of local, national and international activities as one could find nationals from many countries at home in Jos. Little wonder that Plateau State itself adopted the name, "Home of Peace and Tourism". Unfortunately, the 2001 crisis created unprecedented suspicion and animosity between the minority Hausa/Fulani Muslim settler communities and the majority Christian natives. Before now, all had been well as both communities both participated to some extent in festivities: social, religious and political with little or no prejudice or discrimination.

It was incredible to witness what the January 17, 2010 Jos crisis did to the inhabitants of Jos and its environs. Somehow, insanity was let loose, triggering the destruction of churches and mosques with several people displaced as homes and business premises were destroyed. People watched their life's savings go up in flames and loved ones maimed or killed. The communal nature of family life was disrupted as families divided by the crisis were forced to live kilometres away, meeting occasionally to nurse their wounds, then to be separated again.

In the Nasarawa Gwong area and some other parts of Jos, there are areas where Christians or Muslims cannot go to; there are roads where Christians or Muslims cannot follow. I only pray that the Lord of peace and the peace of God will reign permanently over this once peaceful city.

In Bukuru, following the crisis, those who attempted going back to renovate and reoccupy their residences were bluntly told they could never return. This is obviously to gain territorial control, which is basically one of the reasons for the crisis that has unfortunately been simply referred to as a "religious crisis."

The case of Dogo Nahawa was an embarrassment to humanity as some little children and infants were in the early hours of the 7th of March 2010 hacked to death or burnt and their parents were not spared either. The whole community became a wailing valley as sympathizers made their way to Dogo Nahawa. A village that was little-known became famous overnight. I was close to tears when I visited the scene as the whole community was shocked to its marrow.

Solidarity and Interventions

The situation during and after the crisis was too serious for affected individuals to grapple with. Solidarity visits, messages of peace, and prayers for inner healing became very necessary as Jos Archdiocese would not allow the victims to suffer alone. His Eminence, Cardinal Peter Turkson, President of the Pontifical Council for Justice and Peace in the Vatican City, came personally to visit us in Jos and had these consoling words to say: "We live a life of communion and inclusive belongingness, not excluding anyone, but sharing in the life of one another and living for one another. On hearing about what has befallen you, and about the trying moments you are going through, the rest of the family of God could not sit unconcerned." He came to identify with us and to encourage the people and government of Plateau State. He presided at the solidarity Mass organised to beg God for the healing of wounded hearts and the land on the 19th of March 2010. In my homily, I repeated my consistent message of peace through forgiveness and reconciliation. The Catholic Church on the Plateau maintained her leading role as a bridge-builder as over 600 families from different backgrounds were pacified and encouraged through words, prayers and actions. We mobilized the faithful to donate, especially those who had not been not affected by the crisis, and with help from internal and external donors we could assist the affected families with a token amount of money and a greeting card as a symbol of our acknowledgement, appreciation and understanding of the fact that there was a problem and we were in it together. The solidarity Mass helped many as they left St. Jarlath's Bukuru, the arena of the Mass, happier than they came. Healing must have commenced.

At Dogo Nahawa I identified with the people not only in my capacity as the then Christian Association of Nigeria (CAN) Chairman, but as a pastor. We also celebrated a solidarity Mass where I encouraged the people, prayed for forgiveness for perpetrators and assisted the community through the distribution of basic necessities as well as acha (crop) seedlings. We reconstructed the only public clinic, which had been destroyed at Ratsat Village during the attacks. That life is gradually returning to normal in villages that lost so much is nothing short of the miracle of love.

We have ensured that the Archdiocese does not fold its arms at ugly events of this nature. We are undoubtedly present and visible when it comes to dialogue and initiating activities aimed at the common good and promoting peaceful coexistence. We insist on reaching out through our Church organs. Recently the Inter-Religious Dialogue office in the Archdiocese of Jos in collaboration with the Diametta Peace Initiative, also in Jos, organized a football competition where the Catholic Youth Organisation of Nigeria (CYON) and Muslim youths participated, forgetting their differences and sharing the joy and challenges of sports. The trophy was won by the team from Ali Kazaure ward, a predominantly Muslim area. It was quite a delight as I personally attended the finals that took place at St. Murumba's Catholic College football field.

I commend our Archdiocesan Justice, Development, Peace and Caritas Commission (JDPC), which has remained proactive. The body investigates the authenticity or otherwise of rumours and stands ready should there be any break-down of law and order that results in internally displaced persons fleeing from their homes. Its services are available to all without discrimination based on religious or ethnic affiliation. It is interesting to note that the staff of our Archdiocesan Emergency Response Team comprises

Christians and Muslims. They have intervened in all the flash-points of religious, ethnic, social or political crises from Namu, Bukuru, Nasarawa, Fatima Cathedral, Dogo Nahawa, Masallacin Jumma'a and other flash spots. In September 2010, the JDPC distributed grains and other relief materials to Christians and Muslims, especially those whose houses and business places were destroyed during the January 17th crisis.

Efforts at Inter-Religious Relationships

I acknowledge by way of tribute a great collaborator in the person of the late Emir of Wase, Alhaji Abdullahi Haruna Wase, whom I met shortly after assuming office as the Archbishop of Jos. He had come to welcome me and to thank me for the role I played in housing and feeding Muslims who had been affected by the 2001 crisis. As the Chairman of Jamaatu Nasril Islam (JNI) Plateau State, he and I shared common values of peace, reconciliation and harmonious coexistence. In October 2009, at the invitation of MISSIO, we were guests in Germany to participate in the World Mission activities which centred on peace and reconciliation in Nigeria. There we met Christian and Muslim groups, sharing our experience as partners for peace and the challenges we both face in this tedious task of reconciling people from different backgrounds.

For some people who believe that there should be an eternal enmity between Christians and Muslims, the message of peace we propagated hardly went down well with them. Even some of my priests thought I was wasting time, energy and resources by working with a Muslim. The Emir too was doubted and suspected by his Muslim brothers as a sell-out. But gradually there came to be room and some space for reason. When the Emir died on the 17th 0f September 2010 I was away for the Bishops' Conference holding at Ijebu Ode, Ogun State. I asked my Vicar-General, Monsignor Ben Obidiegwu, to mobilize as many priests as possible to go to Wase, in time for the burial, and over twenty priests, some rev sisters and lay faithful were at the burial and brought a message of condolence from the Archdiocese of Jos. It is heartening to note that many messages of condolences from

Muslims and Christians were sent to me condoling me on the death of "your good friend and collaborator for peace". One of such messages came on the 4th of October from the Sultan of Sokoto, Alhaji Saad Abubakar III, the well-respected leader of Muslims in Nigeria, who in a text message wrote: "My dear brother, I just finished reading your very touching tribute to late Emir of Wase. May God bless, keep, and continue to use you in attainment of peace, stability, and progress not only in Plateau, but in our country, amen".

At different times the Archdiocese received Ambassadors, High Commissioners and delegations of Bishops from Germany and America who came to express solidarity with us. The visit of the German Bishops coincided with the death of the late Inuwa Ali, the Turakin Jos and a Muslim leader. Together with the late Emir of Wase, Alhaji Abdullahi Haruna Wase and the Emir of Kanam, Alhaji Mu'azu Babangida, we paid a condolence visit to the family. This is one of the little ways in which we show solidarity not only with Christians but with anyone who needs the warmth of human affection.

Our General Assembly and the Quest for Peace
At our annual General Assembly a pastoral message was issued after days of prayerful reflection and discussion. A Muslim woman, Hajiya Fatima Kyari, a former Commissioner in the State, spoke brilliantly and passionately on "The Social Consequences of Religious Extremism and Negative Religious Indoctrination". She observed that both Christianity and Islam are capable of imparting doctrines in a non-critical way. This she feared may result in negative actions without consideration for the wider society. She encouraged a good understanding of the different faiths and beliefs so that we can co-exist peacefully. She emphasized that we should dwell on our similarities rather than capitalizing on our differences. She harped on the issue of collaboration, citing the occasion of the General Assembly as an example where she, a Moslem woman, is invited to share her experiences with Catholics. The previous year we had invited the Chairman of the Muslim

Pilgrims' Board in Plateau State who gave a talk on harmonious coexistence between the different faiths. It was truly a sober moment for all participants.

Our 8th General Assembly, which was entitled "The Challenges of Religious and Political Conflicts to the Church on the Plateau", helped us to start all over again to seek peace at all costs. Having examined the crises from different angles, we unanimously observed that the love of neighbour has given way to hatred, and only practical love is the solution. (cf. 1 Th. 3:12, Mt. 5:9). The Assembly accepted that the recent crises have generated a lot of mistrust between Christians and Muslims, resulting in a setback to all previous efforts in the area of dialogue. We keep encouraging Christians not to lose faith in God, nor to be paralysed by fear and anger, but rather to renew their love for God and neighbour. We will continue to teach love, peace and reconciliation no matter the cost. In the Catholic Archdiocese of Jos, every Catholic is called upon to be an agent of change, peace and reconciliation. We will want a situation where Christians will be the first to say 'no' to violence. A special prayer for peace was formulated at the end of the Assembly and is currently recited daily by Catholics but especially after communion during Mass. We must all pray and work for peace. While praying fervently for peace, the underlying social causes of this crisis, which only the civil authorities can effectively address, cannot be swept under the carpet. Justice must be seen to be done and the grievances of youths, farmers, herdsmen, settlers or indigenes must be seriously looked into and resolved comprehensively.

Reaching Out

I recently led a delegation of priests and some lay faithful to the Central Mosque to deliver the Pope's Message to mark the end of Ramadan. The Imam of the Jos Central Mosque, Sheik Balarabe Dau'ud, was full of praise for the Catholic Church's quest for peace in Plateau State and indeed in the world. He promised to work in collaboration with all who are sincere in the search for peaceful coexistence. The exchange of gifts and pleasantries, though symbolic at that occasion, signalled a fresh possibility that we can live together.

In the same spirit, the Conference of Women Religious and Men Religious celebrated the last Sallah festival with the Muslims in the Nasarawa Gwong area of Jos. The leader of the community, Alh. Mohammed Magaji, thanked the religious for the sacrifices they had made in the past and the bold measures they had taken in the pursuit for peace. Both the reverend sisters and Muslim women marched through the paths that had hitherto been inaccessible as a result of the crisis. This was very refreshing. We are hoping that with the message of peace sinking deeper on a daily basis, more individuals and communities hurt and traumatized by the recent experiences will discover how love can easily overcome evil, pain and sorrow. Schooled in love, the faithful can be hopeful about the future.

Another milestone was our visit to Mazah village where innocent people were attacked on the 17th July, 2010. It was another show of solidarity with a people in distress. We mobilized the faithful within the city to visit the village and celebrate Holy Mass with the people. The rough, undulating and steep road to Mazah gave the visit the touch of a pilgrimage as we trekked in a long file, crossing mountains and rivers. This village had lost seven people, four were injured and hospitalized, while ten houses were burnt. It was quite a sober moment when a Protestant pastor who had lost his wife and children said he had forgiven the harm done him. This was the same message by the Councillor representing the village. He had also lost relations but publicly declared, "We have forgiven". This visit was as historic as it was therapeutic. In their speeches, the District Head and other chiefs saw the visit as healing the land. It was a day they would not forget in a hurry. Again our JDPC was there with relief materials for those affected. I was particularly moved by the banners members of the community carried with the inscription, "The greatest weapon against violence is forgiveness". What could be truer? Such is the spirit of a people who may be down but not out. Good can indeed overcome evil if there is the will.

WE ARE GOD'S CHILDREN RATHER THAN NORTHERNERS, SOURTHERNERS, MUSLIMS OR CHRISTIANS

Archbishop's Perspective on State of Nation delivered at the Ordination of Nine Deacons on the Sunday of the Epiphany of Our Lord at St. Benedict's Parish, Mista - Ali, January 2, 2011.

We are grateful to God who has given us yet another year – 2011. We pray for a beautiful, fruitful and peaceful year: a year of grace, hope, fulfilled dreams and progress; a year of justice, development and peace; a year free of violence, kidnapping, murders and bomb blasts.

I hope too that despite the fact that our Christmas was rudely disturbed by anti social and retrogressive elements, we still had the spiritual strength to joyfully celebrate the birth of Christ. "Who will separate us from the love of Christ? Will it be trials, or anguish, persecution or hunger, lack of clothing, or dangers or sword?" (Rom 8:35). We discourage all those who seek to fight for God or to promote religion by violence. It actually shows a lack of faith in the Almighty God.

I hope that our Christmas did not only concentrate on those elements that have now come to characterize modern Christmas celebration, namely exchange of gifts/cards/text messages, stylish dresses, social visits and parties. Christmas is about Jesus the saviour who is Emmanuel, God with us. He is the Way the Truth and the Life. One very important lesson of Christmas is that as God loved us and came to dwell with us through his Son, we too must extend our love not only to those close to us but to all human beings (cf. 1 Th. 3:12). We are challenged by the spirit of Christmas to become agents of unconditional love, to become mobile gospels i.e. agents of good news, not bad news; to witness to Christ through our words and actions so that many will see the glory of God the Father through us (cf. Mt. 5:16).)

The social, political and economic structures in our country are meant to serve the common good, but unfortunately they seem to serve individual good and selfish interests. Blessed in so many ways by God it seems it is in our character that each person wants to be comfortable at the expense of others. "I pass my neighbour" is a Nigerian saying that shows that our neighbour is not our priority. The year 2011 should be a fresh beginning to a new solidarity, a new patriotism, a new neighbourliness and a new way of looking at ourselves: children of God rather than merely Northerners, Southerners, Muslims or Christians who treat each other with great contempt. The "we are better than you" attitude creates social problems for us such as election rigging leading to political violence and now bomb blasts causing bodily injury and damaging our collective aspirations as a nation.

What is wrong with us as a nation? Why do we appear to be so religious and yet our behaviours are very ungodly? Let me attempt to identify a few factors:

- Our Religions seem to be focused largely on external practices and sentiments with no corresponding interior renewal. We dwell more on external rituals/prayers, the building and positioning of our places of worship in very conspicuous places to attract attention while neglecting the core religious value of love of neighbour. When we have political economic or ethnic disagreements, we hardly employ our positive religious values to resolve them but allow harmful religious sentiments and irrationality to take over.

- We lack humility and so we do not have the heart to admit our faults even when they are so glaring. We prefer to blame others for even problems we have caused, forgetting that when you point an accusing finger at others four fingers point back at you. We Nigerians hardly admit that our ethnic or political or religious group is ever wrong. We seek to defend them even when their actions are indefensible. We need to cultivate the virtue of self criticism.

- Religion is used as a shield. When criminals are arrested and justice is taking its course the person will say "I am being punished because I am a Muslim" or "I am being victimized because I am a Christian". Even when the authorities know those who are behind various crises as revealed by commissions of enquiries, we lack the political will to punish the culprits which is why such crises tend to repeat themselves with devastating consequences. We wear religious masks when convenient and do evil in the name of religion. Some preachers incite violence and hatred. Some preach at odd hours of the night and keep people awake and if you tell them that they are disturbing public peace they react sharply that you are against their religion. Even when people build a mosque or a church without legal authorization and the building is demolished, they scream that their sacred place of worship has been sacrilegiously destroyed. We do practice "eye service religion" and along with it, there is so much hypocrisy. We speak of love in the public but in private urge attacks on our so-called enemies. Even our security personnel seem to be catching the bug of religious partisanship. Stories have it that when on a mission to quell religious crises, some security agents directly or indirectly take sides with their fellow coreligionists to deal with their opponents and it is alleged that even the postings of some security personnel are done with a religious bias.

- Above the Law Syndrome: Because of their social status some people are treated as if they are above the law. The law seems to be a cobweb where only the weak, the poor and the defenceless get caught. Those who steal or even legally appropriate to themselves billions and millions of Naira get merit awards, chieftaincy titles or honorary doctorate degrees, while the goat thief is jailed for many years.

- Governance in Nigeria seems to be all about "I, me, myself, my people or my political associates". The huge resources at the disposal of our leaders seem to be the primary reason for the acrimonious political struggles, campaign of calumny and character assassination among politicians. Now that we are facing elections, serious issues of governance have come to a halt all over the country, replaced by feverish and negative campaigns and the irresponsible use of public funds to foster personal political ambition. There is so much political paranoia, the type King Herod suffered when he ordered the killing of infants less than two years old to secure his political position. Political opponents are seen as enemies and healthy political competition is almost impossible. Politics is a do or die matter. Worse of all, political office holders are extremely well paid while the poor wallow from poverty to misery because they have no social security and this is what is responsible for the upsurge in crimes.

- There is the failure of elders to form the youths in line with our African values. Respect for elders, life, hard work and honesty are gradually being eroded.

- Youths have become so frustrated and disenchanted that they engage in all sorts of crimes. They are blamed yet there is no alternative of jobs or social security. My advice to youths is that they should not worsen the situation by acts of violence.

- Family values are collapsing. The extended family system which in the past guaranteed social security for family members is fast giving way.

- Ignorance, poverty, violence and religious fundamentalism are the greatest dangers to Nigeria at this time. These monsters must be confronted intelligently.

- Above all, peace in our land is under serious threat. We need permanent peace which can come about only through distributive justice.

The recurring crises in Jos climaxing with a bomb attack on the very holy night of Christmas and those we hear of in several parts of Nigeria does not portend well for our nation. Pope Benedict's message on the World Day of Peace on 1st January must ring in our ears. The path to peace is not violence, but dialogue, truth and forgiveness. Violence only begets more violence. We pray for God's mercy for those who died in or after the bomb blasts in Jos and elsewhere in the country. We should not forget to support the injured spiritually and materially. Please continue to say the *Prayer for Political, Ethnic and Religious Peace in Plateau State.* We want our forthcoming elections to be violence free, fair and honest. I believe that we have a credible INEC in place, so I urge all of you of voting age to register when the time comes and make sure that you cast your votes for only selfless and genuine God fearing persons. May God grant us peaceful elections throughout Nigeria.

MUSLIMS AND CHRISTIANS LIVING AND WORKING TOGETHER

An address at the formal opening of the Inter-Faith Youth Vocational Training Centre, Hai- Hong, Bokkos. January 27, 2011

I wish to thank you for responding so kindly to our invitation and I welcome you very warmly, hoping that your presence here will inspire us more to work for the common good of our young people in Plateau State.

WHY ARE WE HERE? We are here to witness the formal opening of the Interfaith Vocational Youth training Centre, a project of the Catholic Archdiocese of Jos, situated in Hai-Hong, Bokkos, Bokkos Local Government Area of Plateau State.

WHAT IS THE AIM OF THE IFYVTC? It was initiated to be a bridge between Christian and Muslim youths, especially the rural youths who are disadvantaged by reasons of poor education or absence of vocational skills. I had a dream about six years ago of offering an opportunity to Christian and Muslim youths to train together to acquire carpentry, mechanical/ technical/electrical, home management, micro-business skills, etc.; to live side by side, overcoming little obstacles and prejudices and getting a better perspective of each other's religions; to return to their communities not only with some self-employment skills, but to become agents of peaceful coexistence, interreligious dialogue and harmony. I shared this dream with MISEREOR, a Catholic Agency in Germany, and MISEREOR enthusiastically supported my vision and has offered great assistance towards the realization of the project. We have worked together from the concept stage of the project to the building of the structures leading to the formal opening today. MISEREOR is being represented here by Dr. Ernest Sagemueller, the National Advisor to the Justice, Development, Peace and Caritas in the Catholic Secretariat of Nigeria, Abuja. You are welcome, Dr. Sagemueller. Kindly convey our heartfelt appreciation to MISEREOR and all those Catholics who contribute from their personal resources to support projects such as ours throughout the world. We hope individuals here in Nigeria will imitate the example of the German Catholics and help this centre to be self-sustaining.

WHAT HAPPENS HERE? In addition to vocational skills, we train the youths here to cultivate the culture of appreciating one another irrespective of their religious doctrines and traditions. In class they learn the theory and practice of vocational skills, but there is provision for an Islamic teacher who teaches the Muslim students Islamic Religious Knowledge and a Christian teacher who teaches the Christians Christian Religious Knowledge. We also create the opportunity where the teacher of the Islamic religion teaches the Christian students the basic teachings of Islam while the teacher of the Christian religion teaches the Muslim students the rudimentary teachings of Christianity. Both the Muslim and Christian students come together from time to time to be enlightened on the values of inter religious dialogue/harmony and the need to appreciate and respect each other's religion.

WHO ARE COLLABORATING TO MAKE THIS DREAM POSSIBLE? The Catholic Archdiocese of Jos is the key initiator of the project. The Catholic Diocese of Shendam participates in it. MISEREOR is our principal partner. We all believe that young people should receive a training to give them skills and also to foster in them an attitude of respect for their respective religions, so that they can use religion to build positively and not to destroy. My late friend and brother, the late Emir of Wase, Alhaji Dr. Haruna Abdullahi, was very particularly keen about this project. He offered useful advice and gave wonderful moral support towards its realization. He

sent the first batch of Muslim students here. He has gone to be with the Lord. May we rise and offer a minute's silence in his memory please. [*May the soul of Alhaji Haruna Abdullahi rest in perfect peace. Amen.*] He has been succeeded by his son, HRH Alhaji Mohammed Sambo Haruna, who equally is very keen about the issues that his father and I worked closely together on. The Saf Ron Kulere, Da Lazarus Agai, and other chiefs in the Bokkos area gave us this land on which the project is sited, and they are keen in supporting the centre. The Emir of Kanam, HRH Alhaji Muazu Babangida, has also shown great interest in the activities of this centre. We thank all of you.

DEVELOPMENTS: The crises we witnessed recently in the State nearly frustrated the starting of this project. We had to postpone it two times but eventually decided we would go ahead even amidst the crises, to demonstrate our resolve to tackle religious intolerance. Both Muslim and Christian youths were admitted, but the persistent crises made some parents apprehensive about the safety of their children and some were withdrawn. Happily, many have returned and classes are in progress. Some of us believe that genuine Muslim-Christian relationship is impossible. We emphatically say it is possible, and we as Catholic Church are committed to dialogue with other religions and also to the philosophy of "better to light a candle than to curse the darkness". It is this darkness of fear, distrust, suspicion and hatred between Christian and Muslim youths that this centre hopes to dispel. As mentioned, youths who get trained here will hopefully return to their village communities and influence other young people about the dignity of labour, respect for other people's religion, using dialogue as a weapon of settling misunderstanding/ arguments instead of violence. A very important rule here is that no one changes his religion or tries to convert the other. Students are encouraged to practise their religion very well while showing respect and love to the other persons who practise theirs differently.

HOPES: We hope that this modest effort will help to combat idleness, and root out religious fundamentalism and violence in the youths who pass through here. As many of our youths are idle or uneducated and prone to violence, I hope that our leaders will help them to realize their full potentials instead of using their energy negatively. Some political and religious leaders are a bad influence on the youths by inciting them to violence. Youths should be aware of such mischief makers. Those in leadership or aspiring to positions of leadership should know that there is so much that they can do to give our young people a prosperous and happy today and tomorrow. They should plan for, create opportunities, invest in the youths and "give unto the youths what belongs to the youths".

Finally, may I request that you kindly pray for the growth and progress of this project, and support the centre and the students now and when they graduate. Thank you for coming. May God bless your return journey to your respective destinations. Amen.

BETTER TO LIGHT THE CANDLE THAN TO CURSE THE DARKNESS

A report of the formal opening of the Inter-Faith Youth Vocational Training Centre, Hai-Hong, Bokkos. January 27, 2011

Even in the midst of sporadic attacks presently being experienced in the surrounding villages of Jos, Plateau State, the Catholic

Archdiocese of Jos has gone ahead to formally declare open on January 27, 2011 the Interfaith Youth Vocational Training Centre situated at Hai Hong, Bokkos in Plateau State. Established by the Catholic Archdiocese of Jos and with the great support of MISEREOR Germany, the centre is an attempt to tackle the culture of hatred, suspicion and inter-religious antagonism/violence among the youths. The centre is intended to be a symbol of religious tolerance, harmony and peaceful coexistence among young people. The disadvantaged Muslim and Christian youths are helped in the centre during a two-year training programme in vocational skills such as carpentry, mechanical skills, electrical skills, technical skills, masonry, etc., with the hope that they will learn how to live and work together in peace and harmony in spite of their different modes of religious worship, doctrines and traditions. At the end of their training they will return to their village communities and hopefully be self-employed and be a great help in spreading the culture of respect for each others' religions.

Apart from training in vocational skills, the students are helped to mature in their respective religions. They have two religious teachers, one in Islam and the other in Christianity. The Islamic religious teacher instructs the Muslim students in Islamic Religious Knowledge while the Christian teacher instructs the Christian students in Christian Religious Knowledge. Classes are organized for the Muslim students so that the Christian religious teacher teaches them some basic things about Christianity, while the Muslim teacher teaches the Christian students about Islam. The students then have joint classes to learn the art of dialogue, reconciliation and tolerant behaviour instead of resorting to violence at the slightest confrontation or argument.

The ceremony which took place in the training centre, some 70 kilometers from Jos, was well- attended. The Governor of Plateau State, Da. Dr. Jonah David Jang along with prominent Muslim and Christian traditional rulers, Government officials, politicians, youth, women and men groups were in attendance at the simple yet colourful and symbolic ceremony. The Governor, who gave a heart-warming speech, was visibly happy at the initiative of the Catholic Church and pledged his support for the centre, donating the sum of ₦10, 000,000 (to be used to start an endowment fund) and a bus of twenty-eight seats for the students. He also pledged that the Ministry of Education will pay for now the fifteen teaching and domestic staff salaries as part of the local contribution to MISEREOR's support.

There were trees planted symbolizing: Peace, Reconciliation and Forgiveness. The Governor planted the first tree named "Tree of Peace". The Archbishop of Jos planted the second tree named "Tree of Reconciliation" while the representative of the Jama'atu Nasril Islam (JNI), the umbrella Muslim Organization in the State, planted the third tree tagged "Tree of Forgiveness". This symbolic ceremony was well appreciated and applauded by the audience whose good attendance is an indication of the desire of many in Plateau State to help the youths develop positively rather than embarking on violence to solve socio-economic, political, ethnic and religious problems. What we witnessed was a humble effort by the Catholic Church which could be replicated at the District, Local Government, State and National levels. It shows clearly that there is so much that can be done for the youth if there is the political will. In a drama presented by the Muslim and Christian students of the centre, they showed how youths are being manipulated by selfish political and religious leaders and how the youths should resist such manipulations by those who pay them small monetary sums as inducement to violence. We hope that the centre will continue to expand, taking in more students and offering more possibilities in different areas of vocational skills for both Muslim and Christian boys and girls. For now, the facilities only allow for carpentry training for about thirty-five boys. The land is big enough for future expansion. Later the programme will include girls in the training. Certainly, it is better to light a candle than to curse the darkness. So much is being said about youth violence arising from idleness, poor education or poverty, yet very little is being done to remedy the situation. We hope that this little effort will be an eye-opener to Government, non-governmental voluntary bodies, and people of goodwill.

THE PLATEAU STATE GOVERNMENT'S COMMITMENT
An address by the Plateau State Governor Jonah David Jang at the Opening of the Inter-faith Youth Vocational Training Centre, Hai -Hong, Bokkos, January 27, 2011

Protocol
"The surest way to corrupt a youth is to instruct him to hold in higher esteem those who think alike than those who think differently". Friedrich Nietzsche, a German philosopher and critic of culture (1844 - 1900). This quotation by the great German philosopher, captures the substance of the vision of this Centre, anchored on inter-faith training of young people in vocational skills. .

I am particularly drawn to this initiative because it concerns the youth who are instrumental to the growth of any society especially its future. Most critical is the spirit of mutual coexistence among religious faiths which we are all aware is a major challenge globally. Today, this global threat to mutual religious coexistence should serve as a wake-up call for all of us to deliberately work towards building a harmonious society. Failure to do this, and especially by not providing means of livelihood to our teeming youths in the society in which we are allowing the growth of a monster, will impact negatively on the same society which can also consume us in future.

Herein lies the strategic role of the Inter-faith Youth Vocational Training Centre, where we are today witnessing the take-off of the first batch of participants. The mission of this Centre, which is to help the less privileged rural youths of both

Christian and Muslim backgrounds to learn skills together in the same environment, is no doubt a catalyst for promoting religious understanding, dialogue and harmony in the society on completion of their training. This, I must submit, is an answer to one of the great threats to peace and harmony in Jos, which is religious intolerance. I therefore wish to state here that the challenge of guiding the idle youths who are usually exploited to disrupt societal peace, rests on religious leaders and parents. Situations where religious leaders teach, preach and incite intolerance among their adherents while parents encourage their wards not to relate with their peers of other faiths portends danger for our society.

I have always said that none of us asked God to be born into any religion or ethnic group. This therefore requires all us to respect each other's religion and culture wherever we find ourselves. This I believe will mark the beginning of treading the path of peace in our interactions and relations. Government, on its part, is aware of such inflammatory preaching and incitements and will set guidelines to regulate religious preaching.

To our religious leaders, I admonish them to teach and present their messages according to the true meaning of what the holy books say, as no religion preaches violence. Our youths should, therefore, not allow themselves to be used to unleash violence on the society but must say 'no' as the crisis entrepreneurs have their wards in far away high-profile schools or jobs elsewhere, while youths from disadvantaged families are manipulated for their selfish reasons at risk of their lives. It is unfortunate that some politicians are using crises in our society for political gains. I appeal to such politicians who have solutions to peace in our society both nationally and locally to offer such solutions now, and not wait until the damage is done. The business of achieving peace is a collective one.

At this juncture, I wish to state that the Plateau State Government has reconstituted the State Inter-Religious Council on Peace and Harmony which we established as a pivot for peaceful co-existence in the State. The reconstitution followed the death of the co-chairman of the Council, the Emir of Wase, Alhaji.

Abdullahi Haruna Maikano, and the expiration of the tenure of the other co-Chairman, who was also the Chairman of the Christian Association of Nigeria in the State and Catholic Archbishop of Jos, Ignatius Kaigama.

The Inter-Religious Council under their leadership worked relentlessly to promote peace in Plateau State, on behalf of the Government and people of the State, I thank them for their selfless service.

As part of our humble efforts towards youth empowerment, the Plateau State Government has in conjunction with the Federal Government established a Science Incubation Centre in Bukuru where we have spent about 50million naira. The Centre serves for the commercialization of vocational skills. Government believes this Centre will also fill the gap of unemployment in the society.

Our administration will continue to do everything possible towards the promotion of peace and harmony, which includes consultation with various stakeholders. In the same vein, the special security arrangement known as "Operation Rainbow", approved by Mr. President for the State will soon take off, since we are determined to bring back lasting peace and stability to Plateau State.

I congratulate the Archbishop for the establishment of this centre. I pray it will grow to achieve the goals for which it was established for the benefit of humanity and to the glory of God. I assure you the Plateau State Government will be partners with you in this project.

*Below is a handwritten postscript by the Governor at the ceremony:

I have approved the release of N10, 000, 000.00 to the Centre, while the Ministry of Education will take over the payment of salaries of the staff of the school. Similarly, government will donate a 28-seater bus to the Centre. To the new intake, this is the opportunity for you to take your destiny into your hands by acquiring skills for livelihood as well as being advocates of peace in your communities on completing your programme. I wish you every success. Thank you all, and God bless!

DO ALL YOU CAN TO LIVE IN
PEACE WITH EVERYONE
A talk shared with some Catholics in Public Office, Abuja, May 27, 2001

Introduction

My heart is filled with so much joy that you are gathered at this forum in the context of your faith to reflect on issues that are of interest to our church and nation. I appreciate the invitation by Archbishop John Onayekan to share with you on the theme of living in peace with everyone. When I started my apostolate as the Archbishop of Jos I initiated meetings with Catholics in different categories: teachers, lawyers, doctors, politicians, civil servants, etc and found my encounter with them very enriching, and would say it was what helped to define the scope of my pastoral ministry. I am happy that in spite of your very demanding national assignments you consider it necessary and helpful to come here to rub minds. I pray that this will inspire others to take time from their busy schedules to meet even if not to discuss anything, at least to pray together. I was in the UK last year to give talks on the Live Simply spirituality and had the opportunity of addressing some Catholic members of the British Parliament, during which I learnt that they take an hour or so every week to share and pray together.

The Imperative of Peace

Pivotal to the message of Jesus Christ is peace. Being the Prince of Peace, his teachings and actions were predicated on peace. He sent the apostles on a mission and instructed them, "When you enter a house say, 'Peace be with you' "(Mt 10:12). After his resurrection, Jesus' first words of greetings to the apostles gathered in the upper room were, 'Peace be with you' (cf. Jn 20:19, Lk 24:36). Paul's characteristic greeting at the beginning of his letters was "The grace and peace of our Lord Jesus Christ be with you..." (1Cor. 1:3). Peace therefore is the very essence of the

Christian religion and those who work for peace are regarded as children of God (cf. Mt 5:9).

Some Dimensions of Peace

Spiritual peace is attained by being in communion with God. If one's mind is stayed on the Lord, the Lord will surely grant peace of mind (cf. Is 26:3). The Psalmist says "Be still and know that I am the Lord" (Ps 46:11), while St. Augustine concluded that, "Our hearts are restless until they rest in God".

Political peace is attained when there is equity. The absence of justice threatens the existence of peace. Where politics fosters human progress and creates an environment for meaningful and dignified existence, peace will flow like a river. But where governance is characterized by greed, reckless expenditure and insensitivity to the basic needs of the populace, one can only expect a harvest of civil unrest and social conflict triggered by the competition for resources. The pursuit of ethnic harmony in Nigeria can never be separated from the presence of basic social amenities. When there is enough potable water, basic education, health care, accessible roads and fertilizer for farmers, and the youths are gainfully engaged, ethnic rivalry and unhealthy competition will be minimized; farmers and cattle rearers will not have to fight over farm and grazing land; the desire to get into chieftaincy and political positions will largely be inspired by the need to create and foster greater peace and development.

Religiously Related Violence

The country has experienced many crises of a political, ethnic, economic and social nature. The amazing thing is that in the Northern parts of the country, even when it was very clear that a crisis was triggered off by political or ethnic considerations, it was soon made to look like a religious crisis. There is no doubt that there have been religiously motivated crises such as the Maitatsine riots of the 1980s. The fact, however, is that religion is so sensitive an issue that it is easily manipulated. Nigerians are said to be religious and this is evident by the ubiquitous churches and mosques and the outward manifestations of piety either by way of dress, symbols, inscriptions on vehicles, etc. But do we have the peace that religion should bring? We have witnessed violent conflicts in the name of religion. Trivial issues that should not engage our energy end up causing massive destruction and tragic loss of life. The peace that religion should provide is being replaced with hatred, jealousy, and malicious and calculated attempts to outdo the other. For some, religion is brought into governance not with the aim of allowing its values to inspire policies or decisions, but as a way of fostering the interest of a particular religion. Appointments, contracts and other national privileges seem to be dictated by religious affiliation rather than merit. It is wrongly believed that one can be at peace with God and yet do incalculable damage to one's neighbour as long as it is in the name of one's religion. Killing in the name of God is legitimized by some ignorant religious leaders with the promise of a paradise of infinite happiness and peace.

Nigeria Inter-Religious Council (NIREC) and Religious Harmony

We thank God that there is the Nigeria Inter-Religious Council (NIREC) which aims at fostering closer spiritual ties between the two predominant religions in Nigeria. Both Islam and Christianity have failed to arrest the frequently occurring so-called religious crises, in which religious leaders are killed while mosques and churches are destroyed. That such atrocities, especially in various parts of Northern Nigeria, should happen in the name of religion is a disgrace and a contradiction of what true religion stands for. Youths are used to cause destruction in the belief that they are fighting to protect or promote their religion. Some politicians resort to religious sentiments to engineer their political careers, while some preachers either out of ignorance or deliberate desire to cause mischief indoctrinate their adherents with the message of hate. They need to know that one who thinks he is fighting for God believes that God is either impotent or so confused that they have to complement his efforts. It is often said that both Islam and

Christianity are religions of peace, but even if peace exists, it is so fragile that it can easily be broken with disastrous consequences just because somebody is said to have blasphemed God or a prophet, or said an unpalatable thing about the other religion.

Do All You Can To Live In Peace

Our text for reflection is taken from Romans 12:18: "Do all you can to live in peace with everyone." Paul's exhortation in this passage is primarily about the relationship of Christians with non-Christians. He urges Christians not to repay evil with evil even when dealing with those who cause them great harm and inconvenience. Rather, he calls on them to live in peace in as far as this depends on them. Paul realizes that it may not be easy for Christians to live in peace with their neighbours because it does not depend entirely on the Christians. The point here is that Christians should not be the ones responsible for any breach of the peace. Paul's conclusion: overcome evil with good.

The Jos Experience

As pious and nice as this Pauline exhortation is, it is difficult for all to comply with it when confronted with unprovoked hostility. During the 2001 crisis when our cathedral parish house and other Churches were burnt in Jos, some youths came to me and said, "We are being killed, the Church must do something. Give us arms to fight". I took them into the chapel and talked to them about non-violence and they listened. During another crisis they said they were targets of attacks. While the others had weapons they claimed they only had stones. Once again they said, "We need arms, just as others have". My response was, "How do you expect that I order for arms and distribute them to you in the name of the Church?" In the November 2008 crisis, the level of destruction on both sides left us devastated. Many on both sides believe that the only solution is to fight to the end, and that the so-called dialogue and efforts at reconciliation are not yielding the desired results. They claim that some partners in the dialogue are not sincere, saying good things in the public only to retreat to plan evil.

Since 2004 I have been officially involved in the issues of dialogue between Muslims and Christians in Plateau State: first, as the Chairman of the Inter-Religious Council for Peace and Harmony (IRCPH), and recently, with the Emir of Wase as Co-Chairman, leading ten Muslim and ten Christian religious and community leaders. We meet often to encourage peaceful coexistence. We have a "quick intervention committee" which goes promptly to places where there is a tense relationship between Muslims and Christians to intervene. On the whole, we have recorded some successes in mediation.

When the Christian Association of Nigeria (CAN) and the Jama'tu Nasril Islam (JNI) noticed that the Plateau State Local Government elections of March 2008 were going to create problems, we met in my office and issued a statement, urging all to peace. The Local Government elections were however cancelled midway. As the Local Government elections of November 2008 got near we met again twenty days to the time in the Central Mosque, Jos and issued a statement calling especially our youths to avoid violent behaviour and decided we would rotate our meetings to sustain the effort at dialogue. Five days to the elections, the IRCPH met, and the Emir and I issued a joint statement on both radio and television calling our people to vote not according to religious affiliation but for candidates who would improve the welfare of the people. We urged all to conduct themselves peacefully during the elections and let the winner emerge fairly. This was a dream that was shattered in the early hours of November 29. Politics became very hostile and the political storm that broke out soon assumed a religious dimension. In no time churches and mosques were on fire and chaos was all over the place. Deaths were recorded in their hundreds. As our peace efforts went up in the flames, we looked on helplessly. All hopes of reconciliation seemed to be lost. Attempts to convene meetings failed. Even the visit by the NIREC leadership was not enough to allay fears and wipe out the distrust that had been created.

Matters were not helped when some national and international media seemed to be celebrating the tragedy in Jos by dishing out half truths and in many cases very biased information. When it was not possible to convene either the IRCPH meeting or the joint CAN and JNI meeting, I made use of what was possible, my friendship with the Emir of Wase. In the heat of the crisis we remained in contact, thanks to the cell phone. The Emir and I were perhaps the only religious leaders who remained in touch over the sad situation. As soon as the crisis died down the Emir came from Wase to meet me, and on the occasion of the visit of the British High Commissioner, Bob Dewar, we met in my house and proceeded to visit the displaced Christians in St. Michael's Parish, Nassarawa Gwong, where the Emir condoled with them and he and the British High Commissioner encouraged peaceful coexistence. From there we went to the central mosque and met a group of Muslim leaders who were also addressed by the Emir, the High Commissioner and me. It was an emotional event. I had entered the same mosque three weeks earlier with much fanfare as Muslim leaders cheerfully received us. This particular visit was very sombre. I was not sure what they were thinking about me, because being the Chairman of CAN in Plateau State there was no way they could exonerate me from the losses they had suffered. All the same, we were received cordially and even my short speech was applauded. The Muslim spokesman asked me to send their greetings to the Christians.

The crisis has come and hopefully gone. The deep suspicion and distrust still remain, however. The recent hysteria generated by the alleged expulsion of Fulanis from the Wase area of Plateau State is another symptom of that deep suspicion. While the Emir of Wase, the District Head of Bashar where the Fulanis camped and the Local Government Chairman, all Fulanis and Muslims, emphatically said that relocating the Fulanis who had settled there without permission and were a threat to peace had neither tribal nor religious motives, yet experts at whipping up religious sentiments and political opportunists had started shouting loudly that it was a deliberate offensive against Muslims and Fulanis in Plateau State.

Efforts at Dialogue

Efforts at dialogue and reconciliation are continuing, but it is not easy. On both sides people have become sceptical about the usefulness of dialogue. It took some time before some Muslim members of the IRCPH could rejoin us at our meetings. Now that it appears we are together, rumours that are at once ridiculous and at the same time harmful keep circulating the town such as, "There is an imminent plan for an attack, there is a CAN army; a mosque is hiding sophisticated weapons, etc". Every Friday people are very careful about their movements, because all the previous crises originated on a Friday. The other day a man was being pursued by bees, and when he was running for cover everybody started running to nowhere and for no reason in particular. At a recent Archdiocesan Pastoral Council meeting we took a long time discussing dialogue and reconciliation. There were more pessimists than optimists on the issue of dialogue. Some have remained very bitter about what they call "the hypocrisy of these people," and someone believing there are still evil plans warned me to be careful because "these people cannot be trusted". He concluded, "We need you more than they need you, so do not open yourself to great harm in the name of dialogue." The Emir and I have however resolved to stick together despite all the unwarranted attacks and accusations about our motives. We have stated repeatedly that even if everyone around us abandons dialogue and efforts at reconciliation we will not. I have visited Wase twice since the crisis, the Emir has visited my house twice, and we have appeared jointly on TV and radio programmes. At the last NIREC meeting in Jos, 19th May, the Emir and I and shared how we were being perceived by both our respective faith communities over our efforts at dialogue. Some Christian leaders believe that I am "compromising". The Emir says some of his people say he is a "sell-out". On our part, we have decided to do even more than we ever did to foster peace and harmony.

Empty Religion, Hypocrisy, or True Belief?

If you ask me I will say among Nigerian Muslims and Christians we have these categories of believers:

1) *Fire-for-fire believers*. They are very intolerant and are prepared to kill in the name of advancing their religion. They believe in territorial expansion and forceful conversion and can use blackmail, money or arms at will to foster their religion. They never forgive and are fanatical, believing that if they kill in God's name they will be rewarded in heaven.

2) *Indifferent Believers*: They are neither hot nor cold. They are merely happy performing their religious rituals and obligations. They do not care if people are killed in the name of religion as long as it is not one of them. It is of this group that it is said, "What is needed for evil to triumph is for good people to do nothing".

3) *Open and fair-minded believers*: These people are conciliatory in nature. They accept that there are differences of beliefs and modes of worship. They understand that tension can arise but it must be addressed maturely. They can share, relate, talk honestly with others and even appreciate the good in the other religion and condemn the bad actions of their fellow-believers.

It is from the third group that those Christian and Muslim leaders are found, who foster honest dialogue and reconciliation. In this group too one finds good politicians who do not exploit religion, and journalists who are objective rather than sensational, prejudiced and provocative in reporting religious crises.

Light a Candle Instead of Cursing the Darkness

Our Archdiocese is engaged in some ways in the promotion of peaceful coexistence between Muslims and Christians. We have the Department of Inter-Religious Dialogue, the office of the Justice, Peace and Development Commission (JDPC), which houses the Emergency Preparedness and Response Team (EPRT) comprising Muslims and Christians, and the Archdiocesan Women Empowerment Programme, which brings Muslim and Christian women together for peace building, poverty reduction and health issues. The Catholic Archdiocesan Rural Development Programme (CARUDEP) offers social services without discrimination. Very soon we shall start a centre for Christian and Muslim youths in Bokkos to help them acquire vocational skills as well as teach them how to co-exist in an atmosphere of peace and mutual acceptance.

CONCLUSION: People who are divided by prejudicial quarrels, racial and cultural conflicts, tribal sentiments or religious persuasions are prevented from developing. How can one explain that we live in a country blessed with immense natural and human resources, yet the populace wallows in poverty and insecurity? Our diversity should signal strength, wealth, progress and harmony, but on the contrary we are causing harm to ourselves in the name of religion or politics. The gap caused by religious, political and ethnic intolerance seems to be widening unnecessarily. There is need for bridges. We need men and women who can heal the wounds caused by needless political and religious wrangling. We all in our own ways can stop violence from breaking out; if it has broken out we can stop it from spreading.

There is a need for personal conversion, embracing the culture of non- violence by every Nigerian and a practical carrying out of the dictum, "Love your neighbor". We need to seek the common good first instead of narrow ethnic interests born out of greed. Religious fanaticism, ethnic chauvinism and political self-centredness must give way to true patriotism. Where Muslims are in the majority they must respect the rights of non-Muslims to freedom of worship, guaranteeing the right to build churches and carry out spiritual exercises freely, and where Christians dominate, they must give the Muslims a sense of belonging and not treat them as aliens. Our leaders should encourage Nigerians to live and work happily in any part of the country, as proved by Barack Obama's election in the U.S. without the indigene or settler dichotomy. This must be across the entire nation so that an Angas can live as a happy Nigerian in Sokoto, a Yoruba will live with full rights in Jos, and a Kano Muslim fully integrated in Enugu. We expect the media to play a positive role during crises. Unfortunately, some have helped to aggravate the situation by very biased reporting. The major media organizations must exercise restraint in reporting casualties. It would be helpful if the foreign Hausa radio programmes do not use their programmes to incite religious intolerance. The youths must be our priority as a nation. The situation of youths in our tertiary institutions and national youth service programme do not indicate that we want to form a youth that will be useful to the nation. The culture of merit is fast disappearing. Youths are made to bribe their way for everything. Some adopt violent means to get what they want and many resort to cultism, robbery, and prostitution, or even allow themselves to be used as political mercenaries. Religious intolerance in Northern Nigeria, just like youth militant activities in the Niger Delta, must not ruin our country at a time like this when the "gospel" of re-branding is being propagated. Pope Benedict XVI on his recent visit to the Middle East described himself as a pilgrim of peace and reconciliation. You and I too are called to be apostles, ambassadors and pilgrims of peace and reconciliation.

BROTHER AND FRIEND
— EMIR HARUNA ABDULLAHI OF WASE

A tribute to the Late Emir of Wase, Dr. Haruna Abdullahi, a bosom friend.

"Your good friend the Emir of Wase is very sick at the Jos University Teaching Hospital (JUTH)" was a text message I received from one of my priests, which was soon confirmed by the Galadima of Wase, Alh Mustapha Umar in a text he sent asking me to pray for the Emir who had been admitted at the intensive care unit of JUTH. Since I was at the Conference of the Catholic Bishops of Nigeria in Ijebu-Ode, Ogun State, I announced to the Bishops that morning at Mass that my friend the Emir was sick and needed prayers. Immediately after the Mass, I got a text message from the Deputy Governor of Plateau State, Dame Pauline Tallen, informing me that "Your friend the Emir of Wase is no more" To say the least, I was devastated and the whole day was one prolonged time of misery. I knew that I would miss the funeral rite which had already been fixed for 2.00 pm that day Friday 17th, 2010; so I asked my Vicar-General to pass the news of the Emir's death to as many priests in Jos as possible and to make immediate arrangements to be present in Wase. Over twenty priests along with some reverend sisters and lay people cut short their day's activities and headed for Wase, arriving in time for the burial.

The Emir and I began our friendly association one afternoon when he was on his way from Kaduna and branched at my house to welcome me to Jos, upon my transfer from Jalingo Diocese in Taraba State to Jos as the new Archbishop. He said he also wanted to appreciate my role in hosting displaced Muslims on our compound in the wake of the 2001 ethno-religious crisis. He intended a brief visit, but we ended up spending close to two hours. We discovered that we had a mutual passion for peace and inter-religious harmony. I soon paid him a Sallah visit in Wase at the end of Ramadan and was very warmly received by him and his people. During the 2004 Yelwa crisis, I initiated a peace mission to Yelwa. He and the Long Goemai of Shendam, Hubert Shaldas II and I were in Yelwa preaching peace to both the Christians and Muslims. For the first time Christians and Muslims were able to meet face-to-face following the sad crisis that had led to the destruction of life and property. It was a successful mission.

Since that mission, I visited the Emir several times in his Wase palace and he was a regular visitor to my house in Jos. We issued several joint messages of peace and harmony, and I believe that it was in recognition of this that the Chief Joshua Dariye

Government constituted the Inter- Religious Council for Peace and Harmony and appointed us to head it. Subsequently, Gov. David Jonah Jang renewed our mandate and made the Emir and me co-chairmen of the body. In the desire to foster greater understanding, we once initiated a meeting between twenty Christian and twenty Muslim leaders in the JNI office at the Central Mosque to discuss ways for peaceful coexistence and harmony. After the 2008 crisis, the Emir and I jointly received in my house the British High Commissioner to Nigeria and went from there to visit the displaced Christians in Nasarawa Gwong camped at St. Michael's Catholic Church and the displaced Muslims at the Jos Central Mosque. The Catholic German Bishops came visiting and the Emir of Wase and his colleague of Kanam, Alhaji Babangida Muazu, joined me to receive the visitors. We had a fruitful interaction and went on to the house of the late Turakin Jos, Alhaji Inuwa Ali, to condole with his family. We were received by many Muslim dignitaries.

Not long after, the Emir and I were in Germany at the invitation of MISSIO to participate in the World Mission Sunday which was dedicated to the subject of peace and reconciliation in Nigeria. Both of us were happily encouraging a project for the training and formation of both Christian and Muslim youths in vocational skills and inter-religious matters. This is a project of the Catholic Archdiocese of Jos established with the help of MISEREOR Germany and sited in Bokkos with the specific aim of training Muslim and Christian youths together to appreciate the merits of living in harmony by accepting one another without the kind of religious prejudice and hostility witnessed today.

Our friendship and work for peace was commended and encouraged by many Muslims and Christians to the extent that many would say the Emir and the Archbishop were inseparable when it came to peace matters. However, a few did not believe that a genuine friendship was possible between a Muslim and a Christian leader. On our part, we did not need to provide any philosophical proof that our friendship was working well. I spent two full days in his house in Wase and he was such a gracious host, helping me to meet with the Christians of the area and made me very comfortable. He came regularly to Jos to visit me and we had long hours of conversation. Throughout the crises in Plateau State we remained in constant contact, sometimes on a daily basis, and thanks to the mobile phone. We reassured ourselves that our work for peace and interreligious harmony was approved by God. I remember the Emir saying with satisfaction on our way to Germany that even if we died in the process of working for peace at home or abroad the glory was to God.

Nothing good comes easy. On both sides of the religious divide there were sceptics who never believed that we could truly love and befriend each other. There was the constant refrain of "You cannot trust this people" or "They are just deceiving you". That did not frighten or discourage us. Some who prefer confrontation to dialogue did not wish to see us working together with such cordiality and warmth; after all Muslims and Christians are supposed to be enemies, fighting each other through jihad or crusade. We saw things differently. Our religions transcend the narrow boundary erected by religious traditions and doctrines. True religion promotes neighbourly solidarity, care and love rather than hostile confrontation at the slightest misunderstanding. Intimidation, unsubstantiated allegations, malicious rumours and speculations did not stop our work. We were determined and God was with us.

My dear friend Alh. Dr. Haruna Abdullahi, you were a broadminded human being, a sincere Muslim whose love and concern for humanity was unquestionable. Ever since I met you ten years ago I had no cause to doubt, distrust or suspect you. Your utterances and actions were dictated by truth and sincerity. Even when hurtful and malicious rumours came to your attention, you took them with philosophical calmness. You must have suffered deep down when blatant lies were told about your person, yet you bore all with maturity and incredible composure.

I thank you for introducing me to the Sultan of Sokoto, Alh. Sa'ad Abubakar III. The Sultan had come to a function in NIPPS Kuru, shortly after being named the Sultan. We met at his lodge for long hours with the Archbishop of Abuja, Most Rev. John Onaiyekan. I believe that this meeting was the beginning of a loving and fruitful relationship between the Sultan and the Archbishop.

I thank you for the first harvest of your farm that you would kindly share with me: the bags of rice and corn you would send to me annually, knowing that I do not own or work a farm. During my Silver Jubilee of priesthood you surprised me by quietly sending a very big cow to help me entertain my visitors, and when I celebrated the thanksgiving Mass in my village, Kona, in Taraba State, you longed to be there in person. Owing to official engagements you could not attend, but you sent a delegation to Kona not only with prayers and a goodwill message but with a precious basket of kola nuts which was used to entertain all my visitors.

The numerous text messages and telephone calls I received at the news of your passing away from many parts of Nigeria and especially from Germany, where you are fondly remembered because of our two-week visit to Frankfurt, Bonn, Osnabruck, Berlin and Munich, sharing the message of peace and dialogue with the German Muslim and Christian groups, is further evidence that our work for peace is appreciated by many. In all these messages I was being condoled on the death of a friend and collaborator. I saw you not only as a friend but more importantly as a brother. Thank you for believing in me and for your trusting and loyal friendship. We prayed and agonized together on the best ways to avoid crises in Plateau State. Our struggles will not be in vain. May the Almighty and Merciful Allah reward you with heavenly peace, and may Plateau State and indeed Nigeria experience that peace for which you sacrificed so much. Sleep peacefully, dear brother and friend.

Section Five
MEMOIRS/INTERVENTIONS

CHRISTIAN/MUSLIM RELATIONS IN JOS AND NIGERIA: A PERSONAL EXPERIENCE

An input at the Conference organised by CAFOD/Heythrop College, London, October 28, 2009

Introduction

I thank the organizers of this Conference for inviting me to share my experience of Christian/Muslim relations as a pastoral worker in Jos, Plateau State and from my lived experience of the Nigerian situation. Many Muslims and Christians in Nigeria are eager that our respective religions should be instruments of peace and contribute to integral development instead of being the sources of conflicts. I believe that the spiritual salvation and social liberation of Nigeria depend largely on how these two religions cooperate positively. If however they are engaged in merely competing for numerical strength, geographical expansion and claims to superiority, or have a holier-than-thou attitude, they will do a lot of harm to the Nigerian soul, spirit and social existence.

In our West African region, all the countries have been relatively free of religious conflicts except Nigeria. Senegal, the Gambia, Sierra Leone are very good examples of

Muslim/Christian coexistence, even in political life. Relations are cordial and mutual acceptance is of a high degree. Why is Nigeria the exception?

Nigeria and Problematic Muslim/Christian Relations
While the Southern part of Nigeria enjoys relative inter-religious peace and harmony, the Northern part of Nigeria seems to be a boiling cauldron of inter-and intra-religious conflicts.[16] Since the 1980s one can count more than twenty major crises. These crises often begin as a result of some social, ethnic or political misunderstanding and soon assume a religious dimension. It should be noted that apart from some explicit cases involving movements like the Maitatsine of the 1980s and the recent Boko Haram (a fundamentalist/fringe Islamic sect led by one Mohammed Yusuf, which in late July and early of August 2009 denounced Western education and visited carnage and destruction on the people of Bauchi, Maiduguri, Yobe, Katsina and Kano), most of the so-called religious conflicts originate from tussles over control of land, claims to be settlers or indigenes, and politics/elections. Of course, poverty, unemployment, insensitive governance that leads to massive corruption and social injustice are very significant factors. The various movements such as the Movement for the Emancipation of the Niger Delta (MEND), the Movement for the Sovereign State of Biafra (MASSOB), the Ooduwa People's Congress (OPC) and even the Boko Haram Islamic sect are all pointers that social issues are at the roots of the crises especially in Northern Nigeria but are unfortunately often baptized as conflicts between Christians and Muslims. A typical example is the November 28, 2008 Jos crisis, which began as a result of the Jos North Local Government election, suspected to have been fraudulently conducted, but which soon graduated into

---

[16] For the list of major conflicts associated with religion see Rotshak I. Gofwen, *Religious Conflicts in Northern Nigeria and Nation Building (The Throes of Two Decades 1980-2000)*, a publication of Human Rights Monitor, 2004 Kaduna, Nigeria, pp 65-67. Also see "Why North is on Fire" by Ismail Omipidian, in the *Sunday Sun*, August 2, 2009, p. 4.

large-scale burning of churches and mosques and was nationally and internationally reported in the media as a war between Muslims and Christians.

No other issue has kept Nigeria so much on the boil as what has come to be known as the Sharia crisis.[17] The introduction of Sharia in 1999, not so much as a way to enhance religious piety, but to serve the interests of some politicians who are neither clerics nor models of piety, has inflamed religious passion and hypersensitivity, so that even when policies are made or genuine actions taken, the fear by Christians is that of the islamization or "shariazation" of Nigeria; just as Muslims fear the predominance of the Christian religion in Nigeria. Sharia is seen by Christians as a flagrant violation of the secular status of the constitution of Nigeria. The conversion by former President Ibrahim Babangida of Nigeria's involvement from that of an observer to a full member of the Organization of Islamic Conference in 1986 increased the fear of Christians that it marked a new level in the gradual islamization of Nigeria which had started under General Murtala Muhammed in 1975.

Some Christians argue also that right from the inception of Nigeria, the seed of religious discord and conflict was sown by the colonial administration through its pro-Islamic policy in Nigeria.[18] It prohibited the spread of Christianity and the activities of missions within certain areas, thereby laying the foundation of religious conflict.[19]

During the long period of military rule, individuals and groups lacked the freedom of expression, so that these crises, according to Msgr. Matthew Kukah, "represent the cumulative impact of all the negative forces, lack of freedom, expression and arbitrariness with which the military governed Nigeria".[20]

---

[17] Matthew Kukah, *Human Rights in Nigeria. Hopes and Hindrances*, a publication of MISSIO, Aachen, Germany, 2003 p.19
[18] Rotgak I. Gofwen, *Religious Conflicts in Northern Nigeria and Nation Building (The Throes of Two Decades 1980-2000)*, p. 61
[19] **Ibid**. p.60
[20] Matthew Kukah, *Human Rights*, p. 25

The Search for Religious Peace and Harmony

Aware of the sensitive and explosive nature of religion and tribe in Nigeria, the Federal Government excluded information about them from the last national census. These twin issues are the easiest to be manipulated by selfish politicians, ignorant and fanatical religious leaders and ethnic chauvinists. Managing religious conflicts has been more difficult because there is often a mixture of religion and ethnicity in almost all the conflicts in Nigeria. The Boko Haram mayhem was easier to manage because, first, it was mainly intra-religious, although churches and Christians were also attacked. Secondly, given that the current President of Nigeria, Alhaji Umaru Yar'Adua, is a Muslim from the North and of the Hausa/Fulani stock, it was easier for him to give orders to security agents to quell the uprising without raising ethnic or religious sentiments.

The Nigeria Inter-Religious Council (NIREC) came into being in order to help deal with the unhealthy recurring crises that often are attributed to religion. The Council is made up of the Sultan of Sokoto who is the head of the Muslims in Nigeria and the President of the Christian Association of Nigeria as co-chairmen, with well-respected Christian and Muslim religious and traditional leaders as members. They meet often and rotate their meetings in different parts of the country and try dousing tension where crises occur. This body has the potential to inspire a new kind of relationship between Muslims and Christians. The establishment of the Nigeria inter-faith Action Association against Malaria (NIFAAM) is a significant step by both religions to improve the lives of Nigerians. NIREC can help Muslims and Christians to use religion for peaceful purposes and remedy the social situation caused by corruption, bad governance, illiteracy, poverty and superstition. It can help to promote patriotism instead of parochialism and stop the titanic eruption of hostility over trivial issues.

We have seen encouraging gestures such as the building of mosques being facilitated by Christian Governors as in Abia,

Akwa Ibom, Benue States etc., areas considered to be predominantly Christian. In a similar vein, the Christian Association of Nigeria National Youth Wing gave an award of Excellence and Exemplary Leadership to Alhaji Danjuma Goje, the Muslim Governor of Gombe State in recognition of his kind and generous disposition to Christians in his State. The very swift condemnation by prominent Muslim groups and individuals of the Boko Haram sect, that its philosophy and practice are not in consonance with the teaching of Islam, could be attributed to NIREC influence. The recent action of the Niger State Muslim Governor in collaboration with Federal authorities to evacuate about 4,000 or so members of an Islamic group (Darul-Islam), whose activities the State Commissioner of Police, Mr. Mike Zuokumour, labeled as "un-Islamic" and described as a threat to security not only to Niger State but to Nigeria as a whole,[21] is the kind of pro-active security measure that will save Nigeria from the activities of fundamentalists who plunge the country into unnecessary crises.

There are increasing efforts of many Muslim/Christian NGOs in peace-building and conflict resolution. The Catholic Bishops' Conference of Nigeria has a special Committee on Christian/Muslim relations and uses the apparatus of the Justice, Peace and Development Commission to foster greater collaboration with Muslims. Recently, the Conference of Women Religious held seminars and workshops on inter-religious issues, just as Islam is now part of the curriculum in seminaries and many religious houses of formation. The Interfaith Mediation Centre in Kaduna jointly founded and directed by Pastor James Wuye and Imam Muhammad Ashafa, who were both leaders of militant religious groups, offers a faith-based approach to peace-building through the use of non-violent methods. We need many trained

---

[21] Cf. *Daily Trust* Editorial of Wednesday August 26, 2009 p.14; *Daily Trust* of Wednesday, August 19, 2009, p.56.). The Emir of Kano Alhaji Ado Bayero said that the Islamic sects Boko Haram and Darul Islam are threats to peaceful coexistence of the nation cf. *Daily Trust* Monday September 21, 2009, p. 3

peace-makers, who the Bible says are blessed (cf. Mt 5:9). I am happy to say that CAFOD, in addition to its programmes on HIV, orphaned and vulnerable children, water provision, primary health care in our Archdiocese and other parts of Nigeria, is helping me with the training of a priest of our Archdiocese doing an MA in Peace Studies in the University of Bradford, UK.

At our Archdiocesan level we have a Department of Inter-Religious Dialogue. The office of Justice, Peace and Development Commission houses also the Emergency Preparedness and Response Team, comprising Muslims and Christians and headed by a Muslim, with early warning teams across the seventeen Local Governments areas in Plateau State. There is the Women Empowerment Programme which brings Muslim and Christian women together for peace-building, poverty reduction and health issues. Our Rural Development programmes also offer social services (wells, pit latrines, water catchment tanks, techniques of improved agriculture, etc) to Muslims. At the peak of the November 28 crisis the first relief of N1, 000,000 came from the CAFOD office in Jos and it went a long way in providing badly needed water, food, mats and basic drugs to displaced persons camped in schools and parishes. The Archdiocese of Jos is in the process of building an interfaith youth vocational training centre, to teach the idle and disadvantaged Christian and Muslim youths vocational skills, in the hope that they will return to their village communities with such skills and knowledge of each other's faith, to become apostles or militants for peace.

My Experience of Inter-Religious Dialogue
As a bishop I have always worked in conflict areas. My first diocese was Jalingo where there was a long drawn ethnic conflict among the Tivs, Jukuns, Kutebs and Fulanis in the 1990s. Barely one year after I assumed office in 2000 as Archbishop of Jos, a violent conflict broke out on September 7, 2001. Since then, the state has been boiling with a mixture of ethnic and political conflict often masked as religious. I have been living in the middle of it and I have also learnt to face it each time it erupts.

Although some people still view inter-religious dialogue as a watering down of the Christian belief or compromise on the mandate of Christ to evangelize the world, dialogue for me is a Christian obligation. It is either we learn to accept and appreciate our differences or we mutually extinguish each other. My approach to dialogue is basically practical. I do not engage in doctrinal analysis or debates. I advocate the dialogue of life by working with Muslims in the promotion of common social goals. I personally engage stakeholders, politicians and religious leaders in the challenge of peace building in Plateau State and the nation at large. As the chairman of the Plateau State Christian Association of Nigeria and the co-chairman of the State Inter-Religious Council, I see that we have no alternative to dialogue if we are to remain true Christians in our pluralistic society. Why I remain resolute about dialogue, even when there are mounting obstacles, is that peace is a necessary condition for human existence; without peace there will be neither growth nor development. I engage the politicians, traditional and religious leaders at the top, believing that the fruits of our labour for peace will flow to the youths.

The Challenges of Dialogue
Dialogue is a very tedious mission and at times risky, especially in a country like Nigeria where the history of Christian-Muslim relations has been very turbulent. The spirit of distrust and suspicion poses a great obstacle.

I and the Emir of Wase, Alhaji Dr Haruna Abudullahi, who is also the chairman of Jama'tu Nasril Islam (the Muslim umbrella organization) in Plateau State and its Vice- President General in Nigeria, have since 2004 been associates in the search for permanent peace between Muslims and Christians in Plateau State. After the Yelwa crisis of 2004 the Emir and I spearheaded a peace initiative which was very successful.[22] We have since then worked on several peace initiatives and programmes, appeared on TV and

---

[22] See Ignatius A. Kaigama, *Dialogue of Life : An Urgent Necessity for Nigerian Muslims and Christians*, Fab Educational Books, Jos Nigeria, 2006, pp. 29-32

spoken on radio programmes, and have been seen together in mosques and churches so that people now refer to us as brothers or twins. In recognition of our peace activities the Plateau State Government appointed us as co-chairmen of the Plateau State Inter-Religious Council for Peace and Harmony. There are many sceptics on both sides about the genuineness of our relationship. A prominent Christian leader told me to be careful as I was dealing with "snakes". When I invited some Christian leaders to a mosque for dialogue with Muslims some refused to go on the grounds that they were not prepared to become Muslims. The Emir of Wase has been accused by some members of his faith community as being a sell-out and perhaps a possible candidate for conversion to Christianity. We continue to do what we are doing: promoting dialogue and peace. This explains why immediately after the last Jos crisis, when the British High Commissioner, Bob Dewar visited Jos, the Emir and I went with him to a parish where displaced people gathered and then to the mosque, even when the feeling of hurt was still palpable.

The Emir of Kanam, Alhaji Mohammadu Muazu Babangida, impressed by the positive and constructive engagement by the Emir and myself, asked if he could join us, and now he is our partner in the search for peace. About two months ago I got a phone call from him asking for the establishment of a Catholic parish in his Emirate. I created not only a parish in the Muslim dominated area but also appointed a parish priest who has since taken up office even if he has no house, church or other infrastructure . The Executive Secretary of the Muslim Pilgrims' Board, Alhaji Abubakar Dashe, who was invited to give a keynote address at the annual General Assembly of Jos Archdiocese, was very appreciative of the gesture of the Catholic Church in reaching out to other religions. He said he was a beneficiary of Catholic education and noted that he was never forced at any point to change from Islam to Christianity. He told us of a village, Bajama, in Alkaleri Local Government in Bauchi State, in which Muslims and Christians inter-marry, embark on community projects and the council of elders sits often to discuss ways of avoiding crises.

Immediately after the November 2008 crisis, some men, women and youths representing a group called the Dynamic Women and Youth Negotiators for Peace, with a membership of about three thousand made up of Christians and Muslims, came to my office to tell me how they had resolved to work together and never to allow religious differences make them fight each other. They wanted my moral support and to be their patron.

About three weeks ago the Emir of Wase and I, along with three other Bishops and some Nigerians engaged in peace work, were invited to Germany by MISSIO (a Catholic agency) to participate in the World Mission Campaign with the theme "Peace and Reconciliation," focusing on Nigeria, and we spoke on our experience of Christian/Muslim collaboration in Nigeria. Happily, then, I can see those who prefer the "fire for fire" approach and those indifferent to Christian/Muslim dialogue reducing, even if very slowly. It is very encouraging to hear of efforts being made by my colleagues, the Bishops of northern cities such as Kano, Zaria, Maiduguri, Sokoto and Kaduna. The wind of inter-religious dialogue is blowing. We need patience, humility and courage. It is better to light a candle than to curse the darkness.

Conclusion

I took a cursory look at the situation of Muslim/Christian relations in Nigeria and we have seen that events that have nothing to do with religion have often triggered inter- religious conflicts. Cases of intra-religious conflicts are present too. In the name of promoting or protecting either Islam or Christianity many have been killed or maimed and priceless property destroyed. Religion should be a panacea, a roadmap to peace and not a problem. Fundamentalism is a very bad approach to religion, and so dialogue at the level of every day life at the level of spiritual practices, and hopefully at the doctrinal or theological level, is to be preferred. The politicization of religion is what creates more confusion. Negative indoctrination of children and youths must be avoided as well as using idle youths as agents of destruction. It is necessary to emphasize freedom of worship and reciprocity of religious freedom. I suggest that Christians and Muslims should visit each other's places of worship. Name-calling such as "infidels" or "unbelievers" only helps to fuel religious militancy. Swords of religious violence should be beaten into ornaments of devotion and worship (cf. Micah 4:3) so that even in the midst of poverty and social deprivation, religion should be responsible for peace flowing in Nigeria like a river.

Furthermore, I recommend the following:

1) Government and religious bodies need to invest seriously in youth development. The almajiris (Koranic pupils) need to be better formed through functional education in addition to the Koranic training. The youths need to be catered for by the provision of jobs or engaged in micro-economic ventures, or else we shall continue to multiply the number of youth miscreants, especially in the northern part of the country.

2) There is need for a sound formation of religious preachers and leaders, as ignorant and business-minded preachers have the tendency to incite to fundamentalist practices. The attempt by the Northern Governors' Forum to checkmate religious fanaticism is commendable.

3) Inter-religious education must become an integral part of the school curriculum. Some of the crises have started in schools over trivial arguments.

4) The return of Church/Islamic and the schools of other voluntary bodies taken over by the military government in the 1970s will help to accelerate the culture of dialogue and respect, as in the past when Muslims and Christians studied together without great problems.

5) There is no denying the fact that there is poverty in the land. Where social security is absent, one cannot avoid corruption and violence. With the vast available agricultural facilities,

youths could be used to develop that sector. With pervasive poverty and misery in the North and the country as a whole, religious bigotry easily develops into full-blown fundamentalism.

6) The Nigeria Inter-Religious Council needs to be strengthened at the state, local government and district levels with communication equipment, transport, staff and cinema vehicles which move from village to village showing films on peaceful coexistence.

7) National and international media should avoid whipping up sentiments during crises by quoting biased or exaggerated figures of casualties.

8) The "re-branding" campaign championed by the Nigerian Minister of Information and Communication will amount to very little if there is no fundamental change in mentality. Many Nigerians owe allegiance to their tribes or religions first before Nigeria or the common good.

9) Above all, we need prayers and a change of heart. I see light at the end of the tunnel.

Thank you for listening.

RELIGION AND POST-CONFLICT
PEACE-BUILDING IN NORTHERN NIGERIA

*A paper presented at a Seminar organised by the Centre for Conflict Management
and Peace Studies, University of Jos, June 22, 2010*

I commend wholeheartedly the University Community and the Centre for Conflict Management and Peace Studies in particular for giving us this day and moment. The general theme, "Religion and Post-Conflict Peace-building in Northern Nigeria", is timely and appropriate for obvious reasons: incessant upheavals in the North that have stunted development, and in Jos in particular, where crises have become a recurring decimal. The venue is apt – a citadel of learning where education, proper education should be problem-solving in orientation.

Northern Nigeria, like any other region in this country, has had a fair share of crises leaving behind victims, casualties and survivors who lick their wounds. It is a vicious circle that should be stopped, considering the obvious negative consequences we experience each time peace is disrupted. Surely it is far easier to breach than to build peace. A land-mine costs five dollars but it takes over 200 dollars to detonate it so that the community can live without any threat to life.

Most of our crises are triggered by competition for scarce resources, ideological and belief factors, and deep-seated challenges of identity and belonging. The fear of domination by minorities and the perception of alienation and marginalization from independence to the present day still remain some of the causes of social conflict even as we prepare to celebrate fifty years of nationhood.

We acknowledge the numerous institutions and organizations that work hard as peace-building agents. We need nothing short of creative thinking and action for peace. The survival of the whole of the North is hinged on the success we achieve at the level of post-conflict peace-building, given the numerous conflicts we have had. All practical measures should be taken in the entire nation to douse unhealthy religious, ethnic and political impulses which often retard our socio-economic advancement. Attempts at peace-building such as this give the opportunity to hear what the voiceless, the marginalized and excluded of society have to say.

Religion, which stands at the centre of the life of the ordinary citizen in Northern Nigeria, has either been abused or never exploited fully as a tool for peace-building. Religious leaders have the privilege of communicating with the majority of the masses on a daily basis, and experience has shown that our people listen especially when we point the right way. Unfortunately some religious leaders have either abdicated their responsibilities or allowed politics to invade the sacred space of religion to the level that religion is now playing second fiddle.

We cannot afford a situation where religion, which should be a binding factor, the glue of society, is treated with suspicion, bastardized and misused. Religion is not worth its salt if it lacks the capacity to unite people, and things are worse if it becomes an obvious source of perpetual tension and division. The adherents of the main religions in Nigeria, Islam and Christianity, should strive to build rather than resort to the destruction of lives and property at the slightest provocation or sometimes at no provocation at all. We need more apostles, ambassadors, agents of peace and healthy inter-religious dialogue. For some people inter-religious dialogue is a waste of time as they claim persons involved are hypocritical about it, and for some it is a sign of weakness, a compromise of one's religious values; yet we know that it is a veritable way to lessen religious tension and violence in the land. To successfully do this we must substantially do away with ignorance, youth unemployment, and injustice, which are often the underlying causes of all the violence that have masqueraded as religious crises. What begins as a social conflict owing to political or ethnic misunderstanding or differences soon becomes religious with worship places being burnt and unnecessary social tension created.

This seminar has given us a platform for the interplay not only between religion and politics, which is dominant in Northern

Nigeria, but between religion, education and politics. Let this occasion go beyond a talk shop. Once more, I congratulate the university community and urge that there be more funding for research and training of agents of peace-building. Happy deliberations!

THE STATE OF EMERGENCY IMPOSED ON PLATEAU STATE

A perspective of the Archbishop on the State of Emergency on Plateau State, May, 2004.

1) The declaration of a six-month State of Emergency in Plateau State on the 18th May 2004 by President Olusegun Obasanjo should not have been necessary if the Federal Government, which controls the Police Force, the armed forces and the State Security Services (SSS), had in the past three years adopted preventive measures against the recurrence of crises rather than allowing the security situation of the Yelwa area to degenerate to the level it did. That since 2002 the Yelwa area has experienced a series of crises defying solution is an indication of either a very bad security network or the absence of political will on the part of both the State and Federal Governments to tackle the crises. It is ironic that a military barracks situated in Shendam is only a few kilometers away from Yelwa, yet the violence was allowed to degenerate to a very dangerous level. The Federal Government had the authority to ask the soldiers to intervene at each crisis, of course not with unreasonable force, but to secure lives and property. This was either not done or action was taken when it was too late.

2) The imposition of the State of Emergency on Plateau State is a gross political miscalculation which has succeeded in further polarizing Plateau State along ethnic and religious lines. The Yelwa crises were localized, in the sense that the killings of people and the destruction of property were limited to the area. It was mutual. At one time the Hausa-Fulani, who are largely Muslims, would attack, kill people and destroy property, and at another time the Tarok, Goemai and a coalition of other ethnic groups who are largely Christians would attack, kill people and destroy property. Over three-quarters of Plateau State lived and still lives in peace and tranquility. It was surprising that the State of Emergency was imposed on the entire State. The Federal Government should have at best heightened security in the area or imposed an extended curfew on the area or declare a state of emergency only in the area or the Local Government.

3) Figures regarding those killed or displaced have been exaggerated. Perhaps this was what gave rise to President Obasanjo's reference to a state of "near genocide". Genocide as applied to the situation in Plateau State is a misnomer. The situation should have been described as "mutual guerilla attacks and killings." The use of the term "genocide" is capable of creating the false impression that the whole of Plateau State is involved in genocidal practice. Only a few months ago the President and the Vice-President hosted a lot of dignitaries in Jos to launch a new phase of the National Tourism Programme, with Plateau State at the centre of it all. This declaration has made rubbish of the attempt to promote Plateau State as a tourist State. Doubts have been created in the minds of the national and international communities that Plateau State as a whole is unsafe. Such stigmatization has serious economic, political social and security repercussions for the state and the nation as a whole. The views of a columnist in the *Saturday Punch* of May 29, 2404, p.11 summarize the dangerous impressions given and the stigmatization of Plateau State. He writes: "...Plateau State knows no peace. It has been declared a war zone. Soldiers have been called out on the

streets. The state has become one big military barracks. The smell of gunpowder fills the air. The once peaceful state is now a mass grave. The number of refugees is on the increase.... Democratic governance... has become history in Plateau State. An army general has been appointed administrator in place of an elected democrat...." Is this the picture of a State that will attract investors or tourists in the next decade? Great harm has been done to Plateau State.

4) Talking about displaced people who have fled to Bauchi, Nasarawa and Taraba states, numbering tens of thousands, it is important to note that even if the entire population of Yelwa was displaced, the number would not add up to the numbers being bandied around as displaced people. When the President visited the displaced people's camps in parts of Plateau and Bauchi, and when the Sole Administrator, Major General Chris Alli, Rtd. visited these places too, little did they know that the politics of numbers was in play. Street children and hired people are said to have been displayed in these camps in order to portray a pitiful sight. Some idlers found in this situation an opportunity to parade as displaced persons in order to be partakers of the relief materials generously given by Government or NGOs and individuals.

5) The demolition of democratic structures (executive and legislative) during a democratic dispensation, no matter the reason, is a journey backwards to dictatorship and an open statement to the military that they made a mistake by ushering in democratic rule in 1999.

6) Will the declaration of the State of Emergency in Plateau State solve the problems of social discontent, political ineptitude, leadership insensitivity to the plight of the poor masses, financial extravagance by elected leaders in this country? What is needed is an emergency response to the basic needs of ordinary Nigerians and not the declaration of the State of Emergency. It is a diversionary tactic. The cure is worse than the disease. The

perennial problems of poverty, neglect suffered by the poor, unemployment, struggle for fertile land for farming/grazing land for cattle, injustice, insecurity, etc must be the concern of the Federal Government, Hopelessness helplessness and frustration breed social chaos and anarchy.

7) Sophisticated weapons have found their way into Plateau State and other parts of the country. How come they are undetected at the points of entry by Federal Government security agents? It is common to see a vehicle owner giving security agents on our highways ten or twenty naira to be allowed free passage even if the vehicle owner may be carrying dangerous items.

8) President Obasanjo's visit to Plateau State on May 13th, aggravated an already tense situation. His comportment and utterances were most unhelpful to the peace process. His verbal attack on the chairman of the Christian Association of Nigeria (CAN), Rev. Yakubu Pam, was perceived by Plateau Christians as an attack on Christians and Christianity and a portrayal of Christians as the aggressors in the crisis. His utterances gave him away as taking sides.

9) The President should know that the settler/indigene phenomenon is part of the Nigerian sickness. To imagine that Plateau State is guiltier than others in this is to be unaware that this social malady is widespread and is destroying Nigeria. An urgent constitutional solution must be found. The indigene/settler factor becomes more pronounced in Nigeria because the Government insists on the quota system and 'federal character' for appointment, employment, recruitment, admission into institutions, etc. This system, while helpful at times, is what encourages discrimination against others. People of one geographical area see others coming to seek economic fortunes as settlers or outsiders, who therefore should not be allowed to reduce their quota. The whole issue is about fairness. For instance, the Hausas who left Kano State fifty to a hundred years ago and settled in Plateau

State, insist that their children and grandchildren share fully in whatever accrues to Plateau State. In some places they advocate the appointment of Islamic traditional rulers specifically for them instead of subordinating themselves to the existing traditional authority. This is demanded by them in Plateau State, whereas in Kano State, for instance, the descendants of those who have settled for up to one hundred years are constantly regarded as strangers, excluded from Government appointments, denied freedom of building worship centres, and become the objects of attacks and killings at the slightest provocation or no provocation at all. It is also known that Christian religious programmes are not easily allowed in the public media in States that are predominantly Muslim, yet in a State that is predominantly Christian it is expected that Islamic religious programmes be aired freely. When this is not done there is the allegation of persecution. A lasting solution to these discriminatory practices must be found. A Nigerian must be free to live peacefully and happily and practise his or her religion freely wherever he or she finds himself/herself in this country. This must be enshrined explicitly in our constitution and the implications clearly spelt out.

10) The State of Emergency in Plateau State appears to have been an afterthought, hastily executed to prove a political point by the President or meant to pacify some persons or groups. Perhaps Mr. President wishes to use Plateau State to demonstrate to the world that he is not a Christian bigot. He knows that the Plateau people are peace-lovers and therefore do not react violently, as has been the case elsewhere. When many non-Muslims expressed concern about the introduction of Sharia and the serious consequences it would have for Nigeria, Mr. President, perhaps for fear of being perceived as biased in favour of Christians, or for the sake of political self-preservation, simply said the Sharia problem would fizzle out. Events have shown otherwise. Difficulties of inter-religious harmony today in Nigeria can be attributed to the inaction of Mr. President on the Sharia issue.

11) The State of Emergency imposed on Plateau State was ill-advised. The general feeling is that if Mr. President thought Gov. Joshua Dariye had mismanaged the affairs of Plateau State or was incapable of resolving the situation of crisis, there would have certainly been better alternative solutions. Why should the people of Plateau State suffer because the President is unhappy with the Governor? Since the declaration of the State of Emergency, visitors are scared of coming to Plateau State. Seminars and workshops were hastily cancelled. Overseas telephone callers were expressing horror at what they said was happening in Plateau State and the "Are you safe?" remark was common. Somehow today the mere mention of the name "Plateau State" evokes fear and trepidation because of the State of Emergency. The "home of peace and tourism" has suffered a terrible bashing.

12) As the leader of the Catholics of Jos Archdiocese, I have appealed to our people to keep calm despite the State of Emergency, and to cooperate with the Sole Administrator for the period of six months, after which we believe the State will be returned to the path of democratic governance. Concerted attempts must be made by all of us to inspire reconciliation, forgiveness and peaceful coexistence. Though tribe and religion may differ, in brotherhood and sisterhood we stand.

13) The suspended House of Assembly should be recalled immediately. As elected representatives, the members, together with the Sole Administrator, will chart the course for everlasting peace in the troubled parts of Plateau State.

14) Peace and reconciliation must be the main focus and the sole agenda for the Sole Administrator in the next six months. He must ensure that the various reports of the commissions of inquiry set to look into the causes of the previous crises, which for some strange reasons refused to see the light of day, will be published, with the sole aim of reconciliation. People must be helped to ask and receive forgiveness where evil has been perpetrated against one

another. We pray that the State of Emergency, undemocratic though it is, will enable the citizens of Plateau State to do some soul- searching, some critical self-analysis, in order to work together for the unity and progress of the State, transcending political and religious differences. I believe that a lot of good will come when the storm of emergency rule calms down.

A WORD OF ENCOURAGEMENT
Released to the family of God on Palm Sunday, March 28, 2010.

My dear people
of God of the
Catholic
Archdiocese of
Jos,
Peace be with you.

Since the 17th of January 2010, we have been living in moments of tension and anxiety, having witnessed terrible destruction to life and property in the unfortunate crisis. This has dealt many of us a spiritual blow to the extent that some of us ask if it is still possible to love our neighbours and forgive as Jesus did.

For some of us who have suffered pain, loss of means of livelihood and loved ones, it is very easy to give in to despair. This year's Holy Week calls us especially to renew our faith and trust in our loving Jesus and to rededicate ourselves to His fundamental injunction to love all those created in the image and likeness of God. At the heart of the Christian vocation is love, and no matter the degree of violent provocations or attacks, and the hardship that follows, let us unite with Jesus on Good Friday as He pronounces the words: "Father, forgive them, they do not know what they do"

(Lk 23:34).

Because many of us have been deeply wounded physically, emotionally and even spiritually, it is tempting to conclude that there is no need to preach the love of neighbour or forgiveness or to overcome evil with good. The times are rough and tough no doubt, but perhaps it is a test of our faith, as gold is refined by fire. In the end, nothing should separate us from the love of Christ (cf. Rom. 8:35).

In the spirit of this holy season,
I call us all to a renewal of life;
I call us to intense personal prayer;
I call us to family prayer, especially the Rosary after supper;
I call us to Eucharistic Adoration;
I call us to Bible reading and
meditation;
I call us to loving forgiveness.

Our Faith tells us that God can draw good out of evil. We should pray not to be consumed by bitterness and the spirit of revenge. Let us be strong in faith, while praying and watching. We should never opt for violence, for that is not the way of Jesus.

Please listen to your priests and indeed to all people of goodwill who preach the gospel of love rather than that of hatred. Even for pain already suffered, let us remember that the Lord says, "Vengeance is mine, I will repay" (Rom 12:19).

May Mary our Mother, Queen of Peace, intercede for us. She knew pain and sorrow. We trust that she will ask Jesus as she did in Cana to shield us from further attacks and console us with His Holy Spirit.

May the Christ of Easter grant us all his peace, love and healing.

IN THE NAME OF OUR BENEVOLENT GOD, STOP THE VIOLENCE

A statement released to the family of God urging all to stop the violence.

1) The cycle of violence resulting in killings, bloodshed and the destruction of people's hard-earned means of livelihood in Jos and environs is, to say the least, very disturbing, a source of great agony and a terrible embarrassment to all people of goodwill.

2) It is very sad that news about Jos in recent times continues to focus more on the violence manifested in the sporadic attacks on innocent people, deaths and negative religious propaganda.

3) Our two main religions in Nigeria (Islam and Christianity)do not endorse anyone taking the life of another person. "Thou shalt not kill" is a command valid in both Christianity and Islam.

4) We have always affirmed that dialogue with one another is the best solution irrespective of the level of confrontation or provocation. Knives, bows and arrows, guns, explosives and bombs will never bring about the desired resolution; rather, they only heighten mutual hatred, which culminates in a harvest of unfortunate deaths and misery.

5) Rather than reduce the reason for the incessant attacks to religious differences only, the root causes of the incessant mayhem must be identified by the relevant authorities and decisively and definitively addressed.

6) Those who may be encouraging or promoting this unfortunate situation should be made, in the interest of the common good and our beloved Plateau State, to stop instigating violence. Those who are used to perpetrating violence should understand that violence only begets more violence and violence has never brought solutions that genuine dialogue could not bring.

7) We call all men and women of goodwill to prayer, while urging the relevant authorities to decisively act to permanently

bring this trend to an end, save us from further national and international embarrassment and to save precious lives and hard-earned property from wanton destruction. There must be some solution to this problem

8) Plateau State is our home. We must stop destroying one another (the violence carried out against each other) and start exploring better ways of reconstructing broken relationships, rebuilding destroyed infrastructure and healing wounded hearts. We must restore justice in honour of the dead and create a more conducive atmosphere for those who want to invest in Plateau State or come to enjoy our "home of peace" that they may do so without entertaining fears of being attacked or harassed. In truth, no Nigerian of goodwill is proud of our present predicament.

In God we trust and we believe that He can restore permanent peace but let us all do our part by being agents of peace and positive social transformation.

Pope Benedict XVI with world religious leaders

Section Six
DEVOTION TO THE CREATOR

A CALL TO SOBER REFLECTION, PRAYER AND FASTING

Released to Catholic faithful of Archdiocese of Jos, September 6, 2011

The wave of violence we continue to witness in Jos and environs is a cause of very great concern. Each time we think that we are on the road to recovery from the violence witnessed since the 7 September 2001 crisis, an avoidable incident rears its head and before we know it, we are back to the theatre of reckless destruction of life and property.

The crisis seems to degenerate with each passing crisis, and unfortunately it is said to be perpetrated by people who call themselves Christians or Muslims. No good Christian or Muslim will ever engage in such senseless destruction even in the face of provocation.

We denounce violence no matter who commits it. We uphold the sanctity of life. We support non-violent response to issues and we stand on promoting the culture of love rather than the culture of death.

In solidarity with all those families who have been robbed of the lives of their beloved ones and those deprived of their means of livelihood, we have in the past organized Masses and Rosary prayers. We need to sustain our prayers by adding fasting.

I therefore call on all adult Catholics in our Archdiocese to observe a total fast on the Feast of Our Lady of Sorrows, Thursday 15 September 2011, from 6 am to 6 pm. On the following day, Friday 16, we will abstain from meat in honour of those who shed their blood and those who are still nursing various degrees of injuries.

We make these sacrifices to ask God for his forgiveness *(ct. Jonah 3:10)*; that he may touch and change the hearts of those committing these atrocities or those planning to do the same, and also that we shall all realize the sacredness of life and try to resolve issues through dialogue rather than violence.

Kindly continue the "Prayer for Political, Ethnic and Religious Peace in Plateau State" and the frequent recitation of the Holy Rosary for peace to reign.

May Mary the Mother who knew pain, agony and sorrows intercede for us, and may Jos and indeed Plateau State experience permanent peace. Amen.

CALL TO MORE INTENSE PRAYERS
Released to Catholic faithful of Archdiocese of Jos.

My dear Brothers and Sisters of the
Family of the Catholic Archdiocese of Jos,

For some time now we have been living in moments of crises which have caused untold social, physical and spiritual damages to us, to the city of Jos and some surrounding villages. Many have lost their lives, some sustained terrible injuries, while others lost unquantifiable amount of property. We are all traumatized by the unfortunate violence that continues to surface in one form or another.

In the past, I called for personal and family prayers especially praying the rosary in every Catholic home. Please continue the prayer for Political, Ethnic and Religious Peace and redouble your private prayers, recitation of Family Rosary, visits to the Blessed Sacrament and private acts of penance. Prayers coming from many hearts and homes will no doubt attract the mercy of God and hasten the return of permanent peace. We must never despair because the troubled times do not seem to be going away as fast as we want. God's time is the best. Even in these very troubled times, our faith in God must remain unshakable. We cannot seek any other solution to the crises other than the one taught by Christ our Lord and Master: love, reconciliation, and forgiveness. It is easy in this moment of trial for some of us to succumb to the temptation of finding remedies outside what Christ would approve.

At an appropriate time, we shall all come together as a family to offer prayers of supplication/reparation and to pray for the dead. Human blood has been spilt which has polluted our land. Life has been so cheapened that it can be taken without considering that God has said "Thou shalt not kill".

For now, I enjoin all of us to kindly pray for our departed dead brothers and sisters who have suffered violent death at the hands of their attackers. Pray for the injured. Pray for those who have lost their means of livelihood and pray for those who no longer enjoy peace of mind and body.

While we resort to more intense prayers, we must remain security-conscious as those who perpetrate evil are still going around like roaring lions seeking for people to devour. Let us maintain our composure rooted in solid faith and abiding trust in the Lord God who has promised never to abandon His own, and intercede for a total change of heart for those who are bent on destroying our internal and external peace.

I wish to assure you all that the priests, more than ever before, have you, your needs and welfare in mind at the daily Eucharistic sacrifice of the Mass. I personally have you daily in my thoughts and prayers, especially when I celebrate the Missa Pro Populo (Mass for the People) for you all.

PRAYER FOR POLITICAL, ETHNIC AND RELIGIOUS PEACE IN PLATEAU STATE

God the Father our Creator,
God the Son our Redeemer,
God the Holy Spirit our Sanctifier,
we praise and thank You for the precious gift of Plateau State
    endowed with good weather, fertile land and a generous
    people.
We have been plagued by political, ethnic and religious crises, and
    have suffered the destruction of lives and property; we humbly
    ask for forgiveness from You and from one another. Heal our
    wounds with the radiance of Your love and mercy and teach us
    to live in peace and harmony. Use our leaders as instruments
    of peace, social development and love. Help them to be
    selfless in service and to lead us in the path of dialogue and
    reconciliation, so that we can truly be one family, working for
    the common good. Bless and provide for our youth and help
    them to be peace loving. Lord, may the weapons of evil, hatred
    and violence be silenced by love. May we enjoy unity and
    stability as Your children who live, move and have our being
    in You.
We ask this through Christ our Lord.
V: O Jesus Prince of Peace
R: Be merciful to Plateau State and grant us permanent peace.
V: Our Lady Queen of Peace
R: Obtain for us peace in our hearts, peace in our families, peace in
    our State.
All: Amen.

With Ecclesiastical Approval
+I A Kaigama
Archbishop of Jos, Nigeria
20th August, 2010

PRAYER FOR PEACE

Complied by the Archbishop for a group in Germany.

Most gracious, loving and precious Father
May your peace flow like a river in our hearts and homes
Remove the barriers to peace and give us hearts of flesh
So that we your children of all cultures and religions
May truly live in happiness and prosper
May our world be a true neighbourhood
Where no one suffers discrimination of creed or colour
Heavenly Father
We sleep with one eye open and wake with apprehension
Violence, conflict, become our unwelcome guests
Politics, Religion are used for violence
Poverty, diseases, insecurity plague our land
To our broken and suffering world grant peace
A peace which is the fruit of justice.
From the menace of religious fundamentalists, spare us
From insensitive and corrupt leaders, shield us
From ethnic hostilities, deliver us
From political crises and bad governance, free us
From man-made and natural disasters, rescue us
May we know inner peace, solidarity and harmony
So our world becomes a neighbourhood of true brothers and
        sisters.
O God your love for Nigeria and Mother Africa is great
You know of our hunger, diseases and consequences of violence
Children, Youths, Mothers displaced by conflicts
Corrupt governance and injustice the culprits
We are tired of pains and suffering O Lord
Open the eyes of the world to pursue the common good of all
Honour, glory to you through Christ the Prince of Peace. Amen

Section Seven
LETTERS/CORRESPONDENCE

CONGREGATIO DE CULTU DIVINO
ET DISCIPLINA SACRAMENTORUM

Vatican City
2 Dec 2008

His Grace, Most Rev
Dr. I. A. Kaigama
Archbishop of Jos

Your Grace,
    I am greatly saddened to hear
of the violence and tragic destruction of
human life and of property in Jos.
    Please accept my expression of
heartfelt togetherness with Jos in this
moment of suffering, together with my
promise of prayers for God's comforting
grace and also that such tragic
events never repeat themselves.
                    + Francis Card. Arinze

PONTIFICIUM CONSILIUM
DE IUSTITIA ET PACE

MESSAGE OF SOLIDARITY AND CONDOLENCE TO *GOD'S* CHILDREN
IN THE VILLAGES OF

DOGON, NAHAWA, TSAT & ZOT FORON (ARCHDIOCESE OF JOS)

From The Pontifical Council of Justice and Peace, Vatican City.

My Brothers and My Sisters, for some time now, as you know very well, we as members of the Church all over the world have understood ourselves as a family: *a family of God.* God is the head of this family, and through his Son and our saviour, Jesus Christ, we also have become *sons of the God and Father of our Lord Jesus Christ,* and brothers and sisters to one another. The life of this *family of God* is *communion* .... **we live a life of communion of an inclusive belongingness, not excluding anyone, but sharing in the life of one another and living for one another.**

That is why, on hearing about what has befallen you, and about the trying moments you are going through, the rest of this *family of God* could not sit unconcerned. And so the Holy Father, Pope Benedict XVI, our elder brother and head of our Catholic communion has just expressed his condolences to you. Similarly, Cardinal Ivan Diaz, who, as the Prefect of the Congregation for the Propagation of the Faith, follows more closely, on behalf of the Pope, events in the Church here in Nigeria, in the rest of Africa, Asia and Latin America, has also addressed a message of condolence and solidarity to you.

I am a closer neigbour to you, being a Ghanaian and coming from the Archdiocese of Cape Coast. This morning, however, I stand before you as the President of the Pontifical Council of Justice and Peace. This is an office in the Vatican which follows justice and peace issues around the world and promotes the knowledge of the **Social Teaching (Doctrine) of the Church** within and outside the Church.

PONTIFICIUM CONSILIUM
DE IUSTITIA ET PACE

I and my staff, together with the *International Office of Caritas* and the office of *Cor Unum* have also heard of what has happened in this part of the Archdiocese of Jos. Indeed, these offices have

been following for some time now the outbreaks of violence and loss of lives which have afflicted this area and parts of our sub-region, analyzing their causes and trying to understand their nature and motivations. But, again, I am not here to discourse about the revelations and observations of our studies.

No! I have come on behalf of the staff of the Pontifical Council of Justice and Peace and the related office of the Roman Curia to say that we belong, with you, to the *family of God*. Indeed, we belong to the *family of God* with you and with the very many, who at different outbreaks of these violence have lost their lives. We have heard of your affliction, and have come to celebrate this powerful act of healing, forgiveness and reconciliation with you. We heard of this celebration from your chief shepherd, Archbishop Kaigama; and we thought that we should come, at every cost and on behalf of all the members of the *family of God* in Rome to stand by you, condole with you, share your loss and pain and join you in prayer for healing and for forgiveness. Whatever assistance we raise will be transmitted through your Archbishop and his Caritas office.

Finally, we wish to encourage the State, whose citizens you all are, and the Government for whom you pray at your every worship to make your security and the security of all citizens its topmost priority. It should after all be possible in this day and age that *"freed from the hands of our enemies and from fear, we should serve our God and State in freedom all the days of our lives"*.

Peter Cardinal Turkson
President of the Pontifical Council of Justice and Peace
Rome

Archbishop Kaigama

From: "Segreteria Congregazione Evangelizzazione dei Popoli" <Segreteria@PropagandaFide.va>
To: <josarch@hisen.org>
Cc: <rapnig01@yahoo.com>
Sent: Tuesday, March 09 2010 11 50 AM
Subject: Urge

MOST REV. IGNATIUS AYAU KAIGAMA
ARCHBISHOP OF JOS
NIGERIA

E-MAIL: rapnig01@yahoo.com, josarch@hisen.org

WITH DEEP SADNESS THE CONGREGATION FOR THE EVANGELIZATION OF PEOPLES HAS RECEIVED THE NEWS OF THE RECENT VIOLENCE AND ITS HUNDREDS OF VICTIMS WHO WERE PREDOMINANTLY FROM THE CHRISTIAN POPULATION IN THE PLATEAU STATE.

WE EXPRESS OUR HEARTFELT CONDOLENCES TO THE FAMILIES OF THE VICTIMS AND ASSURE OUR PRAYERS FOR THOSE WHO HAVE DIED AND FOR THOSE WHO HAVE BEEN WOUNDED. WE PRAY FOR A RENEWAL OF HARMONY AND PEACE AMONG ALL OF THOSE ENGAGED IN, AND WHO HAVE FALLEN VICTIM TO, THIS TRAGIC EVENT.

WE HOPE THAT THOSE RESPONSIBLE FOR MAINTAINING PEACE AND ORDER IN THE PLATEAU STATE AND IN ALL OF NIGERIA RESPOND QUICKLY AND RESPONSIBLY TO PREVENT ANY FURTHER HOSTILITY.

Ivan Cardinal Dias, Prefect

Archbishop Robert Sarah, Secretary

"The Most Reverend Felix Alaba Adeosin Job
President
Catholic Bishops' Conference of Nigeria

The Holy Father was shocked and saddened to learn of the outbreak of violence, retribution and killing in central Nigeria over the weekend. He sends his condolences to all those who mourn the loss of love ones, particularly women and children, and offers prayers for those who injured and for all who are working to restore security and calm. His Holiness encourages people of different ethnicities and beliefs to replace anger and revenge with forgiveness and charity. Upon all the people of the region, and in a special way those most affected by these atrocities, the Holy Father invokes God's abundant blessings of healing and strength.

Cardinal Tarcisio Bertone
Secretary of State.

Senator (Dr.) Ibrahim Nasiru Mantu, CFR

National Assembly,
Three Arms Zone,
Abuja, Nigeria.

December 15, 2008

The State Chairman,
Christian Association of Nigeria,
Jos, Plateau State

Your Grace – Bishop Kaigama,

CONDOLENCE OVER THE RECENT CRISIS IN JOS

I write to commiserate with the Church in Plateau State over the avoidable crisis that engulfed its membership in parts of the City of Jos.

It saddens my heart that the devil chose to perpetrate this evil at a time the state was fast recovering from a similar incident in the past and peace was gradually taking firm roots. However, we are consoled by the counsel of the living God who we all worship and who through the ages reminds us everyday that vengeance is His. No matter how agents of Satan may traumatize us and no matter the damage they may cause, we should be comforted by the immortal truth that the day of the Lord against them will be worse than the fury of a blazing furnace. This is the promise of God against all evil doers.

In this realization, I urge the entire Christian community not to fret or dwell much on the damages caused the Church in Jos by this mayhem but to commit those who perpetrated the crisis into the great hands of God and continue to pray that they repent before the great judgment upon them comes. Of course as a man of God, I need not remind you to continue to counsel the membership of the Church in Plateau State, in general and Jos City in particular, that it remains the instruction of the Christian Holy Book that we should forgive SEVENTY TIMES SEVEN EVERYDAY those who have wronged us. So, since it is very difficult for someone to wrong another seventy times seven a day, what that portion of the Bible teaches is that we should forgive every second, minute, hour, day, week, month and year of our lives. We must thus forgive at all times and refuse to extend the frontiers of evil by vengeance, which belongs only to the Almighty God.

For those who lost their lives in the mayhem, I pray that the good Lord forgives them their sins and grant them eternal peace.

Please accept my heartfelt condolence and those of the entire Mantu family and friends.

Yours sincerely

SENATOR (DR.) IBRAHIM NASIRU MANTU *CFR*
Deputy President of the Senate of the Federal Republic of Nigeria 2000 - 2007

Plot 451, House No 21, John Kadiyah Close,
Asokoro, Abuja - Nigeria.
Tel: 09-3144373

FEDERAL MINISTRY OF SCIENCE AND TECHNOLOGY
NEW FEDERAL SECRETARIAT
SHEHU SHAGARI WAY, P. M. B. 331, ABUJA, NIGERIA
OFFICE OF THE HONOURABLE MINISTER OF STATE

TEL: 09- 5234391
FAX: 09- 5235204

FMST/HMSST/228/VOL.1
Ref No:................................
14th September, 2001
Date:................................

The Catholic Archbishop of Jos,
Jos,
Plateau State.

His Grace and my dear brethren,

AN APPEAL FOR PEACE

I send you greetings in the name of our Lord Jesus Christ.

2.   My heart is laden with sorrow because of the evil machination carried out against our dearly beloved city, Jos. My concern has been your security and those of your flock. I give God the glory for His mercies on His people.

3.   As the Shepherd of the Lord and one who has been anointed to preach the Gospel of peace, I urge you not to relent in this noble task God has given us, even our Lord told us that in this world, we would suffer tribulation just for his name's sake. Nothing happens without God's consent. My sincere appeal to you is that you should hold your flock and direct them on the path of peace as our Lord Jesus commanded us.

4.   I want to assure you that the Federal Government is highly committed towards resolving this unhealthy and unfortunate incident. The President and Command-In-Chief, President Olusegun Obasanjo is particularly disturbed about this incident and has put a strong security machinery in place to check the situation.

5.   I, therefore, urge you to inform your flock about the Federal Government's resolve to bring lasting peace to restore the good name Plateau State is known for, "Home of Peace & Tourism". Also I commiserate with them on behalf of the Federal Government over the huge loss of lives and properties.

6.   Once again, may the perfect peace of the Almighty God be with you all, Amen.

Sincerely yours.

Pauline K. Tallen (Mrs.)
Hon. Minister of State

From the High Commissioner

19 January 2009

Most Rev. Ignatius A Kaigama
Archbishop of Jos and
Vice President, Catholic Bishops Conference of Nigeria
20 Joseph Gomwalk Road
P O Box 494
Jos, 930001
Plateau State, Nigeria

British
High Commission
Abuja

Shehu Shagari Way

Maitama District

Abuja

Telephone: (09) 413 2010-11,
413 2796, 413 2880, 413 2883, 413 3887,
413 9817
Facsimile: (09) 413 3552

Dear Archbishop

Thank you very much for receiving me last week and for your letter of 14 January. I will be in touch with my visa section about the points you made and will respond to you thereafter.

Meanwhile, thank you very much for receiving me together with HRH The Emir last week and I was glad to accompany you when you gave your Christian and Muslim congregations the joint message of peace, harmonious co-existence, mutual respect and mutual understanding. May I again express my condolences and sympathies to the Christian and Muslim communities who have been tragically affected by the recent events. And please accept my admiration for all the efforts that you and HRH The Emir and other faith leaders are making in the cause of peace and understanding.

Yours sincerely

Bob Dewar

Bob Dewar

Diocesan Catholic Secretariat
OFFICE OF THE BISHOP

Telephone: (048) 550770, 550002
TeleFax: (048) 552442
E-mail: bpokafor@yahoo.com

P.M.B. 5021
Awka
Anambra State
Nigeria

Our Ref:
Your Ref: DCSA/28

January 20, 2010

His Excellency
Most Rev. Dr. Ignatius Kaigama
Archbishop of Jos
Archbishop's Residence
Jos – Plateau State

Your Excellency,

2010 JOS CRISIS

This is to convey our deep sense of shock and dismay at the wanton destruction of life and property in the recent crisis that engulfed Jos. It had happened before and is happening again. One is afraid that this may not be the last if nothing is done by the Government to complement your efforts at facilitating inter-religious dialogue.

The Auxiliary Bishop, Most Rev. Dr. Paulinus C. Ezeokafor, the priests, religious and lay faithful of Awka Diocese and myself send our message of solidarity to you, to the Catholic faithful and to all people of good will in Jos. We feel with you all in this trying moment. We keep you in our prayers and ask God to grant eternal rest to the dead and help the living pull through the difficult times.

Be assured of our prayers and support.

Sincerely yours in Jesus and Mary,

+ Simon A. Okafor
Bishop of Awka

EVÊCHE DE KANDI

L'Evêque

Kandi, ce 21 janvier 2010

His Excellence
Bishop Ignatius Ayau KAIGAMA
Archbishop of Jos
P.O. BOX. 494 JOSS
JOS 93001, Tray State,
NIGERIA
josarch@hisen.org

Objet : Communion of prayer !

Excellence,

I start with reiterating you my most fervid wish of peace and health for the year 2010.

I would like, by the present, to testify you my deep communion of prayer and my spiritual support in the dramas that your city lives these days. I am indeed pained of it, and out the diocese with me. Here is why I didn't hesitate to write you this letter in the name of the brotherly friendship and the ministerial conviviality that unite us. I implore the Lord to make so that peace and understanding come back within the Christian and Moslem between which tension is indeed high. Curiously, the thing happens at the same moment where we are asking for the unit of the Christian of part the whole world. I hope that the Lord won't remain deaf to our supplication and that it will make all so that the rest of the humans has life, and has it in abundance!

Receive, Excellence, the expression of my high consideration and especially of my spiritual support in these sad circumstances.

That Holly Agnès that we commemorate today condescends to intercede in your cause!

My prayers always come with you, you and God's whole people to you confident!

+ C. FELIHO
Evêque de Kandi

Tel. : (229) 23 63 00 05 (00229) 90 02 26 30- Fax +229- 23 63 01 01E-mail : evechekandi@yahoo.fr BP : – République du Bénin
Evêche Kandi (Bank Of Africa –IBAN : BJ11 B006 1020 01001522 0016 3918 SWIFT : AFRI BJ BJ

Le 26 mars 2010

Mgr Ignatius Ayau Kaigama
Archbishop of Jos, Archbishop's House
P.O. Box 494
20 Joseph D. Gomwalk Road
Jos 930001, Plateau State, NIGERIA

Objet : violences interreligieuses

Monseigneur,

L'ACAT-CANADA (affiliée à la Fédération internationale de l'Action des chrétiens pour l'abolition de la torture, ayant statut consultatif auprès des Nations unies et du Conseil de l'Europe, ainsi qu'un siège d'observateur auprès de la Commission africaine des droits de l'Homme et des Peuples), déplore la mort violente de **CENTAINES DE PERSONNES**, tuées lors des affrontements entre chrétiens et musulmans à Jos et ses alentours du 15 au 19 janvier 2010, les blessures et les pertes matérielles infligées à plusieurs autres, ainsi que l'exode d'au moins 18 000 habitants de l'État du Plateau vers celui de Bauchi situé plus au nord, font planer le spectre de graves atteintes aux droits fondamentaux des populations.

Extrêmement préoccupante apparaît la montée des extrémismes ayant conduit aux affrontements de la mi-janvier 2010, ainsi qu'à la vendetta des 6 et 7 mars 2010 contre les chrétiens, où quelques cinq cents (500) personnes ont péri. En dix (10) ans, ces éruptions sporadiques de violence intercommunautaire auraient fait plus de dix mille (10 000) victimes. En septembre 2001, quelque neuf cent quinze (915) personnes sont mortes. En novembre 2008 au moins quatre cents (400) individus avaient aussi perdu la vie. À l'été 2009, l'écrasement par l'armée nigériane des rebelles du *Boko Haram* («l'éducation occidentale est péché»), considéré comme un «groupe religieux meurtrier», a fait plus de sept cents (700) morts.

La déclaration du ministre responsable de la police, *Ebrahim Yakubu Lame*, affirmant que toute cette violence vient de «quelques individus de haut rang qui ont exploité l'ignorance et la pauvreté du peuple pour semer la pagaille au nom de la religion», devrait inciter à la réflexion.

Il en va de même de l'effet explosif du dénuement de larges pans de la population, illustré par les propos qu'on vous attribue, Mgr *Ignatius*, pour qui les troubles récents «n'ont rien à voir avec la religion» et sont plutôt le fait de la «pauvreté».

Nous aimerions vous faire part de notre opinion que l'État nigérian doit, selon le droit international, mettre en place des mesures immédiates afin d'agir sur les causes profondes de la violence et sur les conditions de l'établissement d'une réelle coexistence pacifique entre tous les groupes, religieux et ethniques, formant la population nigériane, ce dont vous êtes sans aucun doute déjà convaincu.

À cet égard, la tenue d'une enquête complète, indépendante et impartiale, devant mener à la traduction en justice des responsables présumés de méfaits, s'impose sur les affrontements survenus dans la ville de *Jos* à la mi-janvier 2010, ainsi que sur les éruptions sporadiques de violence entre chrétiens et musulmans.

Le *Pacte international relatif aux droits civils et politiques* (PIDCP), auquel le Nigeria est partie, à l'article 9.1 stipule : «Tout individu a droit à la liberté et à la sécurité de sa personne». De même, l'article 18.1, reconnaît que «Toute personne a droit à la liberté de pensée, de conscience et de religion (…)».

La *Charte africaine des droits de l'Homme et des peuples*, à l'article 4, dispose : «La personne humaine est inviolable. Tout être humain a droit au respect de sa vie et à l'intégrité physique et morale de sa personne; Nul ne peut être privé arbitrairement de ce droit».

Veuillez agréer, Monseigneur Ignatius, l'expression de notre respect et de notre considération pour votre pays

Roger E. Simon, ing

94 rue McNaughter, Hudson, Qc, J0P 1H0, CANADA

DEUTSCHE BISCHOFSKONFERENZ
DER VORSITZENDE

Dem Hochwürdigsten Herrn
Erzbischof Ignatius Kaigama
Archbishop's House
P.O. Box 494
JOS 930001
Plateau State
NIGERIA

Kaiserstraße 161
53113 Bonn

Postanschrift
Postfach 29 62
53019 Bonn

Ruf   0228-103-0
Direkt   0228-103-290
Fax   0228-103-299
e-mail: Vorsitzender@

AZ:

Bonn, den 27. Dezember

Exzellenz, lieber Mitbruder!

In diesen Tagen der Weihnacht erreichen uns in Deutschland die Nachrichten über die kaum vorstellbaren, schrecklichen und menschenverachtenden Angriffe auf christliche Kirchen in Ihrem Land. Die Fernsehbilder haben mich zutiefst erschüttert. Als Vorsitzender der Deutschen Bischofskonferenz übermittle ich Ihnen mein tief empfundenes Beileid für die zahlreichen Opfer der Gewalt und mein Mitgefühl in diesen Tagen von Angst und Terror.

Die Botschaft von Weihnachten ist eine Friedensbotschaft. Wie weit ist Ihr Land an diesen Weihnachtstagen davon entfernt? Gestern haben wir am Stephanustag der verfolgten Christen gedacht. Ich darf Ihnen versichern, dass ich die Christen in Nigeria besonders in mein Gebet mit einschließe. Jedes Mal frage ich mich beim Anblick der Bilder, wie dieser blinde Fanatismus und diese ausufernde Gewaltbereitschaft möglich sein können? Ich erinnere mich an meinen Besuch bei Ihnen, an die vielen Begegnungen mit muslimischen Gläubigen in Ihrem Erzbistum. Gemeinsam haben wir Totenwache beim verstorbenen Imam von Jos gehalten. Die muslimischen Führer haben uns im Gespräch ihre uneingeschränkte Bereitschaft zum Frieden versichert. Fassungslos stehe ich da und frage mich, ob diese Aussagen noch Gültigkeit haben? Oder ist es eine kleine Gruppe, die terrorisiert und auf die weder politische noch Ordnungskräfte noch muslimische Religionsführer Einfluss haben?

Lieber Mitbruder, wie dramatisch mussten Sie an diesem Weihnachtsfest erfahren, in welcher widerwärtigen Form der Friede auf Erden pervertiert werden kann! Die gesellschaftliche Reife eines Staates zeigt sich an vielen Dingen, vor allem an der

Einhaltung der Menschenrechte. Hier wird das Menschenrecht auf Religionsfreiheit mit Füßen getreten.

Ich versichere Ihnen die uneingeschränkte Solidarität der Deutschen Bischofskonferenz in diesen schweren Tagen. Mein Gebet wird Sie und Ihre unermüdliche Arbeit begleiten, dass die Menschen in der Region von Jos und anderen Teilen Nigerias möglichst bald wieder auf den Pfad des Friedens finden. Der gegenseitige Respekt muss allen gelten, ganz gleich, welcher Religion man angehört. In wenigen Tagen begeht die katholische Kirche den Welttag des Friedens. Wir werden in Deutschland besonders an Sie und die Christen in Nigeria denken. Das Wort von Papst Benedikt XVI. in seiner Botschaft zum Welttag des Friedens 2011 muss Programm sein: „Für die Kirche stellt der Dialog zwischen den Anhängern verschiedener Religionen ein wichtiges Werkzeug dar, um mit allen Religionsgemeinschaften zum Gemeinwohl zusammenzuarbeiten. Die Kirche selbst lehnt nichts von alledem ab, was in den verschiedenen Religionen wahr und heilig ist." Ich bete darum, lieber Mitbruder, dass diese großherzige Bereitschaft der katholischen Kirche auch von jenen in Ihrem Land erkannt wird, die mit Terror den Frieden der Weihnacht zerstören zu müssen meinen.

In stiller Anteilnahme und verbunden mit der Hoffnung, dass die Botschaft von Weihnachten in Nigeria gehört wird, bin ich
Ihr

✝ Robert Zollitsch

Dr. Robert Zollitsch
Erzbischof

Section Eight
CONCLUSION

T he prolonged crises in Plateau State from 2001 to date, though restricted to a few areas, have no doubt inflicted incalculable damage to the socio-economic, cultural and political life of the people and the famed "home of peace and tourism". Where brothers and sisters once lived as one big family and happily interacted and shared the events of life, they have now become polarized along ethnic or religious lines. This is more evident in Jos, where some neighbourhoods have become "no-go areas" depending on which religious or ethnic group predominates there. We hope it will not be too long before full re-integration takes place.

The Imperative of Dialogue and Correct Diagnosis of the Problems

In my booklet, *The Dialogue of Life: An Urgent Necessity for Nigerian Christians and Muslims*, published in 2005, I stressed that dialogue is the best way for trust and understanding to grow between Nigerian Christians and Muslims. No doubt, issues such as Nigeria's joining of the Organization of Islamic Conference, the re-introduction of Sharia Law in some Northern states, the Arabic inscription on the naira notes and Islamic banking have generated unhealthy tension between Muslims and Christians in Nigeria. The new phenomenon of **Boko Haram** is not only a source of great concern to both Christians and Muslims of goodwill, but it can seriously threaten the corporate existence of Nigeria. One notes with optimism however that the very words that appeared to be taboo and which many people were previously allergic to are now appearing regularly in speeches and writings. These are words such as reconciliation, forgiveness, dialogue, peaceful coexistence, etc.

This book, being a compilation of my various write-ups concerning each of the crises in Plateau State since 2001, is a personal reflection and reading of the situation at each occurrence of a crisis. The accounts and interpretation of the crises were formed on the spur of the moment and in the prevailing mood, and written from the perspective of a Christian leader. I am sure that if a Muslim leader were giving a similar account of each of the crises, it would also be likely to be coloured by his or her religious beliefs. I have always stressed that the crises have more to do with social factors than with religion, but not a few people have challenged my opinion. Happily, I now I see a *volte-face*, as many are now saying that the crises go beyond religious conflict. The conclusions of the Solomon Lar Presidential Advisory Committee on the Jos crisis, of which I was a member, acknowledged this fact as well when under the sub theme, "The religious dimension of the Crisis" it states: "The Committee found that religion was not the main cause of crises in Jos; rather it was used by some individuals to gain popularity and win support. It also found that both religious and political leaders in the State used religion in politics to whip up sentiment, passion and emotions. Another finding of the Committee was the improper management of the Almajiri system." (Vol. 1 Report of the Presidential Advisory Committee on Jos Crisis, May 2010, paragraph 2.2.1 p.38. Following the crisis in the Barkin Ladi area, the Plateau State Commissioner of Information and Communication, Mr. Abraham Yiljap on 24th November, 2011, speaking on Plateau Radio (Peace FM) warned people not to interpret the crisis as a religious crisis, saying that there was nothing religious about it. Similar pronouncements by different persons have been made. Having thus established that the crises have multi-dimensional root causes, what is expected now is the political will to permanently address those factors that keep creating the ugly situations. Somehow, we appear to be acting the ostrich by burying our heads in the sand, hoping that the root causes associated with the crises will vanish. It is clear that issues such as the struggle over who owns the land, the indigene/settler controversy, the uneasy relationship between cattle owners and farmers, perceived injustice, etc. are at the root of the crises and of course, this does not exclude the clamour for religious supremacy between Christians and Muslims in the State. These matters must be comprehensively addressed sooner rather than later, and decisive measures must be taken so that peace and sanity will always prevail.

We have painfully realized that permanent peace cannot be brought about by the use of knives, cutlasses, guns, bombs, or the intimidating presence of the military or paramilitary. Only a radical conversion of heart can be the panacea to the seemingly unending crises in the State. Prayers do work and a lot of prayers have been offered and more are being said; but prayers must go along with good works and positive dispositions.

Dealing with the Culture of Violence
Some groups or persons have thought that we could deal with the crises through physical combat, which is perhaps why bombs and explosives suddenly replaced knives, bows and arrows. Not surprisingly, there has been much destruction of physical structures and lives, with consequent psychological traumas. Our young people are now more prone to verbal and physical violence even without any prompting. Innocent children now talk about their "enemies", i.e. referring to those they perceive not to be on their side. I recently met some six-year-old children whose utterances about the crises shocked me terribly. They narrated what they must have heard from their friends or parents about killings and destruction during the crises. What saddened me terribly was the passion and conviction with which they spoke about "those who are against us". The psyche of these children has been bruised, and it needs healing. Correct social re-orientation

must be inculcated in them, and this can be best done by families, schools and positive religious indoctrination in their places of worship.

Religious Extremism

The *Jama'atu Ahlis Sunnah Lidda'awati Wal-Jihad* (Group/community committed to propagating the Prophet's teaching and jihad) but popularly called *Boko Haram* is an Islamic sect which is said to abhor Western education and civilization and wants the application and use of the Sharia instead of the Nigerian constitution, at least in the northern parts of Nigeria "until the flag of Islam rises high," is one phenomenon we must proactively ensure does not compound our problems in Plateau State and further complicate the already wounded inter-personal relationships. Considering the indiscriminate attacks by the *Boko Haram* in Madalla, Kano, Maiduguri, Bauchi, Damaturu, Potiskum, etc on Christian and non-Christian targets, security agents must redouble their efforts to obstruct the plans and strategies of this group. The group may have good reasons for their actions in view of the moral decadence and corrupt social system in the society and the need to correct them, but it is the violent dimension of their approach that is abhorrent. I believe that an objective analysis of the demands of this group may be helpful. Their demands must however be in line with democratic principles and our aspirations, and must be for the common good of all Nigerians. Their detestation of evils such as corruption, injustice, unemployment, or the immoral life-style exhibited by some persons who feed fat on the resources of the country while millions are dying of hunger and disease, must be sincerely addressed. On the other hand, those in Boko Haram who are bent on causing untold havoc to lives and property are to be punished according to the laws of the land. I believe that using modern technological equipment, it should be possible to track down those who instigate, finance and promote violence in the name of *Boko Haram*. Government and security agents must be prepared to invest in arms detection equipment and to efficiently train security personnel for our major highways, airports, motor parks, markets and public/private institutions. Equally, land and sea borders must be well controlled to check the inflow of illegal weapons. It is sad that for a mere pittance it has been alleged that some customs, immigration and police officers are willing to let those carrying very dangerous weapons get away with their cargo. It must be mentioned too that those involved in the manufacture of local weapons should be hunted down with the same aggressiveness as those who push drugs, just as there must be more co-ordinated intelligence gathering among security agencies.

The recent arrest of the mastermind of the 2011 Christmas day attacks on Christian worshippers in Madalla, and the slack nature of handling him by the police which led to his escape, is a symptom of the uncoordinated and unserious approach to security issues. Fortunately, he has been rearrested, and this goes to show that with goodwill, determination and an unbiased approach to security issues criminals, no matter how close they are to authority or how personally connected or religiously affiliated to security personnel, can be apprehended and justice can be done. For as Martin Luther King Jr once said, "injustice anywhere is a threat to justice everywhere".

The Media Impact
It is sad that the news of the Plateau crises has often been blown out of proportion by both the national and international media. The electronic and print media have often created unnecessary anxiety by their reporting, thus scaring people coming to Plateau State, for instance for national youth service, university studies or business. It is very easy to detect where the religious allegiance of some journalists lies from the way they report events or write feature articles. When it comes to religious issues even some of the brilliant journalists who normally write well, suddenly become biased and write with a puzzling lack of objectivity and fairness, obviously because they choose to be blinded by unhealthy religious sentiments. Foreign embassies and High Commissions have added to the elevated level of anxiety and tension by always

warning their citizens not to visit Jos or Plateau State during some of the crises. It must be noted that despite these sensational news and warnings, many people from within and abroad have been visiting Plateau State and finding to their surprise that in spite of the challenges created by the crises, life goes on fairly normally in Jos and indeed in all of Plateau State. The other parts of Plateau State like Pankshin, Shendam, Mangu, Bokkos, Wase, Kanam, etc have continued to live in peace in spite of the impression that all of Plateau State has been on fire. When a crisis took place in Barkin Ladi , a small town [some 20 kilometres] from Jos and a twenty-four-hour curfew was imposed to prevent further violence, newspaper headlines screamed: "Jos burns again...". Barkin Ladi is not Jos! It would appear that some persons were and are still interested in seeing the total collapse of Jos, or in seeing it lose favour and respect in the sight of people of goodwill. I am sure that the over fifty ethnic groups that can be found in Jos, and indeed good Muslims and good Christians in Plateau State will prefer to work out a mode of peaceful coexistence, rather than throw away the baby with the bath water. It must be said that Jos is very safe, but because of the challenges experienced, only positive interpersonal relationships will help to recapture its days of glory and splendour.

The Need for Youth Empowerment

It is imperative for elders, statesmen, politicians, traditional leaders, and clergymen of both the Islamic and Christian religions to speak out in condemnation of violence even if committed by persons from their religious or ethnic groups. Culprits of violence have unfortunately been shielded, as exemplified by the reluctance to release and implement reports of commissions or panels of enquiries into the crises over the years. It is known that some persons caught in acts of violence during the crises, simply because they came from one religion or ethnic group or political camp, were treated with kid gloves and let go. No wonder they often go on to continue attacks in one form or another. Elders seem not to influence the youths with their moral authority any longer and we seem to be in danger of losing a whole generation of youths. They commit acts of violence without any remorse, and some are even alleged to be engaged in cannibalistic practices as a way of showing disdain for their so-called "enemies". The culture of death instead of life is fast developing among them and this may not be unrelated to the fact that most of them are unemployed and have been negatively indoctrinated in their homes or places of worship. The local, state and federal governments must do more to rehabilitate or re-orientate our youths. The Niger Delta initiative is a good one, where militant youths are being equipped with vocational skills or encouraged to do relevant courses in institutions instead of engaging in militancy. No amount spent on the training of the youth, by the provision of good functional education and meaningful employment, is to be regarded as a waste.

Plateau Government Peace Initiatives
In 2004 a Plateau Peace Summit, headed by the late Mrs. Elizabeth Pam was held to discuss peaceful coexistence and fruitful social engagement by the many ethnic and religious groups in the state. Various panels through the years were inaugurated, all in the attempt to seek enduring peace. In recent times, a very notable and positive effort at entrenching permanent peace among other things by the Governor of Plateau State, Da Jonah David Jang, is the appointment of two advisers to the Governor, one each on Christian and Islamic Affairs. This is a very laudable initiative capable of dousing tension and inspiring trust and confidence among adherents of the two religions. By this, channels have been created for easier access to government, and the religious tension sometimes based on rumour and speculation will be highly minimized. Perhaps in the future a ministry dedicated to religious harmony may be considered. Also, the appointment of a Special Adviser by Governor Jang on Peace Building has no doubt gone a long way in reassuring people that the Government is interested in peace and would do anything for peace to be entrenched in the State. The positive outcome of this is reflected in what the Special

Adviser, Barrister Timothy Parlong, had to say: "My office is now like a market where people both Christians and Muslims run to, and we have discussed and found solutions toward building that lasting peace they have been longing to see return to the state." He noted that people were polarized along religious lines, saying: "You had people who ran away from where they used to reside to a place they thought they would be safe" (cf. *The Nigeria Standard*, Wednesday January 25, 2012, pp. 1,2).

A lot still needs to be done to smooth the relationship between pastoralists and farmers, to address the deprivation suffered by those who lost houses, animals, crops and other means of livelihood, the insecurity of not feeling safe to go alone to the farm or to pasture animals for fear of unexpected attacks, or honouring the dead during the crises in a befitting manner.

There is a pressing need at the level of government to encourage a deeper appreciation by adherents of Islam and Christianity to develop a moderate approach to religious issues devoid of unhealthy sentiments, but without in any way compromising the values of the two religions. The Ministry of Education should ensure that in our schools, interreligious studies are made part of the school curriculum. Teachers entrusted with this task need to help students in the proper contextual reading of their sacred scriptures, so as to avoid fundamentalist interpretations. Christians with moderate views and Muslims with moderate views must come together to overcome fundamentalism and politicization of religion and outshine those who spread dangerous religious doctrines and advocates of violence and destruction of lives and property, claiming to do so in the name of God. This we know to be the very antithesis of religion.

Better to Light a Candle: Humble Contributions of the Catholic Archdiocese of Jos

Apart from preaching sermons for peace, encouraging dialogue, holding assemblies and seminars for peaceful coexistence and mobilizing youths/children for peace, the Catholic Archdiocese of Jos has also taken humble concrete steps to ensure that peace returns and life is lived as it should be. The Justice and Peace Department of the Archdiocese with its Emergency Response arm has been very effective in promoting conflict management education as well as relief distribution after each crisis. Houses, clinics and local wells have been constructed or rehabilitated, and medicines and clothing supplied to those affected, irrespective of their religious or ethnic affiliation. An interfaith vocational youth training centre in Bokkos started in 2010 by the Archdiocese of Jos trains both Muslim and Christian youths in vocational skills, at the same time teaching them the culture of dialogue, peaceful coexistence and conflict resolution, rather than violent confrontation during moments of tension or misunderstanding. It is also the dream of the Archdiocese to create a "Dialogue, Reconciliation and Peace Centre" in Jos, where differences can be sorted out, grievances examined, hatred and bitterness diffused and groups of youths, traditional leaders, politicians and women, etc. can be brought together to share edifying messages and to dispassionately analyse issues that lead to conflict and find solutions to them.

The Tripod of Justice, Peace and Reconciliation
Pope Benedict XVI's visit to the Benin Republic from 18 to 20 November, 2011 to sign the post Synodal Apostolic Exhortation on Reconciliation, Justice and Peace was a way of appreciating the peaceful coexistence of the citizens in that country, as the country is known to be fairly stable politically and religiously. Their democracy is said to be in such a healthy condition that an independent candidate was able to win an election as President. Muslims and Christians live side by side and support each other. Adherents of traditional religion practise their religion freely. In Ouidah, where the post Synodal document was signed, I saw the "Temple of Pythons", a sacred place of worship for the traditional religionists situated just opposite the Catholic Basilica; yet there is peace. This goes to prove that once there is goodwill; adherents of different religions can live harmoniously and happily and use their religious values to foster peace, prosperity and progress. We have

similar examples in The Gambia, Senegal, Burkina Faso, etc. People can certainly live together each doing his or her part, practising his or her religion and contributing to the common good. It is very exemplary that in the South-Western part of Nigeria one can find in the same family Muslims and Christians, and also there is the common practice of Christians and Muslims inter-marrying and living in harmony. The question is: If Christians and Muslims exterminate themselves by senseless fighting, who will be left to practise any of the religions or enjoy the beauty and salvific relevance of the two religions, and what credit does that do to religion?

Peace should prevail over war, for God's plan for his creatures (Muslims and Christians) is peace not war (cf. Jer. 29:11). Religion must never be the cause of our inhumanity to one another in Nigeria.

Even with the protracted crises, the beautiful city of Jos "endowed with good weather, fertile land and a generous people", must not be destroyed. The frantic efforts by NGOs and men and women of goodwill will see to a rebirth of Jos and indeed Plateau State. Plateau will rise again: a Plateau where disputes will be settled amicably, spears will be beaten into ploughshares and spears into pruning hooks and no one will raise sword against another or train again for war (cf. Is 2:4). As Prophet Isaiah says, "The wolf will dwell with the lamb...the calf and the lion cub will feed together...." (Is 11:6) and "violence will no more be heard in your land" (Is 61:18). We continue to pray and work harder so that Christians and Muslims in Nigeria and in particular in Plateau State will avoid the path of violence or war against one another so as to enjoy continued peace and harmony.

Postscript:

While this publication was in the press, unfortunate events took place in Jos that were not ever contemplated. The Headquarter of the Church of Christ in Nations, COCIN, was bombed by suicide bombers on the 26th of February, 2012, killing people and destroying Church property, and while we were yet to catch our breath, St Finbarr's Catholic Church, Rayfield-Jos, came under severe attack on the 11th of March 2012, as suicide bombers tried to drive a car into the Church packed with many worshippers. Delayed however by courageous young scouts at the gate, they detonated their parcel of death and the bomb blast resulted in many deaths including the bombers. Many were injured and the Church and the Rev. Fathers' house damaged. In the process of finding lasting peace, a police helicopter carrying a Deputy Inspector General of Police, John Haruna and three other police officers crashed a few days later in Kabong village killing all four on board. The challenge to build peace is enormous. This is further complicated by those who in the name of religion think they will gain easy access to heaven by killing and destroying. They seem to have forgotten their goal while redoubling their effort at causing maximum pain, damage and loss of lives. We pray for conversion of heart for these persons, because if they stop unleashing violence on innocent people, peace will flow like a river in hearts, homes and the larger society.

Pope Benedict XVI with a Jewish leader

APPENDICES

APENDIX 1

http://archive.punchn2.com/Articl.aspx?theartic=Art201104022135298

Saturday, 2 Apr 2011

Plateau crises won't end even if you attach five soldiers to every family – Archbishop Kaigama

Archbishop Ignatius Kaigama is the bishop of the Catholic Archdiocese of Jos and was a member of the Chief Solomon Lar-led Presidential Advisory Committee on the Jos crises. He tells JUDE OWUAMANAM that dialogue remains the best option to resolve the crises in Plateau State as the nation moves into another level in its political evolution.

You have been involved in conflict mediation in Plateau State for a long time. What have been the benefits of such efforts because we have seen the crises not only escalating, but coming in greater degrees?

Well, peace is a gift from God; we only participate in its construction. We do our part in peace building and we allow God to bestow the gift on us. Humanly, we have done what we should. In the last 10 years we have been involved in one activity or the other. We have engaged various groups in dialogue; we have been engaging in inter-religious activities. The late Emir of Wase (Dr. Haruna Abdullahi) and I have for a long time been engaged in ways of promoting peace in the society. On individual basis, there are measures we have taken to create this atmosphere of peaceful co-existence, tolerance, mutual acceptance and a harmonious society. At the level of the church, we have also embarked on so many programmes to ensure peace. Our emergency response programmes; our interfaith programmes are geared towards creating a better atmosphere to ensure that violence is kept at bay and promote a culture of dialogue. This is our style, but as a human society, in some ways we succeed and in some other ways there are failures and these failures are evident in the crises that keep reoccurring in the recent past. Crises that were as a result of minor misunderstandings – political, religious and so on – have now graduated to a level where people are ready to kill and destroy one another, burn each other's property and things like that. We have now reached the level where bombs are being planted indiscriminately and people are not afraid to cause harm and destruction to others. It is very tragic, very sad and unfortunate developments. But we are not giving up. We will continue to do what we can, but we are limited as a religious body. We will continue to work with other bodies like the civil society groups, to do what we should do. So, we hope that there will be a better collaboration with the government and with the people listening to a voice of reason, peace will return to the state.

As we enter the crucial week of the election, what do these crises portend for a state like Plateau?

We just hope that the politicians have the interest of the poor people at heart and I hope they are being propelled by the love for the people that they are supposed to serve; love for the common good. I hope that is their desire because the ferocity with which the politicians compete for power leaves us wondering whether they are out for service; or they are just going there for themselves. We are wont to conclude that it's not all about being there for the people; it is about making it in the Nigerian sense and that is why I feel that issues that should be discussed, whether at the level of the leaders or at the level of the followers, were not things that were given the desired attention. It is very easy when there are problems to hang everything on religion and I have seen elders, political leaders, who for instance, would say that the crises in Jos are all about religion. I keep saying that there are several other social factors on the ground that we don't address and we wish that such problems will vanish overnight. So, there is, in fact, the absence of political will to definitely tackle the problems on the ground. We have just had the Chief Solomon Lar-committee completing its assignment and the report forwarded to the Presidency; there have been several reports of panels of inquiry on the crises that have never seen the light of day. None of them had been implemented and you begin to wonder; are we really serious or we are just playing to the gallery? When there are crises, we go round in fire brigade style, set up panels and in the end, none of the results are used. So, I tell you, we feel worried. I am quite worried that there are no concerted efforts to bring this to a stop. Rather, what we see is the redoubling of personal political activities to the detriment of the common good. We are sad as a church and as religious leaders. I identify with the people, the grass roots. I go round every weekend and meet thousands and thousands of people that I can claim I know where it hurts them. But unfortunately, our voice is limited. When it comes to politics, people are not prepared to hear anything other than the music of their own political games. The music is so loud that they don't listen to any other person. But that doesn't stop us from talking. I still keep doing my work.

I know that the Catholic Church has not taken a stand on the politics of the state, especially in endorsing a particular candidate for the election. What do you make of those religious organisations and leaders endorsing one politician or the other? Are they not contributing to the crises in the state, especially when viewed against the backdrop that religious leaders are not supposed to be partisan?

There was a time traditional rulers were not meant to endorse any particular candidate, just like religious leaders, but now it has changed. Because I have seen traditional rulers openly welcoming aspirants and saying, 'Oh, our votes are 100 per cent for you.' Also in the churches – the church is part of the society – you find people who will tell you this is the candidate to vote for or this is a political party to go into and so on and so forth. I don't know if their own style of church administration allows that, but for me, and the Catholic Church, we are prohibited from playing partisan politics. I am not allowed to adopt a particular candidate or favour a particular political party. What I am allowed to do as a priest is to encourage people, enlighten the people, tell them about good governance and point the way. I am supposed to be the signboard and to say this is the direction. We want peace, we want good governance; we want progress and anybody on the side of good governance and peace should be seen as a good leader and should be voted for. But I have no right to intimidate my followers or congregation to adopt a particular person or a particular political party. It is not in our character as a church. But that does not mean that we are apolitical; that we don't care about what happens in politics. I wrote a pastoral letter in 2007, advising Catholics on what to do and on what not to do; things to look out for. That's our job. We are not to enforce the issue of choosing this candidate or the other.

Talking about panels of inquiry on the Plateau crises, I know that you were actively involved in the Presidential Advisory Committee on Jos Crises led by Chief Solomon Lar. What has surprised many people, including residents of the state, is that the report of that committee is still not known. Is there anything in the report or any aspect of the recommendations you think could be the cause of the delay in releasing or implementing the recommendations of that committee?

I cannot understand because the report is an objective analysis of the situation on the Plateau crises. So, I don't see anything out of the way there. The aim of the report was to bring back peace to the land. I think from the Christians, the Muslims and other participants, we were unanimous. The report was good and well presented. We've been waiting for an action, but as I said earlier, it is not the first time that a report like that is being kept aside.

Why we emphasise this is because of the urgency with which the committee was set up and being a presidential committee set up for the first time on the crises, it would have received a speedy presidential response and so, it hasn't happened and that is why I talked about the absence of political will because I can't see anything concrete being done apart from bringing in soldiers and trucks. What else is being done to maintain security and promote peace that is permanent? What else? Even if you bring two million soldiers here and attach five soldiers to each family, they are not going to bring back peace. Bring in all the trucks to Jos, the story will be the same. Imagine the expenses being incurred on security. The youths are now wild. The language and culture of violence have become part and parcel of their everyday lives. Now, burning, killing and destroying people's property are things of joy. Something is definitely wrong. And nothing is being done to change the mentality of these young people; to re-orientate them. They are becoming wilder and wilder. Killing and shedding of blood have become as easy as taking a cup of tea. It is sad. So, I am still wondering whether there is that political will because I know that these problems can be attacked effectively and drastically too. But are the people ready to sacrifice? Am I ready to do anything for the good of the people not minding the consequences? These are the problems. I am afraid nobody is ready to bell the cat. And as long as this remains, the problems keep circulating. Then the violence will continue to resurge in one form or the other; either in political or religious forms; violence associated with ethnic differences or things like that. There must be a way of addressing this sincerely, objectively and with the fear of God.

So, what is the panacea to the state of violence in the country?

I have said it again and again that dialogue is the answer but unfortunately, many people do not believe that it is the answer. They believe that it is when we fight and bring in arms, bring soldiers and police and so on that they will end the crises. We are only deceiving ourselves. If you look at all the crises in the world, in the end, they were resolved by people coming together to talk. Even our Nigeria-Biafran War was resolved at a roundtable. In Northern Ireland, the Catholics and Protestants were at war for many years. It was resolved through dialogue. In Germany, the local tribes fought many years and it was only when they came together that the issues were resolved. If we say that dialogue is not the solution, I am sure we'll be looking around for solutions that will never come. So, I have always insisted that we should not reduce these crises to religion alone. That it is a multi-dimensional crisis and the factors are also multidimensional and if you reduce it to religion, I tell you, the crises will never end. Let us address the other factors and then religion. Look at the way Jos is so polarised that people are afraid to go to one part of the town or the other. Even if you want to travel to Bauchi or Abuja, you will be afraid of where to follow because of the fear for your life. We are now talking in terms of one being a Christian or a Muslim. It is only when we are ready to listen to the voice of reason that there will be peace. Bring all the soldiers to Plateau State, if the heart is rebellious, poisoned and harbours hatred, I am sorry, we will achieve very little. So, all ethnic groups, all religions should transcend their tribal or religious sentiments to address real issues. The future of our young people is being terribly affected and I hope that this election will provide the window of opportunity for us to elect people that can truly deliver the dividends of democracy, provide good governance and be sensitive to

3

the yearnings and aspirations of the people. With that, I think there is hope. Each time I pray my prayer intentions are on the peaceful conduct of the elections. Now what are my fears? My number one fear is that the President had stated unambiguously that these elections will be free and fair where every vote counts and I doff my hat for him. He made a bold statement. The INEC chairman has also come out to say that it is not going to be business as usual. That it is going to be a radical departure from what used to be whereby election results were compromised and there was corruption. So, we are optimistic with these two personalities reassuring us. But my worry is on whether this message will sink to the grass roots; those who are assistants of the President, those who will be work with the INEC chairman. Would they imbibe this message at the grass roots because they will not be everywhere? What of those subordinates, would they be ready to do things properly?

What is your advice?

This is what I am saying that all these issues should be looked into. I can see in the eyes of my mind, some groups, from somewhere, anywhere going to disrupt the electoral process. Is there an adequate security arrangement? This is my fear number two. Then, my fear number three; when the results are being announced, will the losers accept the verdicts? Even at the campaign rallies, you see that people are so intolerant. I don't think we have developed a civilised political culture, where we make use of words, not necessarily violent actions. Will people be ready to accept the verdict in the end? I just hope that those who are contesting will be able to advise their followers. They may not necessarily be the ones to cause the problem, but you know that at the grass roots, people are more enthusiastic. But as a good leader, you need to tell them that it is not a do-or-die affair that we must shed tears. I hope that those working with the President and the INEC chairman will not compromise their positions and those bent on disrupting the process must not be allowed to do that.

Vanguard

http://www.vanguardngr.com/2012/03/st-finbars-church-bombing-this-is-evil

St. Finbars Church Bombing: This is evil; but we remain strengthened – Rt. Rev. Ignatius Kaigama

ON MARCH 17, 2012 · IN SPECIAL REPORT
7:12 pm
Email7
By Taye Obateru

Anyone who knows the Catholic Archbishop of Jos, the Rt. Rev. (Dr.) Ignatius Kaigama would probably agree that he 'lives' his calling. Not only is he amiable, humble, peace-loving, always with a smile for virtually everyone, those close to him say he cannot hurt a fly.

They attest to his kind and humane nature even in his private capacity. His role as co-Chair of the state inter-religious committee since crises enveloped the state, building bridges and not wasting any opportunity to preach peace, is also outstanding. But last Sunday, the day one of the churches under him – St. Finbarr's Catholic Church – came under a suicide bombing attack brought out the other side of the Archbishop. Despite the genteel mien he showcased as he went round, trying to calm down scores of angry church members, it was obvious that he was deeply hurt by the development. The feelings that did not show on his face were evident in what he said.

Excerpts:

"I want you to see today, for yourself, that this is a practical demonstration of evil. There is evil. This is diabolic; this is a personification of evil. But I assure you that the power of Jesus overcomes. Evil wants to rob us of our faith. These armed robbers of faith will not succeed in Jesus name.

"It's pathetic; it's so sad that this barbaric action should take place, not only here, but in many other places. That someone would wake up in the morning and his intention is to deliberately kill and attack and destroy? This is why I said it is evil and it's a terrible evil. But good will overcome evil.

"We are saddened; we are terribly upset by this barbaric action and I know that no decent human being or religion will allow this. Those who perpetrate evil in the name of religion, God Almighty will deal with them. Judgement and punishment belong to God. If we try to take the path of God, we may not administer the kind of punishment that God Has in reserve for these wicked people.

"And that is why as Christians, when these things happen, we call for calm. Not because we're cowards; not because we are compromising our faith, but we are using reason. Faith that does not go with reason is irrational. Faith that has no place for reason is as good as nothing.

We Christians believe in Almighty God. We believe in using our mental faculties. You cannot just kill yourself or kill another person. That is irrational; that is beastly; that is criminal and our faith does not teach us that. So let's be careful. "If I were to give vent to my anger, what I will do here, none of you can do it. But I tell myself, 'calm down, God is in control'. So my dear brothers and sisters, evil has taken place, but evil will not triumph. We shall continue to do whatever is possible. We will never give up Christianity. If anyone believes that by doing this, Christianity will be eliminated or that we shall give up, that person is the greatest liar on earth. Christianity will grow stronger and stronger.

"The blood or martyrs is the seed of the Christian faith. It is not the first time that Christians have been killed. Remember the Roman times when people were killed and thrown to animals. Did that kill our faith? Our faith continues to grow and grow. Today, the billions of Christians in the world is a testimony of the vibrancy of faith and that is why we should forge ahead even when evil confronts us.

Victims of the bomb blast at St. Finbarr's Catholic Church in Jos being taken to the Hospital on Sunday.

"So I admonish you, don't take the laws into your hands; it doesn't help. My dear young people, let us use reason. God has given us faith and he has also given us reason. Those who are killing like this have what they think is faith and have no reason at all. Let us not be like them.

"We have our Christian faith as a people, to respect one another, not to take lives because life is sacred, not to destroy anybody's property out of malice or any reason. Let us maintain what we have, it's a precious gift. Destruction has happened, lives have been lost.

May the souls of those who lost their lives rest in perfect peace.

"Those people bent on doing evil, it is that same evil that will crush them on by one. We have never taught you to be suicide bombers or to kill. If any religion is teaching that, then I'm sorry. We teach you to be concerned about your neighbours and we will continue to teach this.

"So my dear friends, the worst has happened, but it is not the end. We have our faith, our Christian hope to rely on. Our Christian hope and identity can never be buried. Let's keep that faith alive. Let that faith never be discouraged; let nothing separate us from the love of God. Let us mourn those who have died with correct Christian mentality and attitude."

Meanwhile, the security agencies in the state announced new measures aimed at curtailing the suicide bombings targeted at worship places in the state. A security meeting attended by Chief of Defence Staff, Air Marshall Oluseyi Petirin and other security top notches came up with strategies aimed at checking the trend. Briefing top community and religious leaders on the new measures at a stakeholders' meeting on Tuesday, the state Commissioner of Police, Mr. Dipo Ayeni, said there should be no more preferential treatment for anyone at worship centres.

According to him, "On Sundays and Fridays, all roads leading to all worship centres must be totally blocked or diverted. No vehicle should have access or park near any worship centre during service. There should be perimeter fencing of all the worship centres not only in Jos, but all over the state, to prevent easy access by suicide bombers to the places of worship. Every worshipper must, as a matter of compelling necessity, subject himself or herself to security checks no matter how highly placed.

"We have agreed that to ward off these elements. All of us have roles to play. Every worshipper must subject themselves to search while there must be no accessibility to worship centres. Even if I am the one and I am not a member of that church, please don't allow me to enter. Nobody must be allowed to carry bags to worship centres and when you suspect any object, do not go near. You can carry only your bible or your Qur'an.

"You must avoid clustering worship centres after worship. We observe that after worship people cluster around to gossip. Your business is worship your God and go to your house. After that, please quickly go to your house."

Another measure is that force personnel should also be subjected to security checks or asked to identify themselves in view of the constant use of military camouflage uniforms by the suicide attackers.

However, the state government on its part expressed reservations about the effectiveness of the state of emergency imposed on four local government areas of the state by President Goodluck Jonathan saying it has not had any impact on the security situation in the state. Briefing journalists after an emergency state Security Council meeting, the Information Commissioner, Abraham Yiljab, said enough has not been done by the security agencies to forestall the attacks alleging also that the taking over of the security of the state by the CDS has not improved anything.

"One keeps feeling that the state of emergency declared on the state by the Federal Government has not yielded results. Concerning the management of the security situation in the state as well as management of security information, the office of the Chief of Defence Staff has been fully empowered by the President of Nigeria to be in charge of security in Plateau State.

"The Chief of Defence Staff has delegated that responsibility to the STF that is on ground. Every security operation in Plateau state is being guided and coordinated by the STF. But what the people of Plateau are saying is that the STF must give result; that there should be no silence, that there should be no reason that the people will continue to experience attacks anymore."

The security council also faulted the handling of the suicide bombing at COCIN headquarters church by the Defence Headquarters just as it condemned the shooting of protesters after last Sunday's blast at St Finbarr's Catholic Church.

According to the commissioner, "we expect that the DHQ would be a father to all sides, just as the Plateau Government is a father to all sides. The Defence Headquarters should not have drawn itself into an argument with the victims. It should not have joined issues with the COCIN leadership. One would have expected the DHQ to say that all issues were being investigated when a controversy arose over those that were killed rather than make the victim look like the liar at the end of the day,"

He added: "The Security Council is saying that we should not have a situation where security forces that are meant to protect the citizens are now standing in confrontation with the citizens that they are supposed to protect. Council has directed that security forces must be proactive in maintaining their presence in those difficult areas so that their presence would deter those that are trying to carry out harmful actions against the people."

It urged members of the public to cooperate and work closely with the security forces that have been sent to maintain security.

APENDIX 2

APENDIX 3

HEALING WOUNDS ON THE PLATEAU

PREAMBLE:

A meeting initiated by the National Tranquility Movement was held at the Catholic Archbishop's Conference Hall, Jos on Monday, 17th May, 2004. In welcoming the participants, Archbishop Ignatius A. Kaigama explained that the meeting is a friendly one of concerned leaders, interested in the sad happenings in Plateau State. The hostilities are beneficial neither to Christians nor to Muslims. It is a meeting to talk peace and not to blame anyone. It seeks to emphasize the fact that the spate of killings and hostilities are against the tenets of both the Christian and Muslim religions and **must stop now.**

At the end of the meeting, with the theme, **"Healing the Wounds on the Plateau",** we issue the following communique:

RESOLUTIONS:

We, the leaders agree that factors other than religious are at the base of the crisis. While we admit that there are bad Christians and bad Muslims, the rampant poverty, unemployment, problem of resource, land issues and deprivations are constantly recurring decimals that generate these conflicts.

To find concrete solutions to the crises we categorically condemn what has been done as un-Christian and un-Islamic. We further advocate that as a matter of urgency,

1. Leaders both religious and political who preach but act something else must shun deceit and ensure the implementation of decisions reached at meetings.

2. While in the present situation, we need help from wherever to help us sort out our problems, external forces brought in to dislocate the State and create problems must be condemned and the problem solved at the family level.

1

17.05.04

3. An enlarged forum of Christian leaders outside government structure should meet to talk from the heart if our wounds are to be healed.

4. Ways and means of addressing the elements of mis-trust that have been created are to be sought.

5. We appeal for avoidance of the spirit of revenge. People on both sides have suffered. We must all vow not to revenge.

6. The media is to be more sensitive to what they report. The information reported should be checked and cross-checked before they are sent out so that information is based on facts.

7. We shall avoid rumour mongering.

8. Rehabilitation of the displaced brothers and sisters should be vigorously pursued by individuals and governments.

9. We agreed that this meeting will continue. Archbishop Ignatius Kaigama is to liaise for the Christian side if there are any problems while Alhaji Inuwa Ali is to liaise for the Muslim side.

17. 05. 04

It was attended by:

Alh. M. I. Gashash

N.T.M. National President

....

Most Rev. I. A. Kaigama

Archdiocesan Catholic Secretariat,

Jos.

....

Rev. Dr. A. Lar

COCIN Headquarters, Jos

....

Dr. Haruna Abdullahi

Emir of Wase

....

Alh. Inuwa Ali

JNI, Jos

....

Rev. Yakubu Pam

CAN, Plateau State

....

Alh. Mustapha Umar (Galadima Wase)   C/o Emir's Palace, Wase

Mal. Moh'd Sagir Hamza   N. T.M. Admin. Sec .

Mal. Likita Musa   Representative from Lafia

Mal. Lawal Abdullahi   Representative from Wase

Alh. Iliya Idi   Representative from Shendam

Mr. Menson Dangana   N. T. M.

Rev. Fr. Joshua Daffa   Archdiocesan Catholic Secretariat, Jos.

Very Rev. Fr. Cletus Gotan   Archdiocesan Catholic Secretariat, Jos.

A PASTORAL MESSAGE PRESENTED AT THE END OF THE 8TH GENERAL ASSEMBLY OF THE CATHOLIC ARCHDIOCESE OF JOS, HELD AT THE SACRED HEART PASTORAL CENTRE, JOS

AUGUST 16 - 20, 2010

Preamble

We, the delegates to the 8th General Assembly, at the end of our Assembly send greetings of peace to the family of God in the Catholic Archdiocese of Jos and indeed to all the good people of Plateau State. Gathered together from August 16 to 20, 2010, we prayed and reflected on the theme, "The challenges of religious and political conflicts to the Church in Plateau State". Invoking the Holy Spirit, we reflected on the recurring crises on the Plateau that have resulted in the unnecessary loss of lives and property. These have paralysed economic and socio-political developments in the state, heightened religious mistrust, polarized inhabited areas, and aggravated the suffering of the people.

Condolences

The General Assembly regrets the loss of lives and property as a result of these crises in the State, and we condole with the bereaved families, while praying for the souls of the departed to rest in peace. We sympathize with all those nursing varying degrees of injury and those struggling to rebuild their lives. We appreciate the goodwill of all those who have contributed towards restoring the dignity of life of the affected persons. We appeal to government, NGOs, religious bodies, and concerned groups and individuals to come to the aid of all those who are yet to receive any assistance.

The Church and the Challenges of the Crises

There is no doubt that either directly or indirectly we have all suffered from the crises in the State. In spite of the severe economic, political, social and security challenges that we face in the State and the country at large, we encourage Christians not to lose faith in Almighty God nor be paralysed by fear and anger, but rather to renew their love for God and neighbour. We resolve to step up our teaching of the Church on the culture of love. The

Church continues to teach love, peace, and reconciliation, no matter the cost. Every Catholic is called to be an agent of the change we want to see. We pray for peace in our hearts, our homes, our State and our country. Let us be the first to say "no to violence" and be in the frontline of developing a culture of peace and non- violence. Let us make room for others, respect each other, learn to appreciate our differences and overcome evil with good. No doubt many people are hurting deeply, having been traumatized by the experience of the violence we have witnessed. We must however "Seek first the kingdom of God and his justice", and have the courage to forgive. With St. Francis we pray, "Lord make me an instrument of your peace. Where there is hatred let me show love; where there is injury, pardon, where there is doubt, faith, where there is despair, hope; where there is darkness, light; where there is sadness, joy."

Security
While we commend the efforts of government and the security agencies in maintaining the relative peace in the state, we note with dismay our security situation that allowed sporadic attacks on lives and property to take place. We call in strong terms on those saddled with the responsibility for keeping the peace, to live up to their responsibilities, while urging people to be security conscious and to report all suspicious movements and persons to the relevant security agencies rather than taking the law into their own hands.

Polarization
This is a major concern for us as a people of God. Communities are now identified either as Christian or Muslim. This is an impediment to our interpersonal relationships. We need each other and there is no way that any State in Nigeria can ever belong to only one group. The polarization of our communities leads to further suspicion, mistrust and fear. While it may suit a few for their personal advantage, it will only destroy us and cage our humanity. It will not allow our children to enjoy those days of old when they played together, shared lives together, went to school together, ate food and drank together, celebrated births, marriages and funerals together. Our children no longer mix with people considered to be different. The elders are guilty of passing on prejudices and stereotypes. If this continues, there will only be further division, and only God knows where this will lead us. Let

us begin to build bridges of peace and reach out in some small ways, greet neighbours, invite them to family celebrations and buy goods in the market without fear and discrimination.

Dialogue

We restate the importance of dialogue in conflict resolution. The stand of the Catholic Church is that dialogue remains a veritable means to peace. The dialogue of life means reaching out lovingly to another person, irrespective of ethnic or religious differences. The recent crises have generated so much mistrust that it will take a lot of work to rebuild Muslim-Christian trust and relationships. The lack of clear understanding of the origin and cause of the crises has generated problems even among Christians. While some see nothing in the crises other than the attempt by Muslims to encroach on the sacred space of what is considered a very Christian State, others think that the root causes of the crises are ethnic, social and political, while given a religious coloration.

The causes are multidimensional. The gains we have made in Muslim-Christian dialogue have suffered a great setback. Any attempt to initiate a meeting or dialogue between Muslims and Christians is viewed with suspicion and seen as a sign of weakness and a compromise of one's religious dignity. It is an irony that while some religious leaders are advocating a militant approach to the crises, many non-religious organizations are talking and working for peace. Our Archdiocesan Justice, Peace, Development and Caritas Commission and many other groups are actively engaged in efforts to break barriers in order to restore what was once a beautiful spirit of mutual coexistence between Muslims and Christians. The message of love must override the message of 'fire for fire', the culture of life must overthrow the culture of death, and the spirit of violence must be eliminated by the culture of dialogue. The crises must be put in the right perspective. The causes are multiple and so religion alone should not be blamed.

Love of Neighbour

One thing is clear when we view these crises from all angles: the love of neighbour has given way to hatred. Therefore, the solution to these incessant crises in the country and in the State can be found only in practical love for one another; and not only in beautiful sermons, fanciful churches and mosques, religious titles, visions, prophecies or hateful propaganda, the acquisition of weapons, or unnecessary high spending. Practical love is the solution to our crisis situation. We should be our neighbour's keeper (cf. 1 Th. 3:12, Mt. 5:9).

Nigeria at 50
We thank God that Nigeria will soon be 50, and note the relative progress in our political leadership since independence. We acknowledge and commend our founding fathers. Every Golden Jubilee celebration is a cause for joy and happiness. Our dear country has gone through many challenges owing to the diverse nature of its setting. Yet here we are, still a people. We are increasingly becoming conscious of our differences rather than emphasizing the unity that comes from harnessing our human and material resources. We insist on responsible and accountable leadership. We condemn the culture of "winner takes it all", and advocate an all-inclusive system of government. The Church laments the fact that our democracy is yet to bring the much-needed relief from hunger, insecurity, illiteracy and unemployment and problematic issues of health and housing. The high cost of Nigerian democracy is also a matter of concern, where a lot of resources are spent on elected or appointed senior government officials who enjoy mouth-watering payments, while the common worker can hardly make both ends meet. This has resulted in the emergence of pressure groups that represent sectional rather than national interests. Society continues to witness vicious hostility between ethnic, political and religious groups with daily news of unbridled corruption, kidnapping, women trafficking and youth hooliganism on the rise. We therefore challenge our Christian politicians to be agents of change for a better society.

2011 Elections
The government must ensure a diligent preparation for the 2011 general elections. We commend the Independent National Electoral Commission (INEC) that discovered flaws in the last voters' registration and is making efforts to rectify such flaws. The contentious issue of zoning is a symptom of the absence of a national spirit. We appeal to religious leaders not to allow churches and mosques to be used by selfish aspirants and leaders to incite hatred and violence. The electorate must ensure that they register and vote. Religious leaders, especially priests and

religious, should not dabble in partisan politics. Rather, they have a duty to educate the electorate to vote credible leaders.

Lessons from the 'Year for Priests'

The church has just concluded 'The Year for Priests' in which the whole Church was united in intensive prayer for her priests for one whole year. During this time, priests had the opportunity to realize the seriousness of their vocation within the Church and the world, and to engage deeply in interior renewal for the sake of a more intensive witness to the gospel in today's world. The priest has the responsibility to preach, to teach and to heal. We must avoid, at all costs, using the pulpit to incite religious mistrust and hatred, and we must avoid being politically partial. The solution to the incessant crises in our country and on the Plateau can be found only in the practical expression of our faith: practical love of one another. The teachings of our doctrines, traditions and articles of faith are clear and essential guides to building respect and understanding of all human life. Catholic politicians must remember that they are first Catholic; they must put into practice the Church's teachings on political and social involvement and avoid mischievous political calculations and utterances that will lead to violence.

Religious Extremism

The rising cases of religious fanaticism and negative indoctrination in our country are very disturbing. The activities of religious leaders who preach as well as propagate hatred and invite their adherents to violence are all too common. All relevant agencies of government saddled with maintaining the peace must ensure that such elements are identified and made to face the full wrath of the law. Religious freedom and worship is a human right. Therefore nobody should be harassed or intimidated on the basis of his/her religious profession.

In some parts of Northern Nigeria, places of worship, instruction in religious knowledge, use of the government-controlled media and the free expression of faith are denied. We call for fairness and freedom for all religions.

Reports from Commissions

We commend the Commissions of the Archdiocese: Education,

Communication, Pastoral and Liturgical, Health, Justice Development and Peace Commission (JDPC), Catechetical and Family Life, and Youth, for their sustainable effort to serve not only the Church but the wider society. The education, health and social services provided are without reference to ethnic or religious affiliation. We commend the Catholic Youth Organization in its effort to consolidate and increase its friendship with Muslim youth through sports and peace and reconciliation seminars. The relief efforts by JDPC during and after the crises were distributed to all who were affected regardless of their religious affiliations. The spiritual and pastoral inputs rendered by the Pastoral/Liturgical, Catechetical and Family Life and Communications Commissions are all deeply appreciated. We urge them to continue in this spirit of selfless service and to ensure that, whatever the social or spiritual services given, are with a view to building bridges and promoting peaceful coexistence and the common good.

CONCLUSION

We conclude by first of all thanking God for the success of the 8th General Assembly of the Catholic Archdiocese of Jos. The Assembly appreciates the leadership of the Archdiocese. We commit ourselves to working towards developing the culture of peace and non-violence. The Assembly has formulated a prayer for Political, Ethnic and Religious Peace in Plateau State and pleads with all Catholics to say the prayer in their churches and homes. We implore Our Lady Queen of Peace to intercede for us as a Church and as a State.

Most Rev. Ignatius A. Kaigama   Very Rev. Fr. Emmanuel Ray Ikpa
Catholic Archbishop of   Jos   Chancellor

INDEX

2004 Yelwa Crises, v

Abraham Yiljap, 209

Acting the Ostrich, 110

Alh. Shuaibu Alhassan, 67

Alh. Yahaya Kwande, 67

Alhaji, vii, ix, 20, 40, 83,
84, 104, 129, 136, 137,
146, 151, 164, 170, 171,
173, 174

Ali Kazaure, 51, 81, 135

Angwan Yashi, 72

Archdiocese of Jos, ix, 24,
35, 49, 64, 65, 68, 69, 74,
80, 87, 88, 115, 123, 129,
135, 136, 138, 144, 145,
148, 164, 172, 186, 190,
191, 215, 236, 241

Aso Rock Villa, 44

Awka, vii

Berom, xi

Birth of Plateau State, 8

Bob Dewar, 158, 174

Bokkos, 144, 146, 147, 148,
150, 161, 164, 213, 216

Boko Haram, 38, 110, 168,
170, 171, 208, 211

bomb, 55, 90, 91, 92, 94,
96, 100, 111, 140, 141,
143, 218, 225

Bomb, v, 91

bomb blasts, 91, 94, 96,
140, 141, 143

bombers, 217, 225, 226

Botmang, 53, 59

Bukuru, xi, 52, 85, 86, 87,
133, 135, 136, 152

CAFOD, 89, 121, 167, 172

CAN, 3, 45, 68, 80, 82, 85,
118, 135, 153, 157, 158,
159, 183

Canada, vii

Cardinal Tarcisio Bertone,
vii

CARUDEP, 161

Catholic faithful, 190, 191

Catholic Relief Services, 89

Catholic Youth
Organisation of Nigeria,
135

Catholicism, 77

Causes of Jos Crises, 106

Chief Joshua Dariye, 67,
119, 163

Christmas, v, 3, 27, 34, 90,
91, 93, 94, 96, 97, 100,
102, 109, 111, 140, 143,
212

Christmas Eve Bombings,
v, 3, 109

COCIN Headquarters, 217

communal, 22, 103, 109,
125, 133

communication, 30, 56, 70,
115, 126, 177

communion, 134, 138, 154
condolences, 66, 136
crisis management, 102
CWO, 91
Da D. B. Zang, 67
Dagwom Rwei, 89
Damaturu, 211
David Jowitt, ix
Demshin, 61, 64, 66, 69
Dialogue, iv, 2, 25, 27, 31, 32, 129, 135, 159, 160, 172, 173, 208, 216, 238
Diametta Peace Initiative, 135
Diocese, 2, 145, 163
Dipo Ayeni, 226
Does God allow evil?, 55
Dogon Nahawa, v, 3, 88
Easter, 65, 90, 187
education, 11, 17, 20, 57, 71, 113, 117, 125, 144, 149, 154, 168, 174, 176, 178, 180, 211, 214, 216, 241
Eid El Fitr, 97
Emir Haruna Abdullahi of Wase, vi
Epiphany, 140
evil, 42, 55, 56, 57, 94, 98, 127, 131, 139, 142, 156, 159, 160, 185, 187, 192, 193, 223, 224, 225, 237
Fidelis Tapgun, 67
Fr. Albert Endat, 71, 77

Fr. Blaise Agwom, 90, 93
Fr. Gabriel Gowok, 90, 93
Fr. Innocent Jooji, 18
Fr. John Gyang, ix
Fr. Paul Dajen, 58
Francis Cardinal Arinze, vii
Garkawa, 59, 60, 61, 63, 66, 69
Gbong Gwom Jos, 24
General Assembly, viii, 35, 42, 65, 129, 137, 138, 174, 236, 241
Genuine dialogue, 33
German, vii, 137, 145, 150, 164, 166
Godfrey Danaan, ix
Good Friday Peace Agreement, 43
Good governance, 19
Goodluck Jonathan, 39, 44, 91, 93, 101, 108, 227
Governor Jonah David Jang, 150
Governor Joshua Dariye, 20
Hausa-Fulani, 60, 61, 63, 181
Holy Mass, 69, 74, 139
Homily, 54, 115
Hon. Bitrus Kaze, 109
Hon. Habu Shindai, 67
Ibadan, 16, 18, 117
Imam, 35, 138, 171
In the beginning, iv
Inclusive politics, 19

INEC, 41, 143, 239
intense prayer, 192
Interfaith Youth Vocational
    Training Centre, 148
Interreligious Council for
    Peace and Harmony, 82
Ivan Cardinal Dias, vii
Jalingo Diocese, 2, 163
Jewish leader, 218
JNI, 34, 65, 68, 69, 82, 136,
    149, 157, 158, 164
John Haruna, 218
John Onaiyekan, 52, 153,
    166
John Paul II, 127, 128, 131
Jos Crises, 106
Jos North LGA, v, 3, 84,
    100
Jos North Local
    Government, 44, 78, 92,
    100, 168
Jos South, 39, 89, 109
Joseph Deshi Gomwalk, 10,
    12
Jukun/Kutep/Tiv, 2
Justice, Development and
    Peace Commission, 17
Kano, 117, 162, 168, 171,
    175, 183, 211
Knight, 58
Kurgwi, 66, 69
Kwa, 66, 69, 73
Laity Council, 73, 77
Langtang, 15, 66, 68, 69
Langtang South, 15, 68

Long Gamai, 163
Long Goemai, 65, 68, 69,
    163
Madalla, 211, 212
Maiduguri, 95, 111, 114,
    116, 168, 175, 211
MASSOB, 38, 168
Media, v, 23, 212
MEND, 128, 168
mercenaries, 58, 72, 162
MISSIO, 136, 164, 169, 175
Mission of Peace and
    Reconciliation, v
Moving Plateau forward, 16
Muslim leader, 4, 5, 64, 66,
    137, 158, 160, 164, 209
Namu, v, 3, 15, 66, 69, 71,
    72, 75, 77, 136
Nassarawa Gwong, 84, 158
NIFAAM, 170
Niger Delta, 115, 123, 128,
    130, 162, 168, 214
Nigeria at 50, 239
Nigerian Institute of Public
    Relations, 6
Nigerian Muslims and
    Christians, iv, 2, 27, 31,
    32, 160, 173
NIREC, 155, 157, 159, 170,
    171
Northern Ireland, 43
Northern Nigeria, vi, 3, 104,
    106, 113, 116, 155, 162,
    168, 169, 178, 179, 180,
    240

Nunciature, v

Olusegun Obasanjo, 118, 117, 128, 180

OPC, 38, 168

Open and fair-minded believers, 160

Pastoral Centre, 27, 49, 50, 51, 53

Pauline Tallen, 52, 87, 163

peace, ii, iii, ix, x, 2, 3, 4, 5, 6, 7, 10, 11, 13, 14, 15, 16, 17, 18, 20, 21, 22, 23, 24, 25, 26, 27, 28, 29, 31, 32, 35, 36, 37, 40, 41, 42, 46, 47, 48, 53, 54, 55, 62, 64, 65, 67, 68, 71, 72, 73, 74, 75, 77, 82, 83, 84, 87, 88, 90, 93, 95, 96, 98, 102, 103, 112, 119, 115, 116, 118, 119, 120, 121, 122, 123, 124, 125, 126, 127, 128, 129, 130, 132, 133, 134, 136, 138, 139, 140, 142, 143, 146, 148, 151, 152, 153, 154, 155, 156, 157, 158, 159, 161, 162, 163, 164, 166, 167, 168, 171, 172, 173, 174, 175, 178, 179, 180, 181, 183, 184, 185, 187, 189, 191, 192, 193, 194, 208, 210, 213, 214, 215, 216, 217, 218, 223, 225, 236, 237, 238, 240, 241

Peace building, 126

Peace Forum, 68

Peter Cardinal Turkson, vii, 87, 197

Plateau bloc, 10

polarization, 33, 237

Pontifical Council for Justice and Peace, 87, 134

Pope Benedict XVI, 87, 121, 127, 128, 130, 162, 189, 216, 218

Potiskum, 211

Prayer for Peace, vii, 115

Pre 2001, 14

Priests, ix

Protestant, 51, 79, 107, 139

Punch, vii, 1, 181

Ratsat Village, 135

Reconciliation, v, 18, 36, 40, 42, 65, 115, 127, 149, 175, 216

religious leaders, 22, 23, 25, 28, 29, 30, 40, 43, 46, 54, 62, 67, 70, 98, 102, 103, 111, 118, 121, 147, 149, 151, 155, 158, 170, 173, 179, 189, 226, 238, 239, 240

Religious leaders, 22, 29, 179

religious riot, 3

renewed hostilities, 1

repercussions, 181

Rev. Yakubu Pam, 183
Rise up and walk, 96
Roger E. Simon, vii
Rwang Pam, 115
Senator Cosmas Niagwan,
    67
Shendam, 14, 15, 58, 59,
    60, 65, 66, 68, 69, 73, 75,
    77, 118, 145, 163, 180,
    213
Solidarity Mass, v, xi, 86,
    88
Solomon Lar, 42, 67, 209
St. Finbarr's Church, vii
State of Emergency, vi, 3,
    15, 17, 25, 180, 181, 182,
    184, 185, 186
suicide attackers, 227
Synopsis of Violent
    Conflicts, 13
Taye Obateru, 223
Temple of Pythons, 216

Thuraya mobile phones, 70
traditional religion, 12, 22,
    63, 216
Turaki, 64, 66, 69
Vanguard, vii
Vatican, 4, 129, 134
Vatican City, 129, 134
Very Rev. Fr. Emmanuel
    Ray Ikpa, 241
Violence, vi, 100, 143, 154,
    194, 210
Vision for Plateau State, 12
war, ii, 2, 3, 32, 38, 43, 44,
    45, 55, 71, 110, 112, 118,
    119, 121, 127, 128, 129,
    151, 169, 181, 217
world peace, 2
worship centre, 184, 226
Year for Priests, 240
youth empowerment, 152
Zamfara, 52, 63, 104

www.ingramcontent.com/pod-product-compliance
Lightning Source LLC
Chambersburg PA
CBHW081653270326
41933CB00017B/3152